# AMERICAN DREAMER

# AMERICAN DREAMER

## MY LIFE IN FASHION & BUSINESS

# TOMMY HILFIGER
## WITH PETER KNOBLER

BALLANTINE BOOKS

NEW YORK

Published in the United States by Ballantine Books, an imprint of
Random House, a division of Penguin Random House LLC, New York.

BALLANTINE and the HOUSE colophon are registered trademarks of
Penguin Random House LLC.

Library of Congress Cataloging-in-Publication Data
Names: Hilfiger, Tommy, author. | Knobler, Peter, author.
Title: American dreamer : my life in fashion & business /
Tommy Hilfiger with Peter Knobler.
Description: First edition. | New York : Ballantine Books, [2016] |
Includes index.
Identifiers: LCCN 2016023113 (print) | LCCN 2016024008 (ebook) |
ISBN 9781101886212 (hardcover : alk. paper) |
ISBN 9781101886229 (Ebook)
Subjects: LCSH: Hilfiger, Tommy. |
Fashion designers—United States—Biography
Classification: LCC TT505.H55 A3 2016 (print) |
LCC TT505.H55 (Ebook) | DDC 746.9/2092 [B]—dc23
LC record available at https://lccn.loc.gov/2016023113

Printed in the United States of America on acid-free paper

randomhousebooks.com

2 4 6 8 9 7 5 3 1

First Edition

*Book design by Diane Hobbing*

To Virginia Gerrity Hilfiger, Richard Congdon Hilfiger,
William Henry Hilfiger, James Cirona, and Dee Ocleppo Hilfiger.
And to my children: Alexandria, Richard, Elizabeth,
Kathleen, and Sebastian.
My children are the spice of my life. They keep me young and keep
my spirit alive.
—TH

To Daniel
—PK

# FOREWORD

by Quincy Jones

*American Dreamer.* I like that title for Tommy's book because it's a testament to my friend, to the places and people that shaped his character and the opportunities that were available to us all when we had the courage to try. Without letting my jazz mind run wild, I think it reflects the way he's always gone one step further; no limits, letting cultures clash and making new rules. That was the spirit that connected us when we first met twenty-five years ago.

Think back to the '90s. It was a revolutionary time in music. I remember being at the Hit Factory working with some of my artists, and I had agreed to go to dinner with Tommy after being introduced by my daughter Kidada. I have always had the gift of instinct and there was a moment just then, when hip-hop and the whole urban lifestyle movement were buzzing. The talent I was collaborating with in the studio and featuring in *Vibe* were all expressing themselves in very original, real ways. Kidada was part of that, serving as a stylist at the magazine and as a cool hunter and muse for Tommy, and he was getting a lot of attention. His line was classic, rooted in the clean-cut styles of the Ivy League and workwear, and it felt fresh after all the flash of the '80s. Now, sure, designers have worked with musicians before. Motown was famous for it. But this was different. This was a chance for music and fashion to collide in an authentic way that hadn't been done. I'm not talking about costumes, mind you—this was about accessible, attainable clothes that people could make their own. This was Tommy recognizing the power of music, the science versus the soul, how its power could lift a child like me out of the ghetto and give purpose and hope. He knew that music could be the vehicle to bring his brand to the world. There was magic in that. So as we got into my Lincoln that night in New York, I knew this guy had true soul, and I turned to him and said, "Man, you're gonna blow up."

Tommy and I found common ground from that first day. We came from different worlds—me a raggedy brother from Chicago, Tommy a small-town kid from the sticks—but we both started from nothing and knew how to work hard to develop our core skills and to think big. And after overcoming so many obstacles as I built my own career, I could sense that with his vision and drive, this young man would become a success.

He grew up in upstate New York as one of nine children born to parents who knew a thing or two about a hard day's work. His deeply rooted love of music played a pivotal role in the first styles he offered, from bell-bottom jeans with personalized patches to graphic T-shirts and colorful jackets that were a nod to the artists he admired. He succeeded and then failed, as the bottom line got away from him. I've often said there is music and there is the music business, and if you are to survive, you have to learn the difference between the two. That same principle held true for Tommy, but he took his knocks, learned the lessons, shelved his fears, and most important, he kept going.

I didn't know Tommy in those days, but there wasn't anybody who came to the island of Manhattan who didn't see that billboard in the middle of Times Square proclaiming there was a new guy in town. It looked like the children's game Hangman. It was a bold move, some may have even said reckless, but I think life and certainly business is about never being afraid to do what your heart tells you to do and to follow your dreams. You can't worry about what other people think because it's about building and creating something that didn't exist before. I'm talking about risk-taking. And if you're not scared of it, then the chance for success is much greater. I've heard Tommy say more than once that mediocrity is not an option, and it's as true today as it was then. Anyone with a demanding career will tell you it's hard. Tommy wasn't scared of hard.

I've watched Tommy make time for his children through the years, to encourage them to find their passion. I watched him do the same for my daughter. Tommy gave Kidada the confidence to follow her instincts and gave her a platform to showcase her talents and become the businesswoman she was meant to be.

I look back now to the days when Tommy and I first met and began collaborating, and just smile. Together with all those incredible artists, we were able to create something iconic in pop culture and start a revolution in modern-day marketing. Think about it, it was the King of Pop wearing a Tommy Hilfiger jersey on the cover of *Vibe*; it was Andy Hilfiger and Kidada rounding up Aaliyah, Mark Ronson, and Kate Hudson on a tour bus to put on fashion shows across the country; it was Sheryl Crow, Britney Spears, and the Rolling Stones wearing Tommy's clothes on tour. We were pioneers with a shared philosophy that music and fashion were not only connected, but vital to each other.

Tommy was on top of the world but I think what solidified our friendship was his need to give back. He never forgot where he came from, and philanthropy was and still is a huge part of his life. We've worked together to support Lifebeat, We Are Family Foundation, and the Dream Concert benefiting the Martin Luther King, Jr. Memorial Fund. His Tommy Hilfiger Foundation and now Tommy Cares have supported countless life-changing projects and initiatives over the years. And it's not just Tommy writing his name on a check. It's him inspiring and encouraging his employees to contribute their time, him matching every donation they make, and him putting in the sweat equity.

Somebody once told me there are three phases you go through in life: The quest for materialism, the quest for power, and finally, reaching the stage of giving without expecting anything in return but happiness for having done so. That right there is the American Dream, and Tommy Hilfiger—he's living it.

Congratulations, brother! I love you, man.

# CONTENTS

# AMERICAN DREAMER

# CHAPTER ONE

# IMAGINE

*Dreaming Big!*

was always planning my escape. Mostly I dreamed. I took myself out of where I was and put myself somewhere else. How could I sneak out of school that afternoon? Where was I going that weekend? Where was the party? I dreamed of cars, sports, girls; of making money, enjoying life, being a rock star. I saw myself on a boat in the Bahamas and felt the wind in my face, heard the sails flap as we came about, looked up the mast into the white clouds and blue sky. I was there.

I had eight brothers and sisters, and one Sunday morning my father was driving all of us in the station wagon to Denton Hill, a ski area in Pennsylvania, our gear crammed in the back and on the roof. As everybody vied for attention, I gazed out the window and saw a cabin on the side of a mountain. I pictured myself in that cabin, but in my mind, the cabin was decorated like a Swiss chalet and there was a fire blazing in a big stone fireplace. My skis were on the front porch, ready to go. I wanted to be in the ski patrol, so I pictured my backpack filled with a Swiss Army knife, a first-aid kit, a walkie-talkie, and a fold-up tent. I could smell the pine trees, see the bright white snow, feel the towering evergreens. I don't know where the details came from; I was obsessed with Walt Disney movies, so probably from them or *The Sound of Music*. I dreamed so often I developed a photographic memory. I saw a scene, clicked it in my mind, and it was there forever. The colors, the feel, the shine, the patina. All right there.

My father, Richard, a watchmaker and jeweler, was not a man for fantasies. He said I had to learn a trade so I could have dependable work and make some money in this life.

"What's a trade?"

"You learn to be a mechanic, or work in a machine shop, or be a carpenter."

I didn't want to be a robot, to wake up in the morning and do the same thing every day. Shop was better than sitting in algebra class, but it wasn't a lot of fun. And I was looking for fun.

Home was not fun.

I was born in 1951 and grew up in Elmira, New York, in one half of a side-by-side double house at 921 Laurel Street, off Pennsylvania Avenue. My father's family was German and Swiss; my mom's came from Ireland and Scotland. My maternal grandmother's maiden name was Burns, and on the Scottish side we're supposed to be related to the poet Robert Burns, but that was never spoken about in our house because Robbie Burns had a reputation as a womanizer and a drinker. The whole family, all eleven of us, ate dinner every night around one big table, and chaos reigned. At any given time there were a couple of babies in high chairs; I would be teasing my sisters, trying to make them laugh; one of my brothers could be flying across the floor; the noise level was high and buzzing. But when my father came home and slammed his fist on the table, everybody went silent. He would be the last to sit down, usually in a foul mood. We were all nervous around him, and in our nervousness we would giggle. Which infuriated him, which made us giggle even more, which made him even madder. Every night we tried to hold it together, and every night we made our father furious.

When we were alone, we would ask my mother, "Why is Dad so angry?" My mother, Virginia, a registered nurse who worked the six-to-eleven night shift, came home, made breakfast for all of us, and didn't get a lot of sleep, always found the good in everything. A petite woman with chestnut brown hair and one green eye and one brown, she was kind, warm, sensitive, and loving. Mom was a true saint.

"Dad's store is air-conditioned, and when he comes home it's not air-conditioned here, sweetheart." That was why he was angry in the summer. "The driveway hasn't been shoveled. It's icy, dear." That was why he was angry in the winter. Dad was in a bad mood every season, pretty much all the time.

My father liked to go out with his buddies. They would play cards, shoot skeet, go to the bar, and bet on sports. He had a life outside the home that excited him—he was handsome, impeccably dressed, and loved by everyone who knew him. Around neighbors, customers, and friends, he was perfectly charming. At home he was something else, and no one saw it but us. With a mortgage to pay off and clothes for nine children to provide, home was expensive. He had been raised Protestant and converted to Catholicism when he married my mother, and he followed those rules, but Richard Hilfiger surely did not seem happy with his life, and although with so many children he was a good provider, I doubt he had wanted nine kids. Coming home was facing reality. When his car drove up the driveway each night, we all scattered and hushed.

If I left my bicycle in the driveway, if my shoes were on the stairs instead of in my room where I was supposed to put them, if I kicked my sister—about once a week from the time I was five until I was eleven, my dad punished and spanked me—hard. I hated and feared him, and I never wanted to be in his presence. I became an expert at hiding from my father when he was in the house. I was a phantom, a ghost. I dodged him because I never knew when he was going to find something I had done wrong and go at me.

My mother was so kind and loving, she didn't like the physical punishment. She knew it was wrong. Her way of trying to protect me was to tell her husband quietly, "Enough." She tried to smooth over our relationship, but I was always worried that I would set him off, and every week he proved my fears correct. Whether I was my best self or not, my father scared me every day of my life.

When there are nine kids in the family, things are complicated. Each of us had a distinct role in the household, but I'm not sure there was any rhyme or reason to them. Kathy, the firstborn, was creative and had great taste. She was constantly rearranging the house, a lamp here, a table there, moving the couch to the other wall. She kept everything clean and was every bit the student my father demanded that she be. She was also very aware of the effect of wealth, because we didn't have it. She would point out how other people dressed, where they lived, how they lived: "Oh, look, they have a nice car"; "They have a beautiful home and a swimming pool"; "Their father is a doctor. They must be rich." My older sister passed that awareness along to me. We would look at the children of business owners, and they would be well dressed and well groomed and living in nice houses, and we'd think, "They are perfect."

Kathy tried out for the high school cheerleading squad at a time when cheerleaders were the apex of beauty and was extremely upset when she didn't make the cut. But she was a good gymnast, so they asked her to be the Elmira Free Academy Blue Devil, the mascot. She was very attractive, but she never thought she looked good. She just didn't realize how beautiful she was.

I was the second child, two years younger, and I couldn't do anything right. I failed miserably in school, and though I tried hard and played with passion, I wasn't an athlete. This pained my father to no end. One of Dad's best buddies was Maury Collins, whose son Charlie was a great athlete. Maury would talk about Charlie and his football all the time. I think it got under my father's skin because he couldn't brag about me. Coaches would tell me, "You're too short for basketball" or "You're not big enough for football," and I didn't like baseball. There was nothing I was good at. Dad would tell me all about the other kids in the neighborhood: "Tommy Lynch is brilliant!" "That Scotty Welliver is a hell of a boy!" "Jimmy Rogers is a great basketball player!" Then he would look at me with disdain. I didn't know what I had done to cross him, but by the time I reached junior high school it was clear to me that there was nothing I could do that would ever make him look at me in a positive way. So I stopped trying.

My sister Dorothy, born a year after me and named after my father's mother, liked the name Susie, and requested that everyone call her that instead. She's been Susie ever since. Susie was the smart one. Curious, adventurous, and popular, she was anything but a bookworm, yet she amazed everyone with her consistently stellar grades. She had a quick wit, a big crowd of friends, and an answer for everything. My father had a soft spot for her because she was often ill as a child and finally, in her teens, was diagnosed with multiple sclerosis.

Meanwhile, I was a dreamer. I had to be, because I couldn't understand what everybody else was grasping. English, history, math—

I just couldn't follow the texts. When I tried to read a book, I'd make it two pages into a chapter and start reading from the bottom up. My eyes would jump from one line to another. I would land in the middle of a page and start reading upward. Sometimes I would start at the right side of the page and read backward—and I could not control it.

I wanted to learn. I was curious. I guess you could call me nosy, but I was always extremely interested in what was going on around me. And because I couldn't get information the way everyone else did—my dyslexia wasn't diagnosed until much later in life—I picked up on vibes, facial expressions, and body language and developed my own personal radar to carry me through. I faked it.

I'd sit in Mr. Huber's high school math class and think about everything but algebra. It was so confusing to me—$2x$ over $y$, squares, square roots—and I couldn't help but worry, "If I get through this, I have to go do geometry!" There was no way I could pay attention; every time I tried, it confused me even more. So I just decided to show up, guess at answers on tests, and see what happened at the end of the year.

I saw other kids in the class getting it. When Mr. Huber passed out completed exams, I looked at their test papers and saw they got 90s. Mine would be full of red ink and a grade of 35. And while he was going over the answers and the students around me were correcting their mistakes and making notes for next time, I'd stare at my teacher's Thom McAn shoes, his brown polyester trousers, his white wash-and-wear shirt, his wash-and-wear tie, and think, "Mr. Huber really must be a good Sears customer!"

Some teachers were sympathetic, because they were nice people and I was a likable kid, kind of a jokester. I had a lot of friends, and we had as much fun as possible without getting thrown out. I was good at imitation, and when a teacher would turn around to write on the blackboard, I was the one who would copy his gestures or mimic his voice to get a laugh, mostly to evade the fact that I was not doing well in school. I knew that they thought that for this boy there was probably not much hope.

I would sit in class, look toward the blackboard, and not even see it. What was the point? I couldn't read worth a damn. But I could tell you exactly what the teacher was wearing.

One of my major embarrassments was having to repeat sophomore year. Even worse, I had failed into my kid sister Susie's class; worse still, she was getting 90s, and I was lucky to get 50s.

Susie also had great taste in clothes. She was conscious of how colors coordinated, and she knew and cared about brands and took care of the contents of her closet and dresser. Susie folded each of her sweaters perfectly, was always precisely aware of what she had—my earliest recollection of inventory control—and guarded her wardrobe zealously; she didn't want any of her sisters touching anything. There was a lot of talk among the girls in my family about clothing and style and what people were favoring. Without them I probably would not have paid a lot of attention, but hearing the chitter-chatter all the time certainly had an effect. A boy with five sisters knows things other boys don't.

My sister Elizabeth—Betsy—came along four years after me. She looked like a Hilfiger, but with red hair, blue eyes, and freckles, she was more striking than the rest of us. Not only was she a real beauty, but Betsy was sweet, kind, and caring. She was organized and disciplined, the mirror image of my mother, and became my mother's main helper. When I came home from school and there were fresh cookies or brownies or a cake on the counter, Betsy and Mom had been at it together. Betsy became the Hilfiger historian; anytime anyone wants to know about the family, she's there with the info.

My brother William Henry was born a year after Betsy. Meticulous even as a little boy, Billy loved to sketch and draw, and he was excellent at math. When we first got jobs, my sisters and I would take the money we'd earned and go out and buy something. Billy saved every penny. Sooner or later my sisters and I would outspend our earnings.

"Billy, can I borrow ten dollars?"

"Yeah, but I need it back by Tuesday, or I'll charge interest."

Two years after Billy, Bobby showed up. A ball of pure energy, he destroyed several cribs—he shook and rocked them apart because he just didn't want to be inside!

Bobby was always a wiry, frail kid, but when he got to junior high school he started lifting weights and building muscle. By sophomore year he was pretty buff. He was a great natural athlete and a daredevil with no fear at all. Bobby had a funny and sweet nature, and as he grew older he started getting into trouble. We had a motorized minibike, all of us kids' favorite mode of transportation, and my father would say, "Don't go in the road with it. You're not allowed in the road." Well, Bobby would get on and hit the road. When he'd get back and my father tried to raise a hand to him, Bobby would push Dad off or run away. I could never do that.

Bobby made the football and the wrestling teams. Junior year he was a wrestling star. Senior year he won the New York state championship and earned a junior college scholarship to the State University of New York at Delhi. Bobby was a two-time National Junior College Athletic Association All-American wrestler at Delhi and set the record for the most wins at the NJCAA National Wrestling Tournament. He was selected to the Region III 1970s All-Decade Wrestling Team and earned a place in its Wrestling Hall of Fame. SUNY Delhi named him Athlete of the Year in 1979. He transferred to Appalachian State, in Boone, North Carolina, and won back-to-back Division I national championships. My father finally had a son to brag about. I was happy for Bobby and happy that my dad was in a good mood.

Marie followed Bobby by a year. My mother's sister, my aunt Annie, was living with us at the time, helping with the babies, and she had a way of making Marie laugh hysterically by saying, "D-d-d-d-d-d-d-darling girl!" Very soon, Marie became Dee Dee. Dee Dee grew up to be super popular, and she, Kathy, Betsy, and Susie spent a lot of time obsessing over the fashion that made its way into our house. The style in West Elmira at the time was very preppy. They shopped at all the local mom-and-pop stores—Rosenbaum's, Gorton Coy, Sportogs, Schwartz's, Iszard's Department Store—and wore labels like Villager, Ladybug, and John Meyer of Norwich. I watched what my sisters were sporting, what they were loaning to each other, what they were fighting over.

"You stretched out my sweater!" Susie would yell at Kathy.

"I didn't even wear it for that long!"

"Well, you will never wear it again!"

"Fine, you will never wear my kilt again!"

This was important stuff!

The kids just kept on coming. I never liked seeing my mom in a maternity dress because it meant another Hilfiger was on the way, which meant I would be getting less attention from my mother and the household would become that much more chaotic. Our neighborhood was filled with massive families, as many Catholics had at the time, so if Mrs. Hilfiger was pregnant with baby number six or seven, no one said, "Oh my God, how many kids do they have?" She was more likely to hear, "You only have nine? The Sheehans have eleven!"

My brother Andy was ten years younger than I was, and the eighth baby in twelve years. I think Dad felt he was in the way. Still, he liked my sister Virginia—Ginny—who was thirteen years younger than I and the last of the brood. For the longest time, we called her "Baby Ginny." She was the "cute one."

Dad had his favorites. He was very sweet to Susie, Billy, Bobby, Betsy, and Ginny. Kathy, Andy, Dee Dee, and I got the brunt of it. Later in life I visited a therapist by the name of Roberta Sorvino. I had never seen a therapist before, and she turned out to be an incredible woman of great wisdom and compassion; she is a close friend and confidante even now, thirty-five years later. She pointed out something I found enlightening: all of Dad's favorites were named after members of his side of the family whom he liked, and the rest of us (except for Kathy) were named after ones on the other side of the family whom he didn't. Perhaps psychologically this had an effect on his feelings toward us, though I always thought he hated me because I wasn't who he thought I should be. (I never have figured out why he treated my sister Kathy so poorly.) When I sensed my father beginning to treat Andy the way he treated me, each night when Dad's car pulled into the driveway I took this little boy, ten years younger than I was, and got him busy doing something outside our father's line of sight.

Even my dad's mother was mean to me. Nana Dorothy lived with her second husband, Andrew, in Jacksonville, Florida, and would occasionally drive up to visit. She was mean and crabby and bossy to me but adored Betsy, who stood out as a beauty. "Leave this room," she would tell me, "I'm talking to your mother. You should be seen and not heard." Nana would allow my sisters to sit with them, but not me. "Go out and play."

"But it's freezing out, there's three feet of snow . . ."

"I don't care. You go out there and play."

Good boy that I was, I went outside. When I finally got too cold, I'd come bang on the door, and my mother would let me back in. Nana was angry that she capitulated.

When I was eleven years old, Kathy, Susie, and Betsy (thirteen, ten, and eight at the time) were invited to Florida to spend the summer with her. I was left out. When I asked if I could go, too, there was some discussion and Nana relented. Not happily. While it wasn't unusual for children to visit relatives by bus in those days, we were put on a Greyhound, unchaperoned. Sometime in the middle of the night we reached Charleston, South Carolina, and I had to go to the bathroom. Outside the bus, I saw a couple of sleazy-looking guys staring at me. I didn't know what a pervert was, but they scared me. I rushed in, did my business as quickly as I could, and got back on the bus in a hurry. My sisters were nowhere to be found. I waited, and as time passed and the bus prepared to leave, I got more and more nervous. For a moment I thought I had lost my family. Finally the three of them trotted back from the bathroom. Maybe in the mid-1960s letting your children travel more than a thousand miles by bus without an adult to supervise was acceptable parenting, but it's fifty years later, and I still feel chills when I think about it. That experience many decades ago informs the way I parent; I have always been protective of my children to a fault. Even now I need to be in touch with them at least once a day. I'm sure it feels like a burden to my kids, but that's the way I am.

We spent a good part of that summer with my grandmother. Seems like every day she told me to go out and weed her garden. It was 110 degrees and muggy and nasty with bugs, and I would pull a couple of weeds and think, "Why am I doing this? My sisters are in there watching soap operas and eating bonbons with Nana, and she sent me out to weed the garden." I had to wonder what it must have been like for my dad to grow up in my grandmother's house. (I have heard from relatives that my father had been whipped by his dad as punishment.)

Aunt Annie, my mom's sister, saw what was going on. She and my mother spent hours sitting in the kitchen, smoking cigarettes and drinking coffee, gossiping about people. Aunt Annie did most of the talking. I liked her because I knew she really loved me. "Believe in yourself," she always told me. "You are a good person. You are a smart boy. Stay out of your father's way."

Elmira was in New York State, but it could have been in the middle of Kansas. It was like living in *Leave It to Beaver* land. The city was divided between the wealthy west side and the working-class east and Southside, where we lived. I grew up watching *The Mickey Mouse Club* and *Davy Crockett*. All the kids played out in the street.

The Elliotts next door had three boys—Tommy, Dickie, and Bobby—all of whom were older and tougher than I was. They would taunt and punch and wrestle with me, and I idolized them. I would watch cartoons at their house on Saturdays—*Popeye, Mickey Mouse, Donald Duck, Looney Tunes*—then go outside and play baseball and climb trees. They took me down to the railroad tracks one day, and when cops stopped us and gave us arrest cards, "notices of violation," I was in big trouble at home. I was in second grade when they moved away, and I was devastated.

Mom drove a beat-up 1951 Pontiac station wagon with wood paneling. Now it's a classic "woodie"; then it was a pile of junk. It was so worn down I was embarrassed to be seen in it. One afternoon as we were coming home from the store, Mom turned a corner and a bag of groceries spilled off the backseat and onto the floor. There was a hole where the floorboard had rusted out, so all of our oranges and tangerines started rolling down the road. Mom stopped the car, ran out, and started picking up the fruit. I thought it was funny! "Why do we have a hole in the floor of the car?" I asked.

"Because we can't afford a new one," she said.

My father worked at Shreibman's jewelry store. "Mr. Hoffman just bought Mrs. Hoffman a five-thousand-dollar diamond ring," he told my mom one evening. How could anybody afford that?

My sister Kathy filled me in. "His family has money," she explained. "They live on an estate up in Strathmont. Hoffman Street was named after their family."

I was dumbfounded. "How do people get to that level?"

"They were born into it."

"Why weren't *we* born into it?"

It was at that moment that I was introduced to the idea that there were people who couldn't afford and people who could. I came to the conclusion that the people who could afford nice things lived in special parts of Elmira and were doctors or lawyers or professionals, and in most cases didn't have nine children. I realized that if I wanted a new bicycle or new Levi's or a new pair of Converse sneakers, I would have to buy it myself.

One of the older boys in the neighborhood, Terry Jones, agreed to let me help him with his paper route. We would ride our bikes onto the rarefied streets of the Strathmont area—Euclid Avenue, Hoffman Street, Upper Clinton, Foster Avenue, Garden Road, Fassett Road, Edgewood Drive—where the homes were opulent. I would toss the paper and think, "Wow, people actually live in these houses! They have more than one car, and a swimming pool, and a gardener, and a housekeeper who opens the door in a uniform . . . I want to live that way someday!"

The concept of making money was exciting to me. I had some business experience because somehow I had figured out the concept of bartering. I traded my broken-down bicycle and cash to a boy with a nicer bike. I traded toys. I traded my baseball glove. I'd say, "I will give you my football helmet plus five dollars if I can get your helmet," and would come away with a snazzy upgrade. I raked leaves, shoveled snow, ran errands for my neighbors. I didn't know if I was smart enough to be a doctor or lawyer or own a business, but I was constantly hustling.

When Terry graduated from high school and was about to go off to college, he sold me his paper route for $15, and I became a newspaper boy. Not only did the job put money in my pocket, but every Saturday I would knock on the doors of these great houses to collect, so it taught me how to talk to adults. And they needed someone like me. "What are you doing Sunday?" they'd ask. "Can you come mow my lawn?"

So while my friends were playing sports, I was working. I started making money. I could buy clothes! I could go to the movies! I could buy ice cream and sodas! I thought, "Maybe someday I can have a home like this. People actually live like this!" I couldn't really believe it.

One evening, my father came home from work, took my mom into the kitchen, and said, "We're moving to West Elmira."

"How can we afford it?" I heard her ask.

"Art is selling us his old house for what we can afford, and we can rent this place out for income," Dad explained. His friend Art Welliver was doing him a big favor. I didn't understand any of it, but the next thing I knew, there were trucks backed up to our house taking our furniture, and all of a sudden we were at 606 West Clinton Street in what looked to us like a mansion. Five bedrooms! As we kids all ran through it for the first time, Kathy said to me, "This is where the rich people live!" We would only have to share a bedroom with *one* sibling, not three!

A creek ran through the neighborhood. The houses were bigger, the streets were wider, the area altogether nicer. Larger houses meant larger families, and most were Italian and Irish Catholics, so there were kids everywhere. The Sheehan family on Logan Street had eleven children, and nobody messed with Jack or Pat Sheehan—they were tough. Pat was so tough they called him "Bugsy"! There was another Sheehan family that had ten girls and a boy, and four of those girls became our babysitters. The Rogers family had five kids; the Cesaris next door had six. Dr. Cesari was an oral surgeon and the nicest man in the world. His wife, Lucy, was a second mother to us; her parents owned a bakery and a bowling alley, and she used to give us fresh-baked goods. The Longwells across the way had seven children, and the Smith family on the corner had three. There were softball games on the lawns and Kool-Aid stands; it was like summer camp in the streets all summer long.

The Elmira YMCA ran an actual summer camp near one of the Finger Lakes. I had heard about it for years—Camp Iroquois! It had camping, canoeing, swimming—all kinds of sports and fun. I was dying to go, but my parents couldn't afford to send me. I found a program in which you could earn your way by selling cardboard cartons of saltwater taffy; if you reached their sales goal, you could go to camp for a week. I went to all of my newspaper customers' homes, knocked on their doors, and sold every single carton. I was twelve years old, and it was a dream come true. Not only did I have a fantastic time at camp, but I learned that grown-ups respect and want to help young people who are striving. I was proud. So was my father.

My great-uncle Charlie Kromer was director of the Neighborhood House, the local community center on the east side of town near the projects. It also ran a summer camp, Elneho, this one free, where I was one of the only white boys and met a lot of the African American kids in town. We had a lot of fun together.

Everyone in my west side neighborhood walked to school, so we would see each other morning, noon, and night. Each of my brothers and sisters began to form their own group of friends. John Shingler was the leader of my pack; we thought whatever he did was cool. He had an older brother, Rob, who was the coolest guy in the neighborhood. John took after him, and we followed John. He was the first guy with a *Playboy* magazine and cigarettes. He showed us what a condom was. He dressed cool and had a string of good-looking girlfriends. Andy Sleeper was in our crowd, and Jeff Bloom, and the twins Jack and Jim Colgrove, and Mike French, who was a great athlete and ladies' man.

We graduated from sixth grade and started junior high at the Booth School, where we met even more West Elmira guys: Kevin Delaney, the Hirsches, the Skibs, the Jeromes, Don Nowill, Richie Poes, Mike Straight, and Tim Kennedy. I introduced myself to Larry Stemerman because he was wearing Beatle boots. I thought, "My father would never let me wear those." We became friends immediately. I hung out at the Stemermans'. The first time I visited and saw his mother's emerald-green carpet, I thought I was in a mansion. They took me to my first restaurant. I spent every Passover and High Holy Day with them, which was a revelation: food I'd never tasted, stories I'd never known, words I'd never heard. This was exciting! They became family—they "adopted" me.

Larry and I and the guys hung out on Friday nights. (Larry wasn't so very religious that shul interfered with having a good time.) We would tell our parents we were going somewhere and then we'd go rabble-rouse, drink beer, and make out with girls if we could find them. One night Bloom, French, Shingler, the Colgrove twins, and I got permission to sleep out on the Shinglers' property in a wooden shack, a kind of fort we called The Hut. Around eleven o'clock we decided to sneak out and run around the streets . . . in our tighty-whities. We were hiding in the bushes when we heard our neighbors screaming at each other. The house was lit up and we could see arms flying. I had never seen a husband and wife fight before. My parents never fought.

So we were hiding in the bushes, watching the parents of these kids we went to school with do battle, when a car pulled up behind us. Someone had called the cops. I don't know whether it was because of the domestic disturbance or because a neighbor had seen a bunch of junior high school boys crouched outside in their underwear. The officers shone their flashlights, rounded us up, called our parents, and took us home.

My father was angry and mortified. And let me know in no uncertain terms. I swore I would never do anything like that again.

A year later, my parents gave me permission to stay in The Hut again. Of course we snuck out, but this time we kept our clothes on. We ran over to Linda Stone's house on West First Street because she and Sandy Van Gorder were having an overnight and were going to sneak out and meet us. As we were heading up the driveway of the Stone residence, Mr. Stone and his son Dickie ran out and started chasing us. They caught us at the corner of First Street and Hoffman and called our parents themselves.

Mr. Stone told my dad that matches had been found in the driveway and that he suspected we'd been trying to put them in the gas tank of his car. We were doing no such thing; we were sneaking cigarettes! That didn't cut it with my dad.

# CHAPTER TWO

# UNIFORMS

*my First
inspiration*

My dad wanted me to be the perfect young man. He wanted me to be a great student. I wasn't. He wanted me to be a great athlete. I wasn't. I was never big enough, strong enough, or good enough to make any sports team. I was small for my age, and when they handed out uniforms in Little League, they didn't have anything small enough to fit me. The coaches put me way, way out in the outfield, and it was rare that a ball ever came my way. It was rare that I ever hit the ball when I came to bat.

But I did love the uniforms. I could smell the ink from the numbers and the name of the team printed on the shirts. I thought if you wore a number you looked important, so I kept going out for the teams. In small-fry baseball you got pants with stirrups, sanitary socks, and a real baseball shirt with pinstripes and appliqué letters that were sewn on, not just printed. Game jerseys had blue-and-gold flocked script lettering! I didn't care that I was sitting on the bench the first year or the second year. By the third year I started to play a little, but then football came along, and I lost interest in baseball almost altogether. Football was cooler: you got to wear a helmet and padded pants and shoulder pads.

I loved the Cleveland Browns, with their brown-and-orange uniforms against a white background and stripes wrapping around the biceps, their orange helmets with the stripes down the middle, and number 32, Jimmy Brown, who was the best of all time. (He was still known as Jimmy Brown then, not yet Jim.) The Green Bay Packers had Jim Taylor, the New York Giants had Y. A. Tittle and Frank Gifford. These were heroes. My stepgrandfather was paying attention and gave me a book of photographs by Robert Riger called *The Pros* for Christmas, and I stared at that for hours on end.

At the weigh-in for small-fry football, I didn't make the ninety-pound minimum. I had a friend put stones in my pockets and I still didn't make it, so while I was on the scale another friend pulled down on my trousers to put me over the top. Of course when they handed out uniforms, mine was way too big, but I was thrilled to put it on anyway. The coach, my dad's friend Mickey Collins, was smart enough not to put me in the real fray, because there were some pretty hefty boys out there and I would have been killed. I played deep safety and prayed that none of those guys came running my way too hard.

But I loved being in uniform! How awesome it was to get suited up for a game just like the pros. I had all my equipment laid out on my bed and ready to go for practices after school or our games on Sundays. In my mind, I had big shoulder pads and a game jersey with the numbers and letters actually sewn on, football pants with lace-up fronts and big pads on the knees and thighs, and Riddell spikes and a Riddell helmet with a cool face mask. In reality, the shoulder pads were way too big, the helmet engulfed me, and the face mask probably weighed as much as I did. But I spent a lot of time pretending—dreaming—I was a professional player.

I became obsessed with the sport. I watched the NFL game on TV every Sunday and devoured football magazines. I would hang around the high school practice field for hours, an unofficial water boy, helping out and watching. My nickname was "Hippo," in much the same way you call a three-hundred-pound offensive tackle "Tiny." It had been my uncle Bob's nickname, which was handed down to my dad when he played for Elmira Southside, and followed me to high school at Elmira Free Academy. I guess it was a legacy; another guy my size, Harold Hanrahan, was called "Flea."

In ninth grade I tried out for the high school team, but there was no way; the other players were just too big and too tough. I played small-fry basketball, and while those guys were much faster and taller than I was, I did get to wear the team uniform: royal blue satin shorts with white stripes and a white tank top with royal blue lettering and my number, 13, on both front and back. It didn't breathe too well, but I thought it was very cool.

I was also dying for a pair of low-cut Converse sneakers, the mark of the stylish and serious ballplayer at the time, but they were $13 and I didn't have it. I went into moneymaking overdrive, raking more leaves, mowing more lawns, and delivering more newspapers, and finally was ready to buy a pair. I went to Lou Paltrowitz's sporting goods store only to find that Converse started at size 7 and I was somewhere around a 5. I bought them anyway, put Kleenex and toilet paper in the toes, and for a while was the coolest guy around, the first in my crowd with Converse.

In a small town like Elmira, high school sports was pretty much all that was going on. Elmira Academy athletes were the cool guys. They had all the girls, they were popular, and some stood out as leaders. By eighth grade I came to the conclusion that I was never going to be one of those guys. I was dying to play, but I was a spectator.

In one of the greatest surprises of my teenage years, I found out I could actually buy a varsity jacket: made of wool melton, with leather sleeves, stripes on the cuffs, snaps down the front, and leather piping on the pockets. The epitome of authentic high school cool. I thought I could walk down the street in a varsity jacket and people might really think I was on the team. They were in short supply, and I was lucky enough to get one. I still have it.

I bought the jacket at Lou Paltrowitz's sporting goods store, Lou Pal's. That place was filled with treasures. They sold Converse, they sold Riddell football helmets, they made all the school teams' trophies, and they sold equipment for every sport. One day I said, "Dad, I would really like to work in that store." My father talked to Lou Pal himself, and when I was thirteen I landed my perfect after-school job.

I began by dusting the trophies. I wondered what it must feel like to win one. I loved everything about football helmets: how they felt hefty in your hand and fit snugly between your elbow and your rib cage when you waited to get in the game from the sidelines, like I'd seen on football cards; how they reflected light when they were new and completely unblemished; the solid feel when you smacked them with your open hand; the sound the chin strap made when it snapped onto its grommet. Lou taught me to install face guards. Helmets arrived without them, and when it came time for assembly you could pick either the cage for linemen or the double bar for the backfield. I drilled the holes and made sure each face guard was secure. Once in a while, just for the hell of it, I tried one on.

Lou Pal's sold uniforms to all the local teams, and I would take the jerseys to the printer and bring them back to the store. I loved the spirit of the uniforms. They were bright and shiny and new, they had big numbers and logos, and it felt like if you wore these uniforms, you were a winner. I pored over the catalogs, studied them more carefully and with greater passion than anything I read in school.

Lou was in his fifties. Not that she had been born yet, but Gwyneth Paltrow is his niece. A short, balding man with a high-pitched voice, Lou was in very good shape. He had been a player, a coach, a commissioner, a sponsor, a volunteer. He was a basketball ref at night, he umpired baseball games, and as far as sporting goods went, Lou was the only game in town. He was a very nice man, but he became serious when he negotiated. I listened to him buy and sell goods.

"Yeah, I need fourteen baseballs, but I'm not paying you a dollar per baseball. I'll give you seventy-five cents a ball!" I had never heard this done before.

He would walk customers through the store and say, "Well, this basketball is ten dollars, but I'll give it to you for eight-fifty." He had bought it for $5. Here was my introduction to the 100 percent markup and the whole idea of discounts. When he saw I was interested in the business, he started teaching me retail. My first mentor. I thought of him as a second dad.

Still, sports remained my main interest. The Elmira Pioneers were a Baltimore Orioles AAA farm team—white uniforms with orange and black lettering, just like the big-league club—and my friends and I would go to games at Dunn Field and then hang out near the locker room to get autographs. This was our first contact with real pros, and a lot of fun. Earl Weaver managed the Pioneers for four years and won a championship before becoming the Orioles' Hall of Fame manager. Lou Piniella hit three homers in one game. Things you remember: Mickey Maguire was our shortstop.

The Harlem Globetrotters came to town, and somebody knew

someone and got us inside their locker room. These men were giants! Their red-white-and-blue stars-and-stripes satin uniforms were the coolest things I had ever seen. Meadowlark Lemon and the guys were sporting what looked like zoot suits, with flashy watches and more jewelry than I'd ever seen on a man, and what struck me was how cool these guys were. Cool played a very large role in my teenage life.

Elmira's greatest celebrity was Mark Twain, who summered there in the 1870s and 1880s and worked on *The Adventures of Tom Sawyer, Life on the Mississippi, The Adventures of Huckleberry Finn,* and *The Prince and the Pauper* in a small cottage at his sister-in-law's home. He was buried in Elmira's Woodlawn Cemetery. Every schoolkid was taught that. But our Elmira hero was Ernie Davis, the first black football player to win the Heisman Trophy. He went to my high school, where he was a two-time All-American they called the "Elmira Express." Davis was a two-time All-American again at Syracuse University—uniform number 44—and led them to a national championship. He was quickly acquired by the Cleveland Browns and was all set to become the next Jim Brown when he contracted leukemia and died in 1963 at age twenty-three without ever having played a professional game. I was twelve years old that year. This was a major local tragedy. To this day, I'm sad about it.

I was working at Lou Pal's when I made one of the biggest mistakes of my life. Cartons of Rawlings leather baseballs with the raised red stitching arrived one morning, and when I opened the package the scent of fresh leather wafted up at me. Each ball was individually boxed and wrapped in tissue paper. It was like candy. I decided I needed one. I thought, "He's got tons of baseballs, he'll never miss this one." I took it home with me. Just because I wanted it.

But of course Lou Pal knew his inventory. He probably saw the empty box I left among the dozens in the shipment. That night he went to my father and said, "Look, I know your son Tommy took a baseball. They came in, I looked at them, they were all there. I looked at them this evening and there's one missing. He was the only one in the back room. Do you think he could have taken one?"

As much as I tried to stay out of his sight every day, my father cornered me in my bedroom. "Did you take a baseball?"

I was humiliated. "Yes, I did," I told him. I was so angry at myself, so deeply ashamed.

Lou Pal came to my door. I handed him the ball back and said, "I'm sorry, Mr. Paltrowitz. I know you have to fire me."

But he didn't fire me. I don't know why. Maybe he believed in second chances. Growing up as I had, I was unfamiliar with the concept. But I couldn't forgive myself. I felt so embarrassed and humiliated at work the following days and weeks that I began looking for another job. Lou Pal didn't shine a spotlight on my shame; I did it myself. I'll regret it forever.

I heard that guys pumping gas at the Hess station in town were making $1.25 an hour. I was making 75 cents at Lou Pal's, so I applied and got the job.

The gas jockeys worked almost like a team. When a car pulled in, we would contend for who pumped. Once you got to the window, if you asked "How much?" you'd usually get "Fill 'er up." We were supposed to ask, "How about high-test?" and whether the driver wanted oil, but most guys either forgot to or didn't bother. To spark sales, Corky ran contests; there was a bonus for the boy who brought in the most money. I became quite aggressive. I cleaned everyone's windshield and then asked, "Check your oil?" Eight times out of ten they would be low and I would sell some. I won that award.

I enjoyed the camaraderie, I liked making the customers happy, and the best part was the uniform we all wore: white pants, white shirt with a green-and-white embroidered Hess patch sewn over the heart. Timeless and classic. But the work itself was exhausting. I would get home each night at eleven-thirty and have to bathe to get the smell of gas out of my hair. My face was smudged and grimy, and in the brutal upstate New York winters my hands would crack and bleed. I was supposed to have time to do my homework while we stood around waiting for customers, but there was no way I could study like that. And then I had to get up early and go to school. I liked my friends, but I hated classes with a passion. I couldn't wait to get out on my own. I knew I needed to graduate, but there was no certainty I would get that diploma. And I didn't know what I would do then.

From the time I started working for Lou Pal, I had begun saving to buy a car. The minute I turned sixteen I was going to get a license and be free. My friend Bucky Campbell's family dealt in used cars and found me a good one, a white 1960 Oldsmobile. I really wanted a Volkswagen Bug, but I couldn't afford one. The Olds was $150, so as a down payment, I gave them the $100 I had amassed from my paper route, errand running, and lawn mowing, plus my Lou Pal savings, and paid $10 a week for the next five weeks until it was mine.

I was driving to work one day in my big Olds boat when I saw a beat-up Volkswagen sitting in a parking area near a trucking company. I pulled over, knocked on the office door, and asked, "Whose Volkswagen is that?"

"That's mine," the guy said. "Why?"

"Would you ever want to sell it?"

"No," he told me. "What am I going to ride?"

"Would you ever trade it?"

"For what?"

I looked out the door. "That's my Oldsmobile."

He didn't believe me. "You mean, you want to trade that for this?"

"Yeah."

The guy was suspicious. "Well, I don't know," he said. "What's wrong with your Oldsmobile?"

"Nothing!" I replied. This was my first car. I used to shine it and buff it so I could tool around in style. "It's in perfect condition, original miles." My Olds was pristine. His black 1959 Volkswagen was a little beat-up, but I really wanted one of those Beetles. I talked him into trading straight up.

When I pulled the Volkswagen into our driveway, my father freaked out. "Why did you . . . !"

Our neighbors the Cesaris got it. They always had cool cars. Lucy Cesari gave me a vote of confidence. "Feather it," she said, "sand it in circles lightly, and it will be beautiful!"

"Dad," I told him, "I'm going to paint it; I'm going to clean it up!"

I hand-sanded the whole thing. I saved my money and had the body painted army green. I buffed up all the chrome, polished the engine, took it apart, and put it back together the way my dad did his watches, and then I had the coolest Volkswagen around. Only then, I think, did my father understand.

A few years later, people in my neighborhood started getting sports cars. I fell for the two-seater convertibles with wooden steering wheels and leather upholstery. The noise they made, the double hum as they shifted, was intoxicating. I dreamed about getting on the highway and driving in the sunshine with the top down. I went from loving sports equipment to loving sports cars.

Before I even knew what a Blue Book was, I was in and out of every used car lot in the area, asking, "How much is this? How much is that?" My first love was American cars. The Mustang. The Thunderbird. I watched Corvettes roll down the road and thought, "I'm dying for one of those." Bucky Campbell drove a navy blue Pontiac Bonneville with four on the floor. We'd go out riding with the guys and Bucky would pop the clutch and lay patches on the road. What a thrill!

Flea Hanrahan, who had worked with me at the Hess station, owned a Corvair convertible, Ralph Nader's *Unsafe at Any Speed* death car. Maroon, with a black interior and white top. Flea was running into financial problems and needed money, so I said, "Why don't I trade you my Volkswagen and I'll give you a hundred bucks?" And so I had a Corvair. Four speeds, spinner hubcaps. I thought of it like a Corvette, and driving it was a thrill.

Then I became obsessed with English roadsters: MGs, Triumphs, Jaguars. I loved Austin-Healey 3000s and MGAs, too. Our family friends the Benedicts imported a Mercedes from Germany, and we began seeing BMWs and Volvos. I was fanatical about cars: the looks, the sounds, the speed.

But mostly I wanted a car so I could get out of there. My house was claustrophobic—too many kids, too much noise, too much chaos, too much of my father coming home angry. I felt if I had a car I'd be free.

My dad dressed very well. He wore tweed blazers, Hathaway button-down oxford shirts with Rooster ties, Alden shoes, Hart Schaffner & Marx or Hickey Freeman suits, and always a London Fog trench coat and Dobbs hat. When choosing clothes, I always had him in the corner of my eye, though I didn't want to look as formal or "old." My school wardrobe was a blue oxford button-down shirt, a pair of Levi's, a pair of chinos, a wool V-neck sweater or two, a Baracuta jacket, a pair of Converse, maybe a cotton turtleneck, and a Lacoste polo shirt.

As I said, fashion in Elmira was preppy. I looked at the students who dressed well and wondered how they could possibly afford to have new clothes on a regular basis. My school was filled with Gant shirts, Bass Weejun loafers, and Coach belts. (I have always been brand conscious. I didn't want no-name jeans; I wanted Levi's. I didn't want Thom McAn shoes; I wanted Weejuns. I didn't want unbranded anything; I thought brands meant better products.)

There were some very beautiful girls in my high school, and part of their beauty had to do with the clothes they wore. I'd started looking even earlier. My girlfriend in seventh grade was a sixth-grader named Pam Yunis. (Her cousin, my great friend John Yunis, is a fashion plate to this day.) We used to go to her house and listen to the Four Tops and make out. Pam wore what everyone in school was wearing—John Meyer of Norwich Shetland sweaters with a little grosgrain trim, Ladybug blouses with Peter Pan collars, jumpers. That, to me in those days, was sexy. Plus, she smelled great—she wore *men's* cologne, English Leather!—and I had the best sense of smell. Pam Peterson, Pam Beecher, Susie Peterson, Janet Murphy, Barb Schott, Gayle Schweizer—there were lots of pretty girls wearing cute outfits. I'm not sure my friends looked at the whole package the way I did, thanks to my five sisters. Other guys checked out faces and figures, but I'm not sure *clothes* registered on their radar.

L ike most kids with any sense, in 1964 I had watched the Beatles on Ed Sullivan. I loved the music and thought it was so cool that they had mop tops and were a bit irreverent. I owned one 45: "Love Me Do" backed with "P.S. I Love You." I had a transistor radio in my room and listened to whatever was on AM—Gerry and the Pacemakers, Herman's Hermits. During high school, a friend's brother came back from California with Doors and Cream records, and I got hooked. I loved the music, and I loved how the bands looked. The whole music scene was carefree, a middle finger to adults in ways that had never been done before.

And then the cool guys at my school started growing their hair a little long. My friend Larry Stemerman—the one with the Beatle boots—grew a mustache and sideburns, and I wasn't even shaving yet! I wanted to be like them, but I had grown up thinking I was going to be an athlete like my dad wanted, and the jocks in school had short, neat, Marine-style haircuts. For the longest time I stayed clean-cut and well-groomed.

By my junior year, 1968–69, the fashion and music revolution was beginning, and I really wanted to be a part of it. The problem was, I was seventeen, but I looked twelve. I was dying to have facial hair, a deep voice, and hair on my legs. Elmira College, an all-girls school, was in our neighborhood, and when guys went to the college bars where the coeds hung out, I had to stand on the sidewalk. My friends were dating college girls, and I wasn't! But finally we found one establishment, Bill's Bar, that didn't care who they let in. Once inside, I loved the fact that the music was pounding and there were a lot of cool girls around. We lied about our age and told them we went to Cornell. None of us ever told them we were in high school and living with our parents.

When I told my dad that I wanted to grow my hair—actually, when I just stopped getting it cut for a month or two—he didn't want to hear about it. When I told him I didn't believe in the Vietnam War, he threw a fit. My father thought Vietnam protesters should be jailed. He did everything he could to stop me from looking like a hippie, but it didn't work. I felt so rebellious. I wanted to disagree with anything my father believed in.

The summer of 1969, the summer of Woodstock, a bunch of my friends were going to Cape Cod to find work. I thought, "That's what I want to do!" I quit my job at the Hess station and went with them. I was finally eighteen, I had a car, and there was nothing keeping me in Elmira. I was out of there.

When we drove into Hyannis, the first thing I noticed was how dorky all these New England prepsters looked in their chinos and madras. Walking the same sidewalks was a large sampling of hippie rocker types who looked like they were having a much better time. I wanted to be a part of the cool crowd. I looked at myself. I had some changing to do.

The next morning, dressed in my button-down oxford shirt, Levi's, and Converse, I went out looking for work. Starting at the top end of Main Street, I entered every single business establishment on the right-hand side. No. Nope. Nothing right now. I reached the end, crossed over and made my way back up the other side. No. Nope. Nothing right now. Then halfway up the block I walked into the Sunflower Shop.

Black light, posters, lava lamps, funky jewelry, Steppenwolf blaring out of the hi-fi. The scent of incense combined with candles, the quintessence of gift shop cool, pervaded the place. I loved it. The Sunflower Shop was everything Elmira was not, everything I wanted to be, all in one storefront. I asked if there was a job available. "Have you ever worked in a store?" asked Ken Helleburg, the proprietor. I told him about Lou Pal's. "Okay, come in tonight. Seven p.m."

I worked from seven till midnight. Hyannis was a big tourist town, and people flowed in and out of the Sunflower like it was a club. Despite the fact that I was completely unfamiliar with the products, I waited on people, sold them what they wanted, pointed them toward items, struck up conversations, had a great time. I had never been afraid to pick up a broom or do whatever was needed to help out, and after the first night I was given more hours; by the end of the week, Larry Stemerman and I were in charge of the place.

The Elmira guys—eight of us!—jammed into our rented attic in a small house on Ocean Street. The party started the moment we got there, and lasted all summer. We drank beer, smoked pot, took LSD. I had never indulged back home. I took mescaline once, and it was exciting. I took acid after that, and it was scary. Very scary. So scary that I became extremely cautious about what intoxicants I ingested. I smoked some pot, but it made me increasingly paranoid, and I didn't like being out of control. I was too fanatical about work to mess with something that made me so uncomfortable.

But I loved the rest of the sixties culture! I bought a turntable and started my record collection in earnest. In the attic we played the Doors, the Rolling Stones, Jimi Hendrix, and Steppenwolf till all hours of the morning—loud! Not only was the music enthralling, but I also thought Jim Morrison and Mick Jagger and Hendrix looked really cool. They exuded a sense of danger that I found exciting.

I tossed my preppy stuff in a corner and bought my first pair of bell-bottoms and a thick belt to go with them. I bought a bodyshirt with a long collar. I bought sandals. I was never much into jewelry, though other guys were wearing beads and bracelets, but I found a leather jacket with free-flying fringe and wore it day and night.

We hardly slept, and when I woke up in the morning and went to the Sunflower Shop, our boss would give me and Larry a black beauty, a legendary amphetamine, along with our coffee, and we would be energized for the whole day. Running the store was so much fun that when my friends and some of the girls we'd met said, "They're having this festival at Woodstock. You want to come?" I said, "No, I like my job too much."

These were revolutionary times, and I felt if you weren't into it, you shouldn't be alive! I wasn't living in my parents' house. My father wasn't there telling me what to do. I grew my hair as long as I wanted. I was free!

# CHAPTER THREE

# PEOPLE'S PLACE

The time
of my Life!

The Tommy who had left Elmira for Hyannis was gone. When I got home at the end of the summer, I was decked out in my hippie clothes, my hair on its way down to my shoulders, my eyes a little glazed. I was eighteen and almost out of the house. There was nothing my father could do to change me.

My senior year, I signed up for the easiest courses. The teachers didn't want to keep me back again—they were as lenient as they could be without completely abdicating their role as educators. I was just trying to get by.

The thought of college petrified me. Education was the mark of a successful man, and my parents wanted me to succeed, but they could not afford to send me, and there was no way I was getting a scholarship. How was I going to pay for it? And if I did get in, how would I be able to stay? I needed some other future.

I wasn't so determined to graduate, however, that I was above skipping school once in a while. One October day, Larry and I took off for Ithaca, a forty-five-minute drive up Route 13. Ithaca was a college town, and with its cosmopolitan restaurants and business district, it was a lot hipper than Elmira. Having spent the summer in Hyannis, Larry and I knew a cool store when we saw one, and right in front of us was a stretch that included a leather store (The Beginning), a head shop, and a clothing boutique. Even Hyannis didn't have a head shop! Rolling papers, incense—students in Ithaca had a nice selection! We walked into the boutique and were impressed with their array of bell-bottoms. I had bought one pair over the summer, which I treated like the treasure it was. Here were dozens.

Larry and I eyed the jeans. "There's nothing like this where we come from," I said.

"Where do you guys live?" the manager behind the counter asked.

"Elmira. It's a wasteland. There's nothing to wear," Larry told him. "Why don't you open a store in Elmira? There is no store in Elmira like this."

The manager had no intention of expanding. He looked at both of us and said, "You guys should open it."

Yeah, right.

Jonathan Allen was our third Elmira Musketeer. I was "Hippo," Larry was "Stem," and Jon, because he never spoke, was "Blabbermouth." The next day, as we were hanging out after school, Larry said, "Guys, why don't we open up a store?" It was a Mickey Rooney moment: "Let's put on a show!"

I wasn't so sure. "How do we do that?" I said.

Larry was working at his father's shoe store, The Bootery, in a shopping center downtown. "I think there's a basement we might be able to rent," he said.

"How much do you think it'll cost?"

"I don't know. Let's go ask the guy."

The place was massive. Five thousand square feet. Low ceiling. Below ground, accessible only from the parking lot at the rear of the shopping center. It was dark and probably hadn't been painted or swept in a decade. The landlord, Mr. Edelman, gave us a very good deal: $50 a month, with zero security. On Thanksgiving Day, 1969, we took it.

We began painting the place black, but five thousand square feet was a lot of surface to cover, so we hung burlap bags on a wire and carved out four hundred square feet of selling space, including a changing room. We hadn't quite finished when it was time to go home for Thanksgiving dinner.

I was covered with paint when I walked in. Aunt Annie and Uncle Bill were over, and I knew I was being judged. Aunt Annie was a perfect little Irish Catholic woman, not a hair out of place, with perfectly groomed nails and makeup and stockings. Our own June Cleaver. I loved and respected Aunt Annie, and never wanted her to see me with dirt under my fingernails, but there I was, this long-haired kid with his face smudged, hands and arms slathered in black paint. They must have thought, "What happened to our nice little nephew Tommy?"

"I'm opening a store!" I told the family.

"What kind of store?" my mother asked.

"Kind of a head shop," I told her.

"What's a head shop?"

"They sell incense and candles and hippie clothes," one of my sisters chimed in.

"Oh, how nice, Tommy!" said my mom.

"You can't start a business without any knowledge of retail," said my father. "There's no way you can do that."

Not "What a great idea, I think what you're doing is smart." Not "I think it's great that you're working and trying to make money." My dad wasn't too happy. He wanted me to go to college and get a degree, he didn't want to hear about a store I was opening. If I had told him I was going to jump into a space capsule and go to the moon with Neil Armstrong, he would have looked at me coldly and said, "You are such a loser." After years of his disdain, I expected it and I was ready for it, but that didn't lessen the sting. Now I understand— sort of. But then I really wanted his blessing.

After dinner I met Larry and Jon back at the store, and we finished painting. Then we went to a coffee shop to strategize. We were going to open a week later, on December 1, but first we had to get some goods to sell.

We called our boss at the Sunflower Shop and drove to the Cape the next day to buy some of his leftover jewelry. We drove back to Ithaca and bought twenty pairs of bell-bottoms.

We were ready.

We opened on a Saturday. We were already known as those guys who'd come back from Cape Cod different, and when we told our friends, "We're opening a store!" they all came by to see what we were doing.

We called our store People's Place.

Jon Allen sat silently at the door with a cigar box for the cash— this was way before anyone I knew had a credit card—and every item sold. Every single item. Our friends loved it! We desperately needed to restock. Now we had $200. Where could we find bell-bottoms right away?

New York City!

Two days later, Larry and I hopped in his car and made the four-and-a-half-hour drive.

I had a little history with New York City. When I was fifteen, a group of us had taken a Greyhound bus down for a weekend. Our parents sent us off with frightening stories: "Be careful! There are kidnappers! There are killers!"

The streets were humming with energy, traffic, pedestrians, stores. You could smell the hot dogs and sauerkraut from the pushcarts. You could smell the burn of the subways rising from grates on the sidewalk. We walked to Times Square and saw pimps on the streets, signs for peep shows, and the titles of burlesque movies on the neon marquees. I had never experienced anything like this before! I tried to be cool, but I was truly scared.

We ended up in the Village on Bleecker Street and saw beatniks—guys sitting on the sidewalk with berets, beating on bongo drums. I didn't know what they were smoking, but it smelled weird. We sat at outdoor cafés and were thrilled.

A year later, a bunch of us visited the city again. My friend Larry's mother was from Brooklyn, so his family went back and forth regularly, and his older sister, Lynn, told us where to go. To us, she was super-sophisticated, and she took us under her wing, even letting us sleep on her couch.

John Shingler's hip older brother, Rob, was living in Manhattan on Second Avenue and 84th Street, and we wanted to hang with him because he represented what could happen if we ever got out of Elmira. But while John was growing a goatee and Larry had John Lennon–style wire-rimmed glasses and sideburns, I was still baby-faced. "Rob, let's go hang out," his kid brother said.

Rob looked at me.

"No, I don't really . . ." He had no desire to be seen with some preppy little preteen-looking runt of a kid. I would decimate their cool factor.

So we headed down to the Village without him. The Velvet Underground was playing a club on Bleecker Street. We bought tickets and sat at a round table, waiting for things to begin. I had never been to a show before. I perused the menu and found that Coca-Cola was $1.50 a glass. Cokes cost a quarter where I came from. When the waiter came over I declined. "No," he told me, "you have to have a drink." I nursed that Coke the whole night.

When the burgundy velvet curtains opened and the stage lights went up and the band started, I got chills. Their backs had been to the audience, and when the music started, they all turned around in unison. So this was rock and roll! What power! Loud, driving, unstoppable. I had heard music on the radio and I had my favorite records, but no one had told me about the difference between hearing sounds on vinyl and having a professional band wailing ten feet away. My world was literally rocked!

I didn't want to leave Bleecker Street. Ever. I wanted to hang out and bask in the energy, be a part of the ambience. I no longer had any interest in being in Elmira, New York. And yet I had to go back and finish high school.

So here we were, back in the city again. It was only a year later, but I wasn't the same kid anymore.

We headed straight for St. Mark's Place in the East Village, one of the epicenters of New York counterculture shopping.

To me, St. Mark's Place between Second and Third Avenues was the center of the universe. The Fillmore East was two blocks away. This was where the Grateful Dead, Jimi Hendrix, the Byrds, the Who, Steppenwolf, and Jethro Tull—bands we revered but could only dream of seeing live—headlined nightly. The street was filled with people who, if they weren't musicians, looked like musicians. The beatniks were gone, and New York was filled with hippies. Where even to start? Larry's cousin Sam Wortzel, who owned a children's clothing store on the Lower East Side and knew the game, suggested we check out a shop called Limbo.

We walked up the metal stairs at 4 St. Mark's Place and entered a long, wide room that had been the parlor floor of a brick home owned in the 1830s by Alexander Hamilton's son. The place smelled of old clothes, incense, and musk. Psychedelic rock came out of the speakers. One of the owners, a man in his fifties named Fred Billingsley, was behind the counter. The phone rang, and he answered sharply, "Limbo!" People our age were lined up at the cash register. Marty Friedman, a more soft-spoken gentleman and the other owner, stood across the room behind old-fashioned, wood-trimmed glass cases displaying shirts in all patterns and colors. Trousers were folded on shelves, and black leather car coats, motorcycle jackets, fringed suede vests, purple snakeskin boots, and emerald-green velvet jackets were crowded onto round racks in the back of the room. You really had to maneuver in there. A bunch of colorful shirts on hangers were dangling from the ceiling! There were scarves and torn jeans and hippie fashion at its craziest, and guys and girls were trying on everything, talking to each other about how it looked, making important decisions. There was a Gypsy-like girl named Angel with big earrings and a bandana in her hair; she was working there and wearing all the clothes perfectly, probably the funkiest person I had ever seen in my life.

I was in heaven. We asked whether there might be any stock we could buy. "Bell-bottoms. You know, a lot of them."

Limbo got two hundred to three hundred pairs of jeans each month from a cowboy on the western and southwestern rodeo circuit, which they then embellished with embroidery and leather patches and sold for a bunch of money. However, because of the size of the garments, they often couldn't sell 80 percent of their stock. "Sure," they told us. "You can have six hundred pairs for two bucks each."

We didn't have that kind of money. We had one day's earnings—$200—from selling candles, incense, jewelry, and twenty pairs of pants. We made a quick call to Larry's cousin Sammy, who loaned us another $200. The embellished Western jeans were out of our price range, but we bought bell-bottoms in corduroy, twill, wool, and cotton, in stripes, plaids, and checks. A real assortment. We tried to cover a whole size range, from a 26-inch waist to a 36-inch waist. We crammed eighty pairs of pants at $5 apiece into the back of our car and sped back upstate to sell them for $11 each. Lou Pal would be proud.

We opened the store again on Monday at three-thirty, right after school. By Wednesday we were sold out. We jumped in the car at 4:00 p.m. and raced back to New York. This time we wanted everything we could get our hands on.

Limbo was where David Bowie, Jimi Hendrix, Lou Reed, and all the stars went for their clothes. After a couple of weeks, we, too, became regulars. Marty, one of the owners, would be behind the counter and in a very deep, serious tone he'd say, "What's going on, boys?"

We would ask, "Hey, Marty, do you have any excess merchandise?"

He would get up on a ladder and start pulling stuff out and throwing it down on the counter, some used, but mostly new: men's clothes and women's clothes, striped bell-bottoms from manufacturers like Landlubber and Viceroy, funky vests and shirts from cool brands like Gentleman John and Michael Milea. We learned a lot of brand names at Limbo. We negotiated a little bit. Larry would ask for a better price, and sometimes I would say, "Don't *hondel* with them, just get it!" (I believe I learned the word *hondel* from Larry; it's Yiddish for "negotiate aggressively.") We would pay for the merchandise, throw it in our car, and take off.

We knew next to nothing, but we knew we wanted to do this. We strolled St. Mark's Place and found the Whatnot Shop and hit them up for their excess hippie paraphernalia. We walked Second Avenue and bought from the Naked Grape, across the street from the Fillmore, where we'd heard Led Zeppelin and Jefferson Airplane had shopped. We found Leo Brody way downtown in a factory on Broome and Wooster Streets, when Soho was still desolate. Leo supplied a lot of the army-navy stores with surplus goods, but in addition had his own brand called UFO. He manufactured jeans, overalls, and jumpsuits, and had a line of fishnet vests and other cool things, all of which we snapped up. We found another old warehouse full of peace candles and incense. As our budget increased, so did our suppliers and our inventory. We were becoming more selective as time went on. I loved the editing process, the curation.

We sold out every week. This was Elmira, New York, in 1969. We were importing the counterculture, and everybody wanted some.

We wanted to run the coolest store in town. Since the entrance was a rear door off a parking lot, we put up a small display window out back so people would know we were there. Customers would walk down a flight of stairs and enter a whole other world. The original bare lightbulbs hung from the ceiling, and we'd added black lights and black-light posters. We had incense burning at all times. Many years earlier, the building had been a Montgomery Ward, then the country's largest retailer, and the space still had its raw wood floors and long tables. We put jeans on the tables. As our inventory increased, we built cubbies against the walls and displayed folded clothes. We got wire hangers from a dry cleaner. We bought brown paper bags and invited an Elmira college student named Judy Hanson to write PEOPLE'S PLACE on every single one. Judy was a great-looking girl with excellent handwriting and hair down to her waist. Larry was crazy about her. She added to the vibe by sitting in the store in lotus position, wearing a fringed vest, and painting PEOPLE'S PLACE on everything, including my portable record player. Judy lasted about a year and then disappeared.

One day, a girl we had never seen before showed up and said, "I want to show you my artwork." In her portfolio was a series of paintings of Alice in Wonderland. She was so talented! The hallway leading down the stairs was dark as a tunnel, so we had her hand-paint Alice and the Cheshire Cat and the hookah-smoking Caterpillar and the whole cast of characters in Day-Glo fluorescents on the wall. Welcome to People's Place! I bought a Pioneer turntable and some speakers so that when kids walked in, unlike anywhere else in town, they could count on hearing the Beatles, the Stones, the Who, Ten Years After, Cream, and Blind Faith. The moment we had enough bell-bottoms to spare, we strung them from the ceiling.

Running a store turned out to be a remarkable way to meet women. My most significant girlfriend to that point had been Kathy

Wilson, whom I had met on Main Street in Hyannis on July 5, 1969, walking out of a Friendly's ice cream shop. I had stopped and looked at her, and she'd looked at me, and it was almost as if we knew each other, as if I had known her from school or she was one of my sister's friends. She was very, very preppy and very, very cute. The next day we went to Friendly's and got coffee Fribbles, which is what they called milkshakes. She was in Hyannis for the summer, just like me. She was very sweet, a bit on the innocent side, and all-American, with long blond hair, a beautiful smile, and astonishingly perfect features. I took her to a drive-in movie and a rock concert, and before long I fell truly in love with Kathy. She was the girl of my dreams. My dad loved Kathy Wilson.

That fall, I visited her at her home in Fayetteville, New York, just outside of Syracuse. I got out of my Corvair wearing a turtleneck and a vintage military greatcoat I had purchased on St. Mark's Place that must have been down almost to the ground. My Landlubber bell-bottoms were so long, as was the style, that I was walking on the hems, which were frayed and dirty. My hair was long. When I came to the door, her parents looked me up and down as if I had just gotten off a spaceship from Mars. They were very nice, but I could read from their body language that they were not happy I was there to pick up their daughter. (What I didn't know at the time was that Kathy hadn't told them we were going to drive to visit friends in Worcester, Massachusetts. Mom and Dad were even less pleased when she failed to come home that night . . . and subsequent nights. So they weren't really too happy with me at all.)

Kathy went off to Middlebury College in Vermont. She visited me in Elmira a couple of times, and I visited her. I wanted her to come and spend more time with me, but she was serious about her schoolwork and decided against it. Then she got mononucleosis and couldn't travel. Eventually we grew apart, but Kathy and I remained friends forever.

And now we had every pretty girl in the world coming through People's Place! If I'd ever had concerns about dating, they were gone. I knew all the girls on the Elmira College campus, and I dated the ones I wanted to date, no problem. We'd go to Boss Tweed's at night, where I started seeing the adorable Karen Wolf, who looked like a blond-haired, blue-eyed pixie and was waitressing between classes. We'd put quarters in the jukebox and listen to Rod Stewart sing "Maggie May" over and over, eat the free popcorn, and drink dimies, ten-cent Genesee beers. All the suspense was gone; I was going to have company if I wanted it.

I loved it when I walked around my school and an increasing number of people were wearing clothes I had brought to town. I wanted everyone to look like we looked. Larry and I began making weekly trips to New York to restock. One day we were walking down the hall between classes when our school's vice principal and truant officer, Mr. Fitzgerald, approached. "Hey, boys, you haven't been in school for two days."

"Right," Larry said, "we've been in New York buying goods for our store!"

As we became more savvy, we learned we didn't have to rely on Limbo for merchandise; we could go directly to the manufacturers. Larry's father, Bob Stemerman, gave us a huge helping hand, for which I will always be grateful: he loaned us his line of credit. Until that time we had been required to pay cash for everything and cart it home, but now we could actually place orders and get delivery. By this time, I had been a constant presence in the Stemerman household for years. Larry's dad was calm and steady. He taught me to think things through, to look at all aspects of a problem before making a decision. I was part of the Stemerman family, with Mr. and Mrs. S. and Larry's siblings, Lynn, Steve, and Bruce. I found the experience entirely warming and welcoming. Although I loved my family, it was a different experience at the Stemermans'. They had a close family bond that was missing from my household. As opposed to our dinner table, which was chaotic and noisy and filled with babies and kids and fear of my father's anger, the Stemermans actually had conversations and enjoyed each other's company! I found that wonderful. I loved the way Bob Stemerman thought, and I adopted him as the dad I never had.

Larry and I attended our first boutique trade show, where manufacturers and wholesalers presented their goods, at the Statler Hilton Hotel on 33rd Street on a weekend in February 1970, and found brands such as A Smile, Michael Milea, Gentleman John, Faded Glory, Brittania, Bouncing Bertha's Banana Blanket, Billy Whiskers, UFO, Landlubber, Viceroy, and Cheap Jeans showing their wares. It was a visual explosion. Hand-crocheted dresses and vests, tie-dyed T-shirts, tie-dyed velveteen bell-bottoms—it was all there. Clothes you would see rock stars wearing in *Crawdaddy* magazine, clothes you would see on people in the Village, clothes you would see people wearing at concerts. How I wish I could go back in time and walk through there, knowing what I know now. There were so many wild personalities and great ideas! Fashion was igniting, and all of a sudden we could bring anything we wanted to Elmira!

I still thought Limbo was the best clothing store in the world, and I wanted People's Place to feel just like it, only even cooler, if such a thing was possible. When another store in downtown Elmira went out of business, I bought all their glass showcases, which they were practically ready to throw out. We put them in front of our jean wall and inserted all of our shirts. I wanted people to pore over the glass cases and say, "Can I have one of those in a medium? One of those in a small?" That's the way Limbo did it. I made sure all the shirts were folded perfectly and set in stacks according to color; it made the store look very official, as opposed to being a big mess. I wanted everything to be neat and orderly, like a real professional retail operation. I pinned some shirts to the walls and hung others from the ceiling so people would walk in and be enveloped in a world of fashion. We were selling a lifestyle that didn't exist in Elmira. We were *creating* a lifestyle.

# CHAPTER FOUR

# MAKING IT

*Going
Places*

When I graduated from high school, my escape route was right in front of me. I was in business, and my store was making money. My mom was happy for me. My prayers had been answered: I had something to do that I was passionate about!

My father told me it would never last, and insisted that I either get a real job or go to college. He gave my mother a hard time until she supported him. I caved. I wanted to show my parents that at least I was doing *something* they wanted me to do.

I signed up for Corning Community College because there was no entrance exam: you applied, you were accepted. I paid for it myself with earnings from People's Place, but I had absolutely no interest in being there. When classes started, I was totally distracted, thinking about my business. It was the most wasted time in my life. I met a teacher, Dick Luce, who was a fun guy and whose business partner, David Kastle, helped design my first People's Place logo, but otherwise, going to school was useless. They were talking about macroeconomics and microeconomics, but I was thinking, "The faster I can get back to my store, the more money I'm going to make, and the more fun I'm going to have." I was dying to get back to People's Place and rearrange the jean jackets and create new areas to display the fall sweaters. My parents wanted me to get a college degree so that I could get a good job and make money, but I was making money already, and enjoying what I was doing. What was wrong with that?

I lasted two months. Then I quit Corning and didn't tell my parents. Larry and I rented an apartment that we ran like a party house, with Elmira College girls every night and music blaring. Then we'd get up in the morning and go to work.

Before graduating from high school, Larry, Jon, and I would only open the store after school and on weekends. Now we had a full day to sell. We opened at 10:00 a.m., expanded our lines, opened a record department, and hired more pretty girls and cool guys. We had a head shop, though many people assumed from looking at us that we were selling dope. Parents would call the Elmira police and say, "My kid is going to People's Place to buy leather. What kind of a drug is that?" (We did have a leather shop where we sold Joel Labovitz's handmade belts, sandals, and vests. But we never sold drugs.) The cops thought we were drug dealers, too. But we weren't; we were much more into fashion.

The cops and I went back a ways. When we were in high school and needed a place to take girls, Larry, Jon, and I used the back of People's Place, behind the burlap, to party. We brought in a waterbed and found ways to put it to good use. One evening we'd gone to a concert with some college girls and wanted to keep the party going. But we couldn't take them back to our dorm room because we didn't have one—we lived at home. "Come on," we said, "let's go to the store."

We jumped in separate cars, and Larry arrived first. He was making a racket, pounding on the door, thinking I had already arrived—"Tommy, can you hear me?"—when what he remembers as eight cop cars swooped up behind him.

"What are you doing?" they asked.

Larry couldn't come up with a good answer. "I'm waiting for Tommy!" is what came out.

Then I pulled up. "Hello, officers," I said, and then opened the door, led them downstairs, and gave the squad a guided tour of our establishment. They were dumbfounded. We had a good rapport with the police from then on.

As our reputation and inventory expanded, it didn't take much to increase the size of the store itself. We simply moved the burlap divider a little farther toward the back wall. Jon would sit at the counter with his long hair, floppy hat, and granny glasses, holding his acoustic guitar and taking the money; Larry would run around the store talking to all the girls; and I would be up on a ladder creating displays and making the place look cool. All day, every day. There was no place that was more fun.

By now we were taking in thousands of dollars a day and selling out of everything, but we were still using a cigar box as our cash register. The money was usually Jon's domain, but that changed when our draft numbers came out. In 1969, in order to beef up the size of the armed forces to fight the Vietnam War, the government reinstated the draft and everyone our age was on the line. In the second year of the lottery, Larry and I lucked into high numbers, but Jon's was low enough that he was clearly going to have to serve. He had no interest in fighting that war, so he sold us his piece of People's Place and went to Canada. We missed him—he was a good guy, very steady, very calm, very smart—but we kept on growing the business.

Jon and I stayed in touch, and he is still in Canada. Other guys we knew went to Vietnam. All three of the Elliott brothers, who used to terrorize me in the neighborhood and then invite me over to watch cartoons—went. Tommy and Dickie never came back.

Because there was no other store like ours in the area, we drew clientele not only from Elmira and surrounding towns, but also from New York State's entire southern tier and the wealthy little towns of northern Pennsylvania, which had nothing funky. We would be sold out by Saturday night, and on Sunday we'd jump in the car and drive to New York for more goods. We would always stop in Chinatown, which was very exotic to us Elmira boys, for dinner. Running a very successful operation built my confidence and self-esteem in a way I never could have imagined.

In 1972, with the store generating some money, I took a trip to London. My reason was simple: England was the ancestral home of my favorite rock and rollers. It had brought us Carnaby Street and mods and rockers, or, as Ringo said in *A Hard Day's Night*, "mockers." I wanted to settle there for a while and learn how they did retail. My goal was to design clothes, see people, absorb the British vibe. I intended to stay several months—I wanted full immersion. I don't think my partner, Larry, was too happy, and his cousin Sam Wortzel, who was overseeing our finances, wasn't happy at all, but that didn't stop me.

I went alone and stayed in a rooming house on the Chelsea/ Knightsbridge border. I walked up and down Kings Road every day, looking in the shops and at the people. The Brits were really different—certainly different from my Elmira neighbors, but also a lot more advanced than what I'd seen in New York City. They were more stylish. Their flares were wider at the bottom. Their jackets were shorter, with tighter sleeves and shoulders that were more squared. Their hair was longer. They wore scarves. They all looked like rock stars! In America, you would see a lot of guys wearing bell-bottoms, sandals, and a T-shirt, and think, "Okay, well he's part of the hippie movement, but he has no style." To me, the style was what mattered.

Biba in London was *the* emporium for women. They sold granny dresses and big hats and all sorts of cool stuff. Up and down Kings Road were the most incredible jeans shops and boutiques I'd ever seen. There was denim studded all over with rhinestones and embroideries designed by Marshall Lester. Stirling Cooper had been part of the swinging London scene and sold clothes to all the rock groups and cool people. Jump was owned by Louis Caring, whose son Richard I later had the opportunity to meet. Richard is friends with Sir Philip Green, who owns Topshop and a number of other successful fashion ventures. (Philip and his wife, Tina, are my great friends. He is truly one of the geniuses in the fashion business, with Topshop and Topman being fast fashion at its best.) Also important in that time period was Tommy Nutter, a tailor on Savile Row who made suits for the likes of David Bowie, Elton John, Mick Jagger, Rod Stewart, and others.

I hung out at night at a club called Tramps, which was the Max's Kansas City of London. It was much different from the New York scene. The people at Max's in Manhattan affected an androgynous, glam-rock bohemianism. More generally, American musicians like Kiss had a look of their own, as did Alice Cooper. Lynyrd Skynyrd, ZZ Top, and the Allman Brothers all had variations on a southern vibe going: casual, rural, earthy. And a lot of the American rock stars had a California, granola, hippie vibe. The Brits, on the other hand, carried themselves with a chic formality that was mod, Carnaby Street–like, and extremely groovy. Jimmy Page would wear high-waisted velveteen pants with studs and appliqués. Queen—I mean, these guys were unbelievable. T-Rex was sort of the head of it. Bowie changed personas like he was trying on new suits. And Elton with his suits and feathers and huge glasses and general flamboyance was just so far over the top, he was in his own world!

The New York Dolls picked up the English style in their way, leaning heavily on their own punk androgyny. Lou Reed dabbled in it. But if you looked at English artists like Rod Stewart, Small Faces, Eric Clapton, and the Who, they were not only amazing musicians, but style icons in the making.

I wanted to study this style, take a little bit of this and a little bit of that, and bring it into my idea blender. I decided I would learn as much about jeans as possible; they were the basis of the whole lifestyle. Many restaurants and clubs would turn people away for wearing such casual clothing, and you certainly couldn't wear jeans to work. But I felt jeans were indicative of an entire cultural revolution that was beginning and that they would be a part of our lives forever. I wanted to be an expert.

So I walked into a store called the Jean Machine on Kings Road and asked for a job.

"Do you have papers?" I didn't know what that meant. "Well, if you're going to be working in London and you are a U.S. citizen, you have to get papers."

"Don't worry," I told them, "I'll get them."

"All right. You may begin tomorrow morning."

I found myself standing on the Jean Machine selling floor like a fish out of water. I was accustomed to running my own store, telling everybody what to do, picking out the merchandise that I wanted to sell to my customers, displaying the clothing as I wanted it displayed. I was not British. My style was more informal. Jean Machine employed a system in which the customer was not permitted to touch any of the merchandise. The salesperson was responsible for show-ing his or her client the jeans and, if the sale didn't happen, for fold-ing them up perfectly and replacing them on the shelf. For a supposed purveyor of modness, the store was extremely regimented and uninspiring.

But I did make a great discovery: Made in Heaven jeans, the most unbelievable jeanswear I had seen in my life. Each pair was washed and faded and pieced and patched and detailed exquisitely. Even the label, spelling out HEAVEN with jagged lettering, was sewn memorably. I tracked down the owners and said, "Why don't you let me bring this back to the States? I can sell it in my own store and I can sell it in New York." They agreed.

On my way home from London, I hung out in New York for a few days before driving back to People's Place. What became clear to me as soon as I reached Elmira was that I hated it. The culture shock was profound. After weeks on Kings Road, my store seemed so pro-vincial now, so behind the times. I wanted real excitement. I began looking for something else to do. I dreamed of creating my own brand.

I took the Made in Heaven samples to Barneys, which in the early 1970s was transitioning from a discount department store to some-thing greater and far cooler. (A year after we did business, they were credited with introducing Giorgio Armani to the American public. At that time, the *New York Times* described Barneys as the place "where wealthy hipsters could take pleasure in a $60 bath towel.") I met with Gene Pressman, the son of owner Fred Pressman and grandson of the founder, Barney Pressman. Gene was in charge of the boutique on 17th Street and Seventh Avenue. He looked at the merchandise and gave me an order.

Made in Heaven jeans were the first really cool English jeans in Barneys, and they sold well. But reordering was a problem. There was a VAT tax; there was duty. There was no such thing as email or even fax machines at that point, and we had to do our business by mail, which took weeks. The fact that Made in Heaven was overseas didn't help. The communication between Made in Heaven and me and Barneys was very difficult. Restocking took too much time, and Made in Heaven wasn't really an export company. They expected me to import the clothes and then sell them to Barneys, but I didn't have the money for that.

By June 1972, People's Place had been in business two and a half years. The store was humming. One day when the weather forecast was stormy, Larry said, "Let's take a ride." We drove to Harris Hill, the highest point in Elmira, a pretty spot with a great view out over the nearby towns of Horseheads and Big Flats and the entire Chemung River Valley. Looking down, we could see that the Chemung River, which dominates the valley and flows straight through Elmira, had crested. Larry said, "Tommy, this is huge. All this water is going right into town. It's going to overflow, and it could flood out our store."

We drove back down, and Larry asked his father, whose shoe store was in the same shopping center as People's Place, "Why isn't anybody doing anything?" Mr. Stemerman shrugged. We told our other business neighbors, "There's gonna be a flood!" and they looked at us like we were nuts. People's Place was underground; any water in the streets was going to hit us first. We had to do something.

Fortunately, our building housed an elevator that went all the way down to the basement. The architectural firm on the top floor had extra space and very kindly allowed us access. We called friends and family and began packing and moving our entire inventory, including a huge new shipment of jeans. Our brigade of hippies, high school kids, college girls, and my brothers and sisters spent all day lifting and stacking and loading and unloading dusty boxes. (Even my father, who knew I had quit school and was beginning to believe that maybe what we were doing was a good idea, helped.) Exhausted, we hauled the final heavy cartons to the sixth floor at midnight.

By seven in the morning the whole town was under water.

Hurricane Agnes had stalled over the Chemung River Valley, dropping twenty inches of rain. Just as Larry had said, the water had to go somewhere, and it devastated Elmira. Three of the four downtown road bridges were washed away. Apartments and automobiles were lost. People had to be evacuated from their homes. Sirens howled, and helicopters buzzed overhead. The National Guard was called out. The entire county was in a state of emergency. There were rowboats on Main Street! It was awful. People lost everything.

Then it dawned on us: if every store in the entire valley was wiped out, there were no more clothes in Elmira. Except ours.

Larry's grandfather owned a building on the corner of College and Roe Avenues, an area that had escaped the devastation. His uncle ran a liquor store there, but the storefront next door was empty. "Grandpa," Larry asked, "can we rent this space?" Grandpa was happy to oblige.

To support the devastated community, the American Red Cross provided $100 checks to anyone who could prove they had lost everything, and on the day we opened, we had a line out the door. We were happy to help. We offered discounts. If we were selling jeans for $5.88 each, we did two for $10. We sold more clothes than you could possibly imagine. For months afterward, we saw dads in tie-dye and little old ladies wearing bell-bottoms. People's Place became a household name, and our style, once very outside mainstream Elmira tastes, became the norm.

After months of rebuilding, we rented the main and second floors of the building in which People's Place had originally occupied the basement. Now we had a big corner store. We had a men's department, a women's department, a jewelry department, and cool accessories in Joel Labovitz's handmade leatherwear. The balcony upstairs housed our hair salon, and the original downstairs space was now our record department, still rocking and rolling. We were running a giant Rock Style emporium!

We became pillars of the economic community, mostly thanks to Larry. We joined the Rotary Club. We met mayors, store presidents, people way on the other side of the generation gap. And not only that: because of our economic foresight, Larry was appointed by Governor Nelson Rockefeller to a position on the New York State Urban Development Committee. He really enjoyed playing with the grown-ups, but I had no interest in going to meetings and hearing these people speak. My focus, my passion, was making our store and our business great.

We were twenty-one years old. My excitement was restored!

Rock-and-roll bands began to show up and buy clothes for their weekend gigs. I loved music. I'd bought a bass for $70—a Höfner violin bass, a Beatle bass just like Paul's—and taught myself Cream's "Badge" and "Sunshine of Your Love," but I wasn't really good, so I gave it to my brother Andy, who was eight years old at the time, and taught him what I knew. Andy was a natural. He picked up that instrument and played it every day, never put it down. Rock and roll became his life.

When I still lived at home our whole house had been filled with music. We had five bedrooms and nine kids, so we all shared rooms, each with different sounds coming out of them. Billy would be listening to Uriah Heep and Johnny Winter, Dee Dee played Carole King, Andy would be rocking out to the Stones, and I would be blaring the Doors, Cream, Traffic, Hendrix. Billy played guitar and had real talent, as did Andy. Because I couldn't play, when they got a little older and began to put together bands I managed them, helped them get gigs, and dressed them. When we held a fashion show at People's Place, they were the entertainment. Billy joined a band called Glass Head, and Andy was in Vaudeville and then Fright. Years later Billy and Andy would play together in King Flux, headed up by Richie Stotts after the breakup of the Plasmatics, with Marky Ramone on drums.

Bruce Springsteen and his band bought clothes from us on one of their first tours, in 1973. The J. Geils Band came in as well. The lead singer, Peter Wolf, showed up with an absolutely beautiful wife, Faye, extremely well put together and dressed with sophistication.

Faye immediately took a liking to my handsome little brother Andy, who was about eleven at the time. (It was quickly pointed out to me that this was the actress Faye Dunaway, who had starred in the movie *Bonnie and Clyde*.)

We went backstage at their concert that night, which was a thrill for me. I brought Andy because I thought it would be cool for a little kid to be backstage, and because he and Faye had hit it off so nicely in the store. We were sitting at the side of the stage when Andy saw our brothers Billy and Bobby out in the crowd smoking pot. He said, "I'm telling Mom and Dad!" I had to convince him otherwise.

Somehow afterward, as he was walking past a stack of equipment, Andy cut his finger on a piece of metal and began to bleed. Faye quickly called for a Band-Aid, put Andy on her lap, and treated his boo-boo. I was trying to have a serious conversation with Peter, but I saw him watching his wife carefully. Peter Wolf was actually jealous of the attention his wife was giving an eleven-year-old boy! I found that funny. I don't think I'd realized yet that, while they might be famous and successful, performers were real people with real insecurities. That was a lesson worth learning.

Our store manager and high school friend Dino Pisaneschi understood the connection between the music and fashion worlds. He suggested we form a company to sponsor rock concerts. People's Place could sell the tickets, which would drive traffic into the store and be a great way to get our name out there. We called the company Further Adventures. Dino was CEO. Larry and I were presidents.

Our first concert was held at the Elmira College athletic complex, The Domes, and the headliner was B.B. King. We drew a large number of customers to the store because we were ticket agents, and the show sold out.

When King arrived on his tour bus, his business manager came to us directly and said, "How many tickets were sold? Where's the money? Before B.B. goes onstage, we want to be paid." B.B. and his crew were considerably older than we were, and I realized immediately that they were very serious businesspeople, and extremely buttoned up. They may have played the blues, but these guys opened my eyes to the fact that they were in the music *business*. They had decades of hard-earned experience; I had none. Until that moment I had simply been a fan, but this was a crash course in how the entertainment business worked, and I was impressed.

I had missed out on Woodstock, but when I heard that the Band, the Grateful Dead, and the Allman Brothers were all on one bill at the Summer Jam at the Watkins Glen Grand Prix Raceway, I was determined to be there. The raceway was about a half hour up Route 14 from Elmira, and the concert was being touted as the "next Woodstock," so we contacted the promoters, and People's Place became an official ticket distributor.

I knew something about Watkins Glen because my friends and I would go to watch the Formula One races. The Grand Prix was loud, exciting, spectacular. After the 1972 race ended, we had jumped some fences, gone into the pits, and headed straight for the Lotus John Player Special garage, our favorite. We sauntered inside and found all the mechanics and drivers standing around in black cotton JPS jumpsuits, just the coolest jumpsuits in the world. I thought, "These would be very cool to sell in the store . . . or to wear!" I had seen Pete Townshend in a white jumpsuit, or what the British called a "boiler suit," onstage at the 1970 Fillmore at Tanglewood music festival, featuring Jethro Tull, It's a Beautiful Day, and the Who. He had jumped four feet into the air playing "Summertime Blues." I felt this could be a very cool fashion trend.

I thought, "No way, they will never sell us these suits." How to get them?

My girlfriend at the time was a blond beauty from Ithaca named Laurie Brown. I said, "Laurie, go up and ask if you can have one of the suits." So Laurie batted her eyes at one of the guys, and he said, "How many do you want? We have a whole trunk full of them back here." She grabbed an armful. All that summer, every time we would go anywhere, people would say, "Where did you get those suits? They are incredible!" We felt a whole vibe happening.

I had samples made in denim that I hung in the store to see how many people wanted them—this was one of my first forays into market research. We could have sold a bunch, but I couldn't get them made. There was a lesson in that, too.

We sold tens of thousands of Watkins Glen tickets at $10 each, and made and sold hundreds of Summer Jam T-shirts, so Larry and I became honored guests. Six hundred thousand music fans showed up and, as with Woodstock, the roads became jammed with Volkswagen vans and campers. I spent the morning at the store, but Larry landed backstage by helicopter and found paradise. While festival goers couldn't even get close enough to see the stage and were sweltering out front, the backstage area featured an above-ground swimming pool, chefs barbequing, and garbage bags full of pot. There were no cellphones in those days, but a telephone system had been established, and Larry called the store to say, "There's no way you're getting here by car, and you missed the last helicopter."

"Don't worry," I told him. "I've got it."

The father of a kid who was a regular shopper at People's Place was flying back and forth from the concert as a doctor, shepherding injuries and drug overdoses to the Arnot Ogden Medical Center in Elmira. My mom was a nurse, and I knew my way around. I went to the hospital, walked into a supply closet, grabbed a pair of scrubs, and boarded the next chopper out. I landed backstage among the trailers. Right away I heard, "Doctor! Doctor!" Someone had fainted. I wasn't a doctor, but I played one at Watkins Glen—only for a moment, until a real one showed up. I scooted off, removed the scrubs to reveal my cool jeans underneath, and found Larry.

We had the time of our lives! Backstage was crawling with guys with very long hair and beards. They weren't hip New York hippies; they looked like California hippies or Georgia hippies, very earthy . . . and dirty. They seemed so far out of it—just so stoned.

We tried to stay out of the legendary concert promoter Bill Graham's way. Bill had a security squad with him, pushing people back to make sure that everyone was making enough room for Dickey Betts and the Allman Brothers to get on stage.

We hung out with some guy named Robbie Robertson. At the time I didn't know who he was; it turned out he was with the Band.

I was surprised he could perform—he wasn't the most coherent person in the world that day.

Word was going around that Watkins Glen was the largest gathering of people in the history of the United States. I don't know if that is true—the *Guinness Book of World Records* called it the "largest audience at a pop festival"—but it was pretty crazy.

To keep People's Place sharp, and also to have a good time, Larry and I would visit New York and head down to the Village. We'd go to Boston and Cape Cod. We'd go to Ithaca, L.A., London, anywhere people were having fun. We started going to New York's boutique shows and to manufacturers' showrooms. While our friends were going to college, Larry and I were building a brand.

I had an epiphany at a Statler Hilton boutique show. The Statler was a classic old hotel at the corner of 33rd Street and Seventh Avenue, right across from Madison Square Garden, with narrow corridors, worn carpet, and plaster walls that hadn't been painted for years. It was crumbling around me, but I didn't care. I was pleased to be a part of the industry. Each room on the floor was taken by an individual manufacturer and filled with merchandise. Salespeople in various degrees of desperation eyed the traffic and stood ready to attend. We bought jeans from UFO, patchwork madras Western shirts made in India from Gentleman John, and shirts in baby pajama prints with snaps and round collars from Michael Milea. Baby prints! We bought silky print shirts with long collars from Nik Nik, and shirts with big, rounded, dog-eared collars by Bon Homme.

Landlubber, a jeans manufacturer that had originally supplied bell-bottoms to the U.S. Navy and then hit it big when hippies adopted the look, had rented out the ballroom and was a major presence. The young businessman Lenny Rubin was running the company under its original owner, Martin Hoffman. When Landlubber became fashionable, it had expanded and hired Courtney Chan Sing as designer/creative director. Courtney had long hair and wore hip suits. When I found out what he did, I thought, "I want his job." I had never given real thought to designing, but at that moment it came to me: "This is what I want to do in life. I want to create a line of clothes. I want to be the one who picks the colors, the fabrics, who designs the pockets. I want to be that guy!"

Landlubber jeans were low-riding hip-huggers with little slit pockets, a short fly, and wide loops for thick belts. Their Chelsea jean had four patch pockets and was made from ten-ounce denim. People's Place was one of their biggest customers in the Northeast. We were selling a lot of Landlubber. But I thought I could do better.

The jeans shipment would arrive, and as I put them on the shelves I'd wish the pockets were located higher or the bells were a bit wider at the bottom. It didn't matter which company we were buying from; I kept thinking I could design better jeans. I had no training; I just felt what was right. The coolest people at the time were wearing bell-bottoms that were noticeably frayed and beat-up. The wear and tear meant that these guys had owned their jeans and been in the scene for a long time. Everybody wanted to be that hip. It occurred to me that we should take some of our jeans and bleach and wash them to make them look old and capture that essence of cool. This had rarely been done.

We bought navy surplus pants in white and took them to Second Avenue Cleaners on 12th Street, where Stanley, the proprietor, would dye them for us. Then he put our dyed jeans into the wash with more bleach than anyone would think advisable. The results were erratic but striking. Some pairs came out spotted; sometimes one leg would be whiter than the other. We could never predict what exactly we were going to get, only that every pair would be an original. When we took them back upstate, they sold in a hurry.

Next, I came up with the idea to wash the bleached jeans in machines with bricks and stones to really wear them down. We were speeding up and exaggerating the aging process, giving whoever wore these jeans the look of someone who had lived the life, who had been around. We were stonewashing our own jeans.

When Courtney left Landlubber two years later, I thought, "Okay, now they're really going to need more creative help." In my spare time I had designed denim vests, denim jumpsuits, skirts, and jeans with the intention of selling the ideas to Landlubber. I rough-sketched them and found two girls in Elmira—a Fashion Institute of Technology (FIT) graduate named Catherine McPherson and an artist named Rosie Larimer—who drew them for me more professionally. I took the designs to Lenny Rubin at Landlubber and was so anxious to get them into production that I gave them to him outright. "I hope you can use these," I said, and asked for nothing in return, though what I really wanted was the opportunity to continue.

The designer was not impressed. He flipped through my sketches and said, "We've already got a Landlubber vest."

I didn't know. I was only familiar with their jeans. I thought I was giving them a brand-new idea.

I knew what every other jean company was offering, I knew what young people wanted to wear, and I knew what *I* wanted to wear. I wanted to see if my ideas were as good as I thought they were, and Landlubber was telling me they were not. In my heart I knew I had it right. I knew it the way a musician knows the right riff or a chef knows the right taste. It came to me naturally. But here were the pros telling me I was wrong. I went home and cried.

Ultimately, Landlubber did use some of my designs, but they watered them down. The denim in their versions was too light-colored, too stiff and heavy. Not washed enough. I was trying to achieve a very specific look, and I knew how to achieve it. Landlubber had begun to lose its luster and did not create the clothes with the quality or attention to detail that I had expected.

Lenny Rubin left Landlubber and started a company called Succotash, and he asked me to go to Europe with him to find new ideas. In spring 1974, on a shopping trip I will never forget, we explored new boutiques in London, Paris, and Saint-Tropez, where I found unusual and incredible ideas that had not yet come to America. We sat in Saint-Tropez's Café Sénéquier and I sketched ideas for him as if they were coming from heaven. I was possessed! I thought that if we launched these ideas in the States, we would have the best jeans company in the country. Back home, I showed him how I would interpret the samples we had purchased to create a stunning brand.

Unfortunately, Lenny's partner, a former department store buyer, had her own design concepts. She wanted to make lightly washed jeans with basket-weave pockets that I thought looked very dated. Because she had experience in the industry and I had none, Lenny decided to listen to her. A year later, they had to fold the company. Not long thereafter, the brands Brittania and Faded Glory developed ideas similar to the ones I had proposed, and launched them to great fanfare and success. I was tremendously disappointed: I'd had a shot, I'd been there first with an idea that was right, but I had no brand to show for it. I still feel that if Lenny had taken my direction all those years ago, Succotash might be in business today.

This unfortunate experience made me realize I had to do it myself. I took real workwear worn by carpenters and mechanics and tinkered with it. I bought dark denim in bulk. I found orange thread—not as thick as I would have liked, but acceptable nonetheless. I found local seamstresses in Elmira, showed them the materials and designs, and had them create my clothes.

I was proud and excited when I saw the samples. In one of my first market research endeavors, I showed the clothes—under a NOT FOR SALE sign—to a wide range of customers in my store and asked, "What do you think?"

People were excited. I could have sold a bunch if I had any stock at all. I was dying to go into production, but I couldn't find the right factories. I didn't know how to get it done. We were retailers, not manufacturers. My "homemade" samples hung in People's Place as a challenge.

Larry and I were running around buying merchandise, and we needed someone to mind the store. My sister Betsy took over and did an amazing job of managing and overseeing everything in Elmira, where we had Scott Parker and a group of very pretty, very switched-on girls working the floor, including Mary Pat Spanbauer, Debbie Stanko, Lisa Parker, Tina Bateman, and Sharon Pritchard. My sister Dee Dee was our jeans expert and worked there with her school friends Debbie and Darcy Crumb, "the D's." We intuited, and it turned out we were correct, that people are more comfortable and more likely to buy in an attractive environment.

Next, we began expanding. Our second store opened in Corning, New York, and was run for a time by my sister Susie, who had just graduated from college. She was disciplined, smart, and well organized. When Susie moved on, we hired Mary Chely, a long-haired folk singer who would sit in the store and play her acoustic guitar.

We opened a store in Ithaca that could handle hipper and cooler merchandise, since its large customer base was made up mostly of Cornell and Ithaca College students with more informed tastes. We bought excess inventory from Barneys and Saks. We also contacted the Liebeskind family, who owned Ann Taylor at the time, drove trucks to Boston, and bought everything they had left from their warehouse sale at a dollar per unit for clothes and ten cents per accessory. We drove back to Ithaca and opened an off-price store we called The Wearhouse and sold a ton of stuff. We were T.J.Maxx before there was T.J.Maxx!

We opened a fourth store in Cortland, New York. Both Larry and I wanted to spend time in Ithaca because the scene there was so much cooler than back home, so we took turns, neglecting the other stores because we were kids. Larry's brother Bruce became manager of the Corning store, and he was a star. He showed such business acumen that for the first time, we felt we had someone we could trust managing the entire People's Place empire. That would have freed us even more! But Bruce decided to go to college.

There were other places we wanted to be. We were in New York City buying merchandise so often that we sublet an East Village apartment from Larry's cousin Sam Wortzel at 225 East 12th Street, near Second Avenue. At night, we went out clubbing. We had heard of Regine's, the chic private club on Park Avenue, and when we arrived we found a line of limos parked out front, dropping off Liza Minnelli, Halston, and other notables. We were eyed through a sliding peephole in the door and somehow allowed entry. Our first surprise was the admission fee; we hadn't expected one, and to us it seemed substantial. We drank as we usually drank—not grandly, but with gusto—and at the end of the evening were presented with the bill: $200! We were blown away. "Okay," I said, "we can't come here again."

Then we found Studio 54.

It was by no means a guarantee that we would get in. We had heard the stories, and they were true. When we arrived, there was a huge crowd of people pouring out of limos and waving money at the doorman, yelling his name: "Marc! Marc! Marc! Keith invited me, he's inside!" The drill was that you would stand on the sidewalk, and he would look over the mass of potential partygoers, point to some lucky person, and flag him or her in, editing for age, style, looks, and whatever else he had been instructed to consider. His job was to make sure the crowd consisted of people whom the owners, Steve Rubell and Ian Schrager, wanted to represent Studio 54. It helped to be with a bunch of people who all fit the description. Then he would point to another person and loudly say, "No, you're not coming in." Being on Marc's bad side was brutal.

Somehow we connected with Marc and the guys at the door. Maybe they liked our look, which was no longer hippieish but still showed a good sense of style. Whatever the reason, the first time we showed up, we got the nod. "Oh," we thought, "this is too good to be true." We had Elmira confidence, but this was New York City, and we were newbies. We couldn't believe he'd actually flagged us in.

The excitement and energy we felt walking into the club that first time was beyond exhilarating. The music was pounding: Gloria Gaynor, Diana Ross, Donna Summer, the Bee Gees, Nile Rodgers and Chic, KC and the Sunshine Band. Synthesized electronic disco and heavy-duty dance music had taken over, and while I still loved the original English rockers, I had to admit this was a lot of fun.

From that point on we showed up almost every weekend and often on Mondays after a full day of buying. We would walk up to the stanchions, wave and say, "Hey, Marc"—no screaming, no jumping up and down—and immediately be admitted.

Inside, Larry and I and our small group would get a booth or a place to sit, order drinks, check out girls, and dance. The sound system was amazing, mixing pulsating disco with seventies soul. Stevie Wonder was at the top of his game. Harold Melvin and the Blue Notes. The O'Jays.

We would see Andy Warhol, Bowie, and Bianca and Mick. We hadn't yet met them—there was a scene going on in the basement at Studio 54 that I was never invited to join—but we had met Halston, and Halston's boyfriend was a friend of a friend, so we had a few connections. Halston had his regular booth, and he was very friendly, so we usually got the next booth over. The problem was, you couldn't really hear people talk in the club. Even if you were screaming at the top of your lungs, the music was so heavy and so loud, and the lights on the dance floor so intense, that it was impossible to hold any kind of conversation. Most communication was done by hand gestures— a kind of club sign language. We rarely got home before five in the morning. This was our life!

We spent money like crazy. In Elmira we threw huge parties and had tons of girlfriends and other people around. We smoked more pot than you could ever imagine. We did our share of acid, speed, and Quaaludes. And of course we sampled mushrooms. I ate some at the Tanglewood festival, and it seemed to me like It's a Beautiful Day played for twelve hours, not just forty minutes. I got separated from reality and swept up in the crowd. I finally found my friends, but I was lost for hours. There was some cocaine around, but it didn't do much for me except make me grind my teeth and get sweaty palms. One day I was up, couldn't sleep, fidgety, and I asked myself, "Why am I even doing this?" When I didn't have a good answer I stopped everything. I had a kind of automatic shut-off valve. I would get to a certain point and say, "Okay, no more." I recognize that I am very fortunate to have survived it all, because I was living right in the heat of the seventies drug culture. There were a lot of people who didn't survive, who either lost their minds or OD'd or never made anything of themselves. I think Larry and I were very lucky: we were serious enough about making money and being successful that the drugs didn't become a high priority. I'm sure our parents worried about us, and I'm sure that some friends may disagree with me, because there were times when we were definitely on the edge.

Still, with or without drugs, we felt untouchable. In June 1977, I had bought a new Dodge van, and my girlfriend, Susie, my brother Andy, his bandmate Michael Houghton, and I were headed for the Blue Oyster Cult/Lynyrd Skynyrd/Ted Nugent/Starz all-day outdoor concert at Rich Stadium in Buffalo. On the way there, Andy asked, "Do we have tickets?"

"No," I told him, "but don't worry about it."

"How are we going to—"

"I got this. Don't worry about it."

"How—"

"We're going backstage."

We all looked the part. We drove up to the back gate.

"Credentials," said the guard.

I told him, "We're playing tonight. We're one of the bands."

He was not convinced. "You are?"

"Yeah," I said. "Look."

He stuck his head inside and found a van full of the most rock-and-roll-looking kids on earth.

"Go ahead."

We parked next to the limos and buses and headed to the wings. People with passes gave us "Who are these guys?" looks, but nobody had the balls to challenge us. We were standing offstage right, looking out at the eighty thousand people in the crowd, and who was down front but my brother Bobby. He was a great music fan and always had a way of ending up in front of the stage. Between sets he shouted up to us, "How did you do that?" I shouted back, "We're with the band!"

People's Place was making a lot of money, but we weren't saving any of it. We paid cash for a silver Porsche 911 right off the lot. We chartered a plane to take us and all our friends to a Stevie Wonder concert in Syracuse, and hired a limo that got us backstage. One time, Larry and I and our dates were zooming up to Rochester in our beautiful new Mercedes-Benz to see the Rolling Stones when we were pulled over for speeding. "Officer," Larry said, politely suggesting he look in the backseat, "I've got rock-and-roll stars." I rolled down the window. "We need to be there." We got a police escort.

Our friend Eddie Ravelson owned a cool boutique in Boston and had connections with a travel agency, International Weekenders. He routinely found space available on group tours that had not sold out. Eddie would call up and say, "Guys, you wanna fly to Brazil? We've got two seats empty" or "You want to go to Machu Picchu?" For sixty bucks we would get onboard. We flew to Hong Kong on a propeller plane, were put up in a decent hotel, and had a couple of days to explore the city. We went to the yacht club, where I asked to see a boat captain. We picked out an eighty-foot yacht and said, "We would like to try this for a day; we are interested in purchasing." They gave us the yacht and crew. There was nothing we couldn't do.

# CHAPTER FIVE

# FROM CHAPTER 1 TO CHAPTER 11

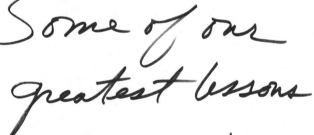

Some of our greatest lessons are learned from failure!

was in one of my stores when Larry called from New York and said, "I think I got us a design job."

I said, "Wow, cool!"

Santa Cruz Imports, a California company with a showroom at 1407 Broadway, was run by a bunch of hippies who were bringing in mostly womenswear from India: peasant blouses with embroidery and beads. Larry was in there buying when they mentioned they wanted to start a men's knitwear line, and David Hirsch, the owner, said they'd give us a chance to show our stuff. I put my jeans work on hold for a moment and started designing shirts. We designed knit shirts with plaid gauze collars, madras checks, and plackets with checks, in fabrics that were familiar and easy for their Indian factories to produce. I suggested combining the Indian fabrics with knit materials that were not readily available from India. Hirsch agreed. In homage to Santa Cruz's SoCal lifestyle, they called our line Ripple Knits.

Our first collection wasn't spot-on. We were making the goods at Milsan Mills in Lebanon, Pennsylvania, which was owned by a man named Larry Green. At the time, I thought he was an old-timer, but in reality, he was probably around fifty. Larry knew the knit business inside and out, having manufactured product for decades, and he taught me about the grades and weights of knitted fabric and garments. Milsan made large quantities of men's shirts, but they were golf shirts. Mine had to be hipper—they had to be skinnier and more fashionable. I wanted my ribbed knit shirt to have baby snaps, overlock stitching, prints, and a soft, brushed fabric from India that would feel like the Michael Milea knits coming out of Hong Kong. But when we arrived with our designs, the old-line Milsan pattern makers didn't understand how to make them. It was very hard to get our ideas across because in their minds they were experienced manufacturers of *real* men's shirts—and we were these young, upstart kids who didn't know what the hell we were talking about. They didn't realize we were making clothes for guys with hair down to their shoulders, who wore hip-hugger velvet bell-bottoms and blouses and high-heeled platform snakeskin boots and hung out at Max's Kansas City. In the end, Larry Green turned out to be a fatherly type, and I believe he thought we had potential, but when he saw us coming, I think he wasn't too happy.

We also had a run of production problems: we couldn't get the exact hand feel of the cloth I wanted, and the checks and plaids came from India late. It just didn't flow right. And in this business, everything has to really flow well. We knew we wanted to design our own collection, create our own brand. The Santa Cruz team turned out to be a bunch of surfer dudes, smoking a lot of weed and drinking a lot of beer. Yet they also wanted creative control, while *we* wanted creative control. I *needed* creative control. It quickly became clear that Santa Cruz Imports was not the right place for us. When they ran into some financial issues, we moved on. Another stepping-stone, another learning experience.

Next, Larry Green introduced us to Marvin Kleinman, an owner of Brentwood Sportswear. We had bought their sweaters for People's Place. Sol Nadler, their upstate New York salesman, was a cool old guy who would come to our stores with his sample line of sweaters. We would edit the Brentwood catalog and buy an assortment that fit our customers: reindeer and Fair Isle sweaters and whatever else we thought we could market with bells and flares. When we were done, he would take us to dinner at Pierce's or Moretti's, the best restaurants around, tell jokes, and have fun. We thought this guy was great.

Another Brentwood salesman was a different story. He looked at me one day and said, "Are your heels rounded?"

I had no idea what in the world he was talking about. I looked down at the high heels on my English rock-star snakeskin boots. "What do you mean?"

"I know you like girls. Do you swing both ways?"

"That's not my thing," I told him.

"You could always try it out."

I said, "TNT."

"What does that mean?" he asked.

"Thanks. No thanks."

Larry and I went to the Brentwood facilities in Philadelphia, and I started showing them sketches. Times were changing. The hippie look that had reigned for ten years was starting to wane, and I had begun thinking about a more fashion-oriented customer. I wanted skinny fits; I wanted heavier-gauge nautical-inspired sweaters with buttons on the shoulder; I wanted high-waisted sailor trousers, striped T-shirts, and military numbers. My tastes were developing, and I wanted to produce clothes that I would wear and that my partner, Larry, thought we could sell.

My ideas were not greeted warmly. The older manufacturers told us, "We can't change Brentwood Sportswear—it is already a great business."

So I suggested, "Why don't we do our own division?"

The co-owner, Marvin Kleinman, a very pleasant and soft-spoken guy, said, "Okay, let's do it." He allowed us to brand the new company.

This was 1976, and people were beginning to dress up, go to discos, live a more polished lifestyle. To reach these men, we created an aspirational fashion line under a designer name. My middle name is Jacob, Larry's is Alan. So was born Jacob Alan Sportswear.

My dream at that point was to build Jacob Alan to compete with Giorgio Armani and the other real designer companies, but I quickly realized how difficult that would be. In order to make garments of the proper quality and at the right price, you had to manufacture either in Europe or in Asia, and we were making our clothes domestically. American factories couldn't add the details that I wanted to focus on: many were not equipped to do this level of work, and others didn't want to because of the increased handwork and skill required. At the time, American manufacturers were primarily making mass-market goods for operations like JCPenney and Sears. I wanted better stitching, better ways of inserting the pleats on the trousers. I wanted to use European fabrics and do fine knits with cashmere and silk and linen, and at the time these could only be made in European or Asian factories because only they had access to the raw materials and expertise. To do the work in the United States, I would have had to import the raw materials and then scour the country for people able to construct the garments.

We found factories in New York and Pennsylvania, and Jacob Alan got off to a nice start. Our line consisted mostly of sweaters, a few trousers, and a couple of T-shirts. The department store B. Altman & Co. was very supportive and gave me the windows on Fifth Avenue and a whole department. B. Altman launched Jacob Alan, and we started to get some traction.

I was like a sponge. Anytime I went to a factory or store, I wanted to learn more, more, more, because I knew this was not the last stop on the train. We sold to Wanamaker's in Philadelphia, and a few others around the country. I called Gene Pressman and got us into Barneys. We designed a second line and it sold the same. Still, Jacob Alan needed more sales in order to survive, and we needed salespeople who could really go out and knock on the doors of all of the top stores. That demanded expertise and connections that were not easy to come by for a couple of guys from Elmira.

We lobbied Brentwood to find great salespeople, and they hired Pete Markow from McRae's department store in the South, a man with a notebook full of contacts. In one of the great eye-openers of my younger years, in 1976 Pete took Larry and me on a road trip and introduced us to the southern department store community. Jackson, Mississippi; Birmingham, Alabama; Nashville—we went all over. I showed each buyer the line. Sometimes we got orders; sometimes we got "Well, I'll think on it."

I had never been to the South, and I was blown away. I found the store executives to be very stiff and rigid, very southern in ways that fit my preconceptions. And they didn't quite get the fashion. It wasn't conservative enough for them—and neither was I.

Sales increased, but it was made clear to us that the Jacob Alan line wasn't quite broad enough. Plus, our relationship with Brentwood was not ideal. Even though we had our own label, there were rules and regulations and operational details that I found excessively traditional and old-world. I needed to be in an environment where I made my own rules and wasn't encumbered by unnecessary structure. For instance, lead time. We had to submit our designs in July and wouldn't see samples until January. I thought, "By the time January rolls around, that design is going to be passé!" I wanted instant gratification; I wanted to deliver a design, see the sample the next day, and put it in the store two weeks later (which, by the way, is how Zara, H&M, and Topshop operate so successfully today). I realized it was all about speed to market. It was then, and it is now.

There were a lot of old-timers in the corporation who I suspect were thinking, "Who are these whippersnappers, trying to design something today and market it next week? Why are these kooks from upstate New York trying to change our whole design philosophy? And they're designing sweaters with elbow patches—my grandfather wore that!" Well, we wanted to bring those classics back in a new way.

Ultimately, Marvin came to us and said, "Guys, I don't think it's working out that well."

We said, "Fine, give us back our name." Which he did. Brentwood also sold us our excess Jacob Alan merchandise, which sold nicely in our stores. Marvin was always very fair with us, and he was a very nice guy, but I think his organization held him back.

The mid-1970s was an exciting time to be in New York City. Max's Kansas City was open seven nights a week, and there were always parties and fun people there. One night we saw David Bowie at a table with Debbie Harry and Lou Reed. Another night I ate downstairs with Lou Reed and the New York Dolls' David Johansen, and then cabbed a few blocks to Ashley's on Fifth Avenue, where Billy Preston and Ronnie Wood and the Stones showed up. A seriously exciting time! I had access because we looked the part and people would not turn us away. Rock style was becoming paramount and powerful.

English style was also coming into New York around this time, with Led Zeppelin and the Who and other big bands on tour. Zeppelin and Robert Plant's frilly shirts had a spectacular effect. The bands were surrounded by their entourages, and the scene was androgynous, funky, and fun. It was the era of Marc Bolan and T. Rex— the beginning of glam rock. Larry and I bought a lot of glam rock clothes—silver motorcycle jackets, platform boots, frilly blouses, all the glitter and shine—and brought them back to our shops in up- state New York.

And that's when we had a rude awakening: people just didn't get it. We'd had an unerring touch until then, but what was fashionable in New York City within a certain sector did not travel well. I thought this thrilling scene was going to take hold in other parts of America, but I was wrong. The number of people in college towns in upstate New York who wanted glam style was minuscule. Because we were spending most of our time in the city going to clubs at night and not working as hard in the daytime, we took our eye off the ball. We bought too much inventory. Plus, it was 1976: the country was in a recession. Discount retailers woke up and figured out that they should also sell bell-bottom jeans, but at very low prices. The novelty of our hip style faded.

So did the novelty of driving around New York State visiting our stores. I didn't want to stay in Elmira and watch our business floun- der. Larry wasn't around much, either. We had both gotten bored. After ten years, I needed a bigger and better horizon—my dream of building my own brand.

Our division of labor put me in charge of designing and deco- rating the stores and Larry concentrating more on the buying. He was good at it, as was evidenced by the six-year string of successes People's Place enjoyed. In the mid-seventies, Larry met buying agents who worked in New York at the offices of the Stuart Mandel- baum company, whose job it was to give stores of all sizes access to an array of manufacturers. They would take Larry and me around the marketplace, and we would place orders for our stores. We were two young guys going into a New York showroom run by these glam- orous, sexy, somewhat older girls, and they seemed sort of impressed with these two boys running a business. We thought it was cool to brag to them about our commercial success: "Yeah, we're going to open stores in Syracuse and Rochester and Binghamton. We're going to open a store in New York City!" But when we told them business was booming, I think they were thinking, "Oh, they must sell thousands of units per week," when in reality we were selling hundreds. Both Larry and I made our suppliers believe we were a bigger operation than we were, and we allowed them to place orders for larger quantities than we could digest. We began to receive large shipments every day from dress houses and sportswear companies, in part because we were believing a lot of our own bullshit. Thinking big brought us success, but thinking *too* big would hurt us.

Some of these new suppliers suggested that we be on an automatic reorder system, and we were basically too embarrassed to say, "Hey, enough," or "We don't need all of that," so the goods kept coming, and our inventories kept building up. Larry's father had a store in Auburn, New York, and he shared half the space with us, so now we had People's Place, Auburn. And then some guys came along and said, "Hey, we have space in Lake George, and it's a summer location, everybody goes to Lake George. Why don't you share a space with us?" So we opened in Lake George.

Things were getting out of control. The credit line from Larry's dad was used up. We couldn't borrow any more money from the bank; they were already breathing down our necks to get paid on time. And we weren't selling enough merchandise to cover our expenditures.

To help us figure this whole thing out, we brought in Larry's cousin, Sam Wortzel, as a salaried partner. Sam, who was about ten years older than we were, was a real New Yorker: smart, fun, and funny, but with no real sense of style. He didn't care about style at all, which at the time I found to be a major flaw but now realize doesn't matter. He tried to help us organize and discipline our business, and I hated that. I didn't want to go through a formal restructuring process, because we were used to doing things our own way and coming and going as we pleased. Sam wanted to install inventory control systems. We were getting a lot of pilferage, so we put Sensormatic tags on our clothes. As a result, our expenses actually rose, but Sam was trying very hard to show us how to control them. And we were fighting it. Then he brought in Marty Levinson, a proper accountant from New York, to help us with our taxes.

Marty sensed something was wrong when he reviewed our inventory levels and our buying. He said, "Unless you bring more money in, you're going to have to make some big decisions."

I said, "Like what?"

"Let's talk to a lawyer," he told me.

"Why do we have to talk to a lawyer?"

He was very direct. He said, "There are different things that you can do."

I was not understanding. "What?"

"You can dump more money into the business . . ."

"Or?"

"Or you can go Chapter 11."

"What the hell is that?"

"It's a form of bankruptcy."

"*Bankruptcy?*"

"Unless you bring fresh money in," he explained, "you owe more money than you could possibly earn in the next six months. You have people who have sold you merchandise who want to get paid. And you've got employees and you've got overhead."

I said, "This is all bullshit. Are you kidding me? Why don't we just have a sale?" We were opening new stores, there were new streams of revenue. This had to be a mistake.

A sale, the accountant explained, was not going to do it. We were way too deep in a hole for a good week to dig us out.

We went to our banker, who told us, "We've already loaned you money, and you haven't paid it back. We will not loan you any more." The economy was starting to sour; competition was coming on; our stores were overstuffed with too much merchandise and not enough point of view. We would go to the boutique shows and buy cool stuff, only to get back and find it overshadowed by the bulk of our other inventory. This was Retail 101: Work within a budget. Be the editor with buying agents. Be up to date on the history of what has recently sold. And we were learning it the hard way.

So we filed for Chapter 11.

It was a terrible day. It was a huge slap in the face; it was embarrassing. I woke up and asked myself, "What the hell did I do? If we hadn't taken our eye off the ball, if we hadn't over-inventoried, if we hadn't bought too much glam and glitter, if we had closed two of the stores that weren't doing that well and put the focus on better management . . ." There was a litany of things we could've, should've done. We had been driving Porsches and Mercedes-Benzes, living in cool places, buying tons of clothes and expensive watches, and traveling to Europe and South America. We'd been living like multimillionaires when we weren't there yet. Nowhere near. I had saved nothing. All I could think was, "Oh my God, how am I ever going to start my own brand now? I can't leave the premises. I have to stay here and make sure that everybody gets paid." It was beyond depressing.

We talked to the lawyers, who told us we could stay in business but had to operate under specific terms and conditions. I learned all about preferential treatments and court filings. My friend Stu Komer, who owned the direct-mail marketing company Artistic Greetings and had been through Chapter 11 several years prior, said, "Look, I'll help you. The first thing you have to do is, you've got to really learn how to read a balance sheet. And you've got to look at your sales and expenses on a daily basis and know where you stand." We met at his office at seven-thirty in the morning three days a week, and he showed me how to track my business. This was the MBA that I had never earned.

With our credit gone, all incoming merchandise had to be paid for in cash. A trustee was assigned to review every penny coming and going. I was embarrassed to settle with our creditors for 25 cents on the dollar. Our Chapter 11 was public knowledge and in all the newspapers, and we had to go hat in hand to those with whom we wanted to continue doing business and offer to pay a little more. "Listen, we can't pay you now, but we really need merchandise. Is there a way we can work it out?" Some treated us poorly; some had faith that we could pull it together and were supportive. When we went to New York to buy goods for cash, we no longer spent two weeks partying. We had to go down and come right back.

But worst of all was having to face my father. When my business started taking off, my dad had found a respect for me, which made me feel secure and strong. I'd begun to see my folks more often, even gone home for dinner once in a while. The relationship had begun to strengthen. Of course, along the way, my father had said, "I hope you have systems in place. I hope you're watching your inventory." And I'd told him, "Yeah, yeah, yeah, don't worry, we've got everything under control." Now, only a few years later, I was very embarrassed. My first thought was, "What is Dad going to think?"

I found out soon enough. He gave me his "I told you so" look. My father had finally taken pride in me, and I had let him down. Again. There was nothing I could say that would satisfy him. Or me.

# CHAPTER SIX

# 20TH CENTURY SURVIVAL

a
Fresh Start!

While running People's Place I was seeing a woman named Susan Cirona. Susie had left home at age fifteen and ended up at Larry's mother's friend's house in Ithaca. Larry's mom called her son and said, "You've got to hire this girl." Being a good son, Larry did, and Susan started in the Ithaca store, vacuuming, folding clothes, and generally making herself useful. When we discovered that she had a great sense of style, we had her hang clothing and create window displays. She was very attractive—Greek, Hungarian, and Italian, petite, with dark hair and big brown eyes, perfect skin, and a beautiful smile. And she had great taste! But she was seventeen, and I was in my mid-twenties. She wanted nothing to do with me.

Still, we hung out as People's Place devotees and friends, talking about fashion and music and the world around us. Her senior year in high school, 1975, I convinced Susie to apply to the Fashion Institute of Technology in New York City. "You could learn fashion design, and eventually we could design together for other people," I told her. I was very pleased when she was accepted. I was back and forth to New York on buying trips all the time, so we saw each other often. Unfortunately, she hated FIT. I said, "Why don't you stay at least for the semester and then come with me and we'll set up our own design team?" She put in her semester and then headed back to Ithaca.

I was at the Gramercy Park Hotel in Manhattan in February 1976 when I got a call in the middle of the night. "Your Ithaca store is on fire."

"What?"

The college kids who were renting an apartment upstairs had been smoking in bed and the whole building had gone up in flames and burned to the ground. I drove to Ithaca in the morning. There was nothing left. The place was charred; the clothes were stalactites of frozen water from the fire hoses. Susie met me out front.

"What can I do? Can I help you clean it?"

"There's no way—we've got to bulldoze the store down. There's nothing we can do. We need to get the insurance people here first." I crossed the street to look at the store, trying to get a long view, and walked between two parked cars. At that moment one of them started and crushed my leg between it and the back bumper of the sedan in front of it. My leg broke immediately.

I was rushed to the hospital. Susie went with me. I had a broken femur. The doctors put me in a cast from my toes to my thigh, reducing my mobility to next to nothing. Susie came with me to the party house in the country that Larry and I had rented, and stayed there for several weeks nursing me back to health. She was so devoted, and I was so grateful, and we were on such a wavelength, that as I recuperated, we fell in love. That was the beginning of our relationship.

In 1978, Susie and I bought a former one-room red schoolhouse that had been converted into a house with a little living room, a little kitchen, and two upstairs bedrooms, in the town of Pine City, outside of Elmira. We began making a home. I asked her to marry me, and she said yes. Susie was a great partner because she dreamed with me. We would talk for hours about what a great collection would consist of, how it should fit, where and how it should be shown and sold.

We thought it would be romantic and fun to get married in Venice, but after arriving there and visiting several Catholic churches, we found that we needed baptismal records in order for the ceremony to proceed. We had both been baptized Catholic but, this being before the time of fax machines, there was no way of getting the certificates from Elmira to Italy in time. We settled for a great pre-honeymoon trip but never made it to the altar.

Once home we decided on a more traditional wedding and were married before a small group of family and friends at St. Mary's church in Pittsford, New York, on August 25, 1979. My brother Andy was my best man.

Susie's dad, Jim Cirona, was a successful, rather reserved banker. Her mother, Connie, was not so quiet but very gracious. I wasn't so sure either of them was excited about our getting married, but they did accept the idea.

I met Muna Baig in New York at one of the clothing shows during a buying trip. He was a manufacturer showing dresses and Indian-made goods, and he told me he had a factory. I asked whether he could make my designs. He said, "I can make anything."

"I've got a lot of designs."

"So come to my factory."

How? Where? When? I was intrigued.

Susie's father had said, "I can buy you a wedding present, throw you a big party, or give you a check." We took his check for $1,000 and bought plane tickets, and two weeks after the wedding, we flew to India to develop our first fashion collection together. That was our honeymoon!

When the plane door opened in Bombay, we descended a set of stairs and walked to a bus for the ride to the terminal. It was the middle of the night in September 1979, still summer, and we could see the lights of the city twinkling in the distance. But the funk in the air was startling. Throngs of homeless Indians had built a shanty-town at the perimeter of the airport. Their plumbing was outdoors, and between the cooking and the environment, the heat and the smell were unbelievable.

We picked up our luggage from the terminal carousel and found hundreds of people with their faces pressed against the plate glass windows, staring at the arrivals. Many looked desperate and poor. I had heard that India was intense, and I had tried to prepare myself for it mentally, but seeing this shook me.

We exited customs with our suitcases full of ideas, samples, and our own clothes, and as soon as we reached the sidewalk, beggars surrounded us, pleading for money. Muna pushed them away. "No, no, no," he told us. "If you give to one, everybody is going to come." One of Muna's workers, a Sikh with a beard and turban, drove us to Muna's house near Juhu Beach.

Muna showed us to our bedroom. No curtains, no blankets, one bed with a mattress and a sheet covering it. No closet. A ceiling fan. A bathroom in the hallway with no toilet paper. A sink with one faucet: cold. The shower was a little spout—also cold. No shower curtain, no shower door! Muna gave us each a towel. The flight from New York had taken eighteen hours, so in the middle of the night we both took cold showers. I thought, "This is going to be an experience." I slept like a rock.

The sun was starting to come up when Muna knocked on our door.

"Do you want to go and see the beach?"

Of course we did.

We walked about two blocks to Juhu Beach, then strolled waterside past the Sun and Sand Hotel. Muna said, "You know, a lot of movie stars live on this beach." A sizable number of homeless-looking people also seemed in residence, and when the sun started coming up, many of them went into the water and did their business. Then the waves came up and washed their waste away. The Arabian Sea was like a big open outhouse.

I knew cows were sacred in India, and I had heard that they walked the streets with freedom. Sure enough, they shared the beach as well. A couple of camels stood their ground. Goats ran about. Chickens crossed the road or stayed in the middle of it, as they wished. People were roaming around in traditional Indian saris, kurtas, dhotis, and pajamas.

As the sun came up, the streets came to life, a blur of traffic, bicycles, and peddlers selling their wares. Many people looked at us as if they had never seen white people before; others gave us blank stares. In New York, if someone gives you a blank stare, you think, "I've got to watch that guy because he has his eye on my wallet." I didn't know whether this was the same in India, and I wasn't taking any chances, so our first morning was a little scary. But that walk was a revelation. The country was exciting. I wanted to see more. I truly loved the energy, and the more time I spent there, the more I loved India and its people.

Back at the house, we met Muna's parents, who were wonderful. His entire extended family lived under the same roof. Muna's father was a heavyset, balding former Bombay police detective and an excellent storyteller. His mother was a tiny, chatty woman in control of everything, bossing a staff of two around and asking us all sorts of questions. Not only did she ask us about ourselves, but she listened intently when we told her. I found myself surprisingly forthcoming with this wonderful stranger. She was warm and loving.

After breakfast Mrs. Baig said, "Now you must get some sleep." An excellent idea, since we were exhausted. We took a long nap.

I woke up, sweating, to the sun blazing through the window and the sound of cars honking and cows mooing. We took another shower just to cool down, and then we went to work.

Muna's factory turned out to be in his basement. He took us downstairs to his sample room, where they were making garments. When I heard the churning of the sewing machines, I got excited. I thought, "Okay, we've come to the right place. This guy has a cutting table, a pattern maker. He's got sewing machines, and I see a lot of fabric on those shelves." So I got right into it.

The tailors, pattern makers, and sample room workers didn't speak any English. How was I going to give them my ideas? Mohan, the Sikh who had picked us up at the airport, turned out to be Muna's right-hand man as well, and both men began translating. I laid the fabric out on the worktable and the sample-making team proceeded to cut the fabric according to our specifications. In a matter of minutes, they started making samples.

Each morning Muna took us to the fabric market. We brought the fabric back to the sample makers in the afternoon, they would start cutting and sewing, and our ideas would instantly take shape. In twenty-one days, we made approximately fifty samples. In America, fifty samples could take two months. We were knocking them out!

The first night for dinner, as with all nights thereafter, we sat down at the table and Muna's parents put out pots of food and began serving. I was unfamiliar with Indian food and had no idea what I was eating, but it was delicious. There were no knives or forks. When Muna's father started eating with his right hand, I looked at Susie, she looked at me, and we started giggling, then burst out laughing uncontrollably because we had never seen anyone do that; we had always been taught never to eat with your hands. And as we were giggling and laughing, Muna's father asked, "So, you are liking India? You are having a good time?"

You know, we were!

Susie and I stayed with Muna and his family for almost four weeks. It was a very productive visit. We designed a line of shirts, pants and jackets in the style of 1950s bowling shirts, plus Hawaiian shirts with embroideries on the back. I loved the way the Indians embroidered: you could give them a sketch or a photograph and they would sit down with their machine and just make it. We didn't speak the same language, but they were incredible at translating our ideas.

The Indian makers were very dedicated. Each day, the tailors traveled miles and miles by rickety train from villages and the outskirts of Bombay to come to work. They sat at manual sewing machines, powering them with their feet. They ate lunch in place, opening their containers of curry and working right through to make sure we had our samples.

I gained a lot of respect for the Indian work ethic. Even amid the buzzing of the teeming cities, perhaps because of their religion or philosophies, the people seemed serene. It appeared to me a spiritual nation, and I felt very comfortable there.

At first we were going to call our line Pook, because that was the nickname Susie's parents used for each other, and I thought it looked kind of cool when written out. Then we thought, "Why not call it Tommy Hill?" With a name like that, we could present our work as a designer line. I thought of calling it Hilfiger, but I didn't think people could pronounce it.

We returned to New York via Paris, where we sat in cafés and soaked up the atmosphere. As I watched Parisians stroll their streets, I took photographs in my head, as I had done since I was a boy. I was certain that sooner or later I would put the mental snapshots to good use. I studied the windows of Galeries Lafayette, thinking that someday we would see our clothes in those windows.

I was ready to take our samples to department store buyers and start getting orders. I told Muna I needed some payment for the design work I had already performed. He told me, "You don't get paid until after we manufacture and after we ship and after the stores pay us."

I couldn't wait for months; I needed some sort of revenue immediately. I said, "I can't do it this way."

Muna told me, "This is the only way you can do it if we are going to be partners."

"I have no money to survive," I said. "I need to work."

He did not relent. It became clear to me that we would not be able to work together. I needed someone who could pay me.

I felt the Tommy Hill line was mine. I'd created it; I'd designed it. But when I sent in the forms to register the name Tommy Hill, I found that Muna had already claimed it as his own. How was that possible? It was my name! I thought we should at least have had a discussion about it beforehand. So we had a falling-out. I told Muna, "I can't work without being paid." He still didn't budge.

We had been working on a handshake agreement. I was a young, inexperienced designer, this was my first time out, and I thought this was the way things were done. In hindsight, we should have had clarity before starting the whole project, but I didn't know enough to insist on it. Every time I went to Muna's office I would ask when we were going to schedule out the deal and put it on paper. He'd say, "Don't worry, don't worry, don't worry." So I didn't worry. But when it came time to put the deal together, it was his way or no way.

Even worse, Muna had my samples. He took my designs and sold them. One day I walked by the corner of 59th and Lexington, and there were my shirts in the windows of Bloomingdale's. It should have been a big day, but it wasn't. I got no credit and I got paid nothing.

So that was that. Muna was a nice guy, and it was very generous of him to open his home to us, and my trip to India was a great experience. But he now had a line of my clothing with my name on it, and he owned my designs.

I was more than a little upset, but I didn't have any recourse. I didn't have money for a lawyer, so I couldn't sue. Muna pointed out that Tommy Hill was not my real name, indicating that he was sure to put up a fight. I didn't want to battle with him. I didn't want to have anything to do with him.

As for Tommy Hill, the line was very strong at first, but without a designer, they couldn't produce a successful follow-up, so the brand fell apart. That did not upset me. I wanted to transform all my negative energy into positive energy and move on, which I did.

We slowly cleaned up the mess at People's Place. With Chapter 11 protection and a laser-like focus on the bottom line, Larry and I got the business back on track. It took time, but we finally paid everyone and started fresh.

In 1979, after ten years together, Larry and I split the business. He took the Ithaca store, I took Elmira, and we closed the rest and went our separate ways.

My new goal was to rid my store of legal burdens and inventory issues, build the business back up, and sell it. As we righted my People's Place, all I could think was, "I want to get out of the retail business, head for New York, and create my own brand. I've had enough of this."

My brother-in-law, Christopher Fredo, my sister Betsy's husband, had worked at the Elmira store and managed the one in Corning. I told him, "I'll sell you the store."

He said, "I'll buy it."

We arranged to come up with a number that satisfied us both.

In the late 1970s, Jordache was the hottest jeans brand in the world. Its Syrian owners, Ralph, Avi, and Joe Nakash, were very smart guys. On one of my final People's Place buying runs in the city, I showed them my designs and said, "You should have a shirt line to go with the jeans. And you should hire me and Susie to do it." They contemplated and contemplated and contemplated. I kept calling the company president, Russell Hartman, saying, "You guys want to start? Let's get started, let's get started, let's get started!" All I got was, "We're not ready yet."

One day, after weeks of not hearing from them, I told Susie, "I've got to call this guy again. I really want to go to New York and design. I've got to do this." I was leaning against the brass bed in our little red schoolhouse. My brother-in-law had not yet finalized his agreement to buy the store, but at that point I didn't care. I said, "I'll take whatever I can get for it; I really want to go."

Susie felt differently. We had just bought the schoolhouse and were enjoying living out in the country. It was cozy. We had a fireplace, and there was a stream going through the property. We jogged on dirt roads and had barbeques in the back yard. The Elmira store was very manageable; I only had to go to New York every couple of weeks. We had a nice, comfortable life.

But I wasn't satisfied. I wanted to get to New York and start designing and learn how to manufacture in a big way with the big boys, and then start my own operation.

Susie found the whole idea—giving up everything we had and moving to New York to start over—frightening. I was asking her to leave our idyllic home for the grit and grime of late-1970s New York City.

But she also understood. She loved fashion, too, and wanted to be a part of whatever I was doing. As we talked about making it in New York, the idea grew intoxicating. Finally, she agreed.

I called Russell Hartman again and said, "Look, we're going to design for somebody else." It was not a complete lie; we *were* going to go design for somebody else. I just didn't know whom.

"Okay," he said, "let's try it."

I called Chris and said, "How much can you pay me for the store?" He told me, "I don't have the money, but I can give you five thousand dollars, and then I can make payments." We verbally agreed on $5,000 a month for about twenty months, approximately $100,000.

I thought Chris would be great at running his own shop. He had a big, funny personality and loved to entertain people. His plan was to remake People's Place as a menswear store and rename it Christopher's. But I never should have done business with family. Chris made a couple of payments and then stopped. Apparently his lawyer told him there might have been liens on the property or that people were still owed money and that I might have intentionally left him with those debts. Chris became convinced that I was taking advantage of him, and I guess they wanted to collect evidence for a lawsuit. His lawyer told him to stop talking to me, and Chris listened.

So I wasn't getting paid. I couldn't force Chris to live up to the contract, and on general principle, I refused to sue my sister's husband. I needed the money but I never got it. Within a short amount of time, Christopher's went out of business.

The closing was a big disappointment for my sister Betsy. She had managed People's Place successfully and had hoped to establish a menswear business and support her family. Soon after, she had two boys, Michael and Joe. Eventually, Chris and Betsy divorced. Chris moved to Florida, and some years later he was killed in a terrible car accident. Michael and Joe were teens at the time, and their dad's death was very difficult for them, as well as for Betsy. They are both great boys and have felt the pain ever since. I have tried to stay close and be there for each of them. Michael and Joe have both worked for me at different times, and I remain available to them in every way possible. They are now in their thirties, and I feel their pain still; they were so close to their dad, and they looked at him as if he were a god.

negotiated a $30,000-a-year contract with Jordache—total for both of us. Susie and I found a one-bedroom apartment in Manhattan at 31 East 31st Street, between Park and Madison Avenues, for $700 a month. Coming from Elmira, we thought that was quite an overhead, but I rented out the schoolhouse for $200 a month, then got a U-Haul and packed everything in it with the help of my brother Andy and Michael Houghton, who had grown up with us and was so much like another brother we called him Michael H. We drove to New York City on a Friday night in the pouring rain, unloaded on 31st Street, and set up the apartment.

Susie and I stayed in that weekend, mostly because we had no money, but also to strategize how to succeed in this new life. We met neighbors on our floor, Joe and Suzanne, who were pleasant. As we got to know them, we'd often all stay in on a weeknight and order Chinese food together. To outsiders, New York seems impenetrable sometimes, and it was nice to meet real people right off the bat.

Susie and I went to work for Jordache bright and early Monday morning. First thing, I showed my designs to a woman named Liz. I presented jeans, a jean jacket, and the Tommy Hill bowling shirts. When we finished, she said, "I'm not sure whether we need men's designs or women's designs. Let me ask Ralph."

Ralph said, "I don't know, I don't know."

I told Liz, "Look, the best way we can get this started is for you to send us to Hong Kong, to your factories, and we will come back with a line for you." I'd been to factories and was dying to go to theirs and see what they were capable of.

A few weeks later, Susie and I were in Hong Kong, staying at the very posh Excelsior Hotel on the Hong Kong side of the harbor.

Larry and I had been to Hong Kong as tourists a few years earlier, and I had loved the entire landscape. The energy had been exhilarating! The traffic on the streets. The stores open late at night. The lights. The Star Ferry shuttling back and forth to Kowloon. The Chinese junks and sampans in the South China Sea.

This time, I headed for the markets. Hong Kong had not yet been modernized, and in primitive marketplaces on small streets, people were selling everything from live snakes and chickens to eels in tanks and all sorts of other seafood. Pharmacies sold everything from herbs to deer antler to shark fin.

And the fashion! Some markets sold goods from factories that manufactured for designers and brands throughout the world, and others sold these factories' overages. Those outlet markets were a gold mine: that's where I could find ideas and see what everyone else was making. After even a brief look at the merchandise, I could tell that the Chinese were making products with details that American factories could not approach. It quickly became my dream to manufacture there and incorporate that kind of stitching, pocketing, and design innovation into my garments.

I was hoping to explore new resources and expand into jackets, shirts, and blouses, but Mr. and Mrs. Lee, Jordache's Chinese partners, made it clear that they did not want us going to anyone else's factories or designing anything other than what they were already manufacturing: jeans and bottoms. They attempted to be polite, but we could tell that they were not happy with us at all.

Rather than accept a stalemate, I began designing alternative embroideries for the jeans. Jordache made only one style of jean, with the Jordache horse logo stitched on the back pocket. I said, "I think you need more jean designs. I think you need more pocket designs." They made some samples of my work, albeit reluctantly.

I brought out my design for a jean with a houndstooth check lining; turn up the bottom cuff and you would see the contrasting fabric. The pocketing matched the cuff, and the jean jacket that I designed as a companion piece had the houndstooth check under the cuff and collar. The Lees were hesitant to make my samples because their plant was automated, and inserting the lining in the various places wasn't an automatic operation. But I was there to do a job, and they made what I required. I was very proud of those pieces. If nothing else, I thought, when we showed them on our return, the people at Jordache would be impressed.

Susie and I stayed in Hong Kong for two weeks and got home just before Thanksgiving. We drove up to Ithaca to visit Susie's family for the holiday, and then to Elmira to visit mine. It was very cozy, and we both missed the simple life. We thought, "Maybe if we get going, we could get a house up here and come on weekends." We saw a very modern house on the lake that had been built for Carl Sagan and thought perhaps we could put a design studio in it and eliminate the need for one in the city, which would bring down rent costs. The house was not far from the Ithaca airport; we could fly into LaGuardia and maybe spend three days in New York and four at home! We were always dreaming.

On Monday we walked up Seventh Avenue to the Jordache show-rooms on 35th Street. Susie prided herself on being psychic, and she said she felt something strange. It was extremely quiet as we entered the office. "Well," I mused, "everyone is just getting back from vacation."

Susie said, "I think they're going to fire us."

I told her, "No, no, no." I didn't want to hear about the negative.

That's pretty much the way I am: I don't like to talk about anything bad, and if something negative does enter a conversation, I try to avoid it. Why? I was immersed in negativity as a child and couldn't wait to get out and be positive about everything. I'm always looking for ways something can be done successfully, and I believe that's one of the reasons I have succeeded. If we're in traffic, I'm sure it will clear up soon. In a restaurant, I'll say, "Well, the food's not good, but the atmosphere is nice." Airport? "The flight is delayed, but at least we'll be on time for tomorrow's meetings."

I don't like taking no for an answer. I believe there is always a way. I think this outlook is a gift from God, I really do.

"I've got to talk to you guys," said Russell Hartman, Jordache's president. I thought he was going to tell us he had a meeting that day and would look at our designs the next. We went into his office. He closed the door.

"It's just not going to work out," he said. "We don't need designers; we have our jeans that are selling. I don't think we are going to go into other areas right now. But thank you very much." Russell couldn't have been nicer. The brothers who were the company's owners were nowhere to be found.

Back on Seventh Avenue, Susie said, "I told you, I told you." She was scared.

"You were right," I said. We'd been in New York only three weeks and already we were out of work. "Let's not waste any time. I've got to go find a job, and you've got to find a job." Susie looked in the back of *Women's Wear Daily* and got work right away at a skirt shop, Ms. Montage, at 87th and Lexington, making $200 a week. I kept pounding the pavement.

One evening, Susie and I arrived at 31st Street to find our building cordoned off with police tape. FBI and people in law enforcement jackets were swarming around the place. We tried to go upstairs, but they wouldn't let us inside. A government agent showed us his badge and checked our IDs, then asked who we were, where we lived, and whether we knew our neighbors. We said, "Sure. Joe and Suzanne."

"That's not their real names," our interrogator told us. "He's one of the FBI's Most Wanted criminals, and she's an accomplice. They're in jail now." The agents had found guns and silencers and all sorts of ammunition in the apartment. Apparently Joe was a big drug dealer and who knows what else!

The FBI interviewed us at length. "How long have you known them? Did you know their real names? Was there any unusual activity?"

Somehow I'd known it! I had told Susie that I'd sensed a little something but couldn't put my finger on exactly what it was. We told the FBI that Joe, or whatever his name actually was, had had a facelift recently, because we could just tell. And that the couple were very secretive—they never went out in the daytime, only at night.

When we were allowed back in the building, there was police tape crisscrossing everything. Joe and Suzanne's door had been broken down, and inside we could see detectives roaming around, looking for stuff. Drug dealers down the hall—that was an eye-opener! And it certainly didn't sit well with Susie, who'd been hesitant to move to New York in the first place. We couldn't wait to get out of that apartment, but we were having trouble pulling together the rent. We had to stay put.

About two months later, we got a call from Suzanne. She wanted to borrow money. I said, "We have no money, and we can't get involved with you because we don't know what's going on. We just can't get involved."

Two days later, all over the news was a story about a woman who, along with an accomplice, had chartered a tourist helicopter, held the pilot at gunpoint, landed on the roof of the Metropolitan Correctional Center downtown, jumped out with wire cutters, and attempted unsuccessfully to cut through the steel mesh on top of the roof. She had lowered a gun to the convicts waiting below and tried to break her boyfriend out of the pen. It was Suzanne!

We certainly weren't in Elmira anymore!

Hartley Goldstein, who had been hired by Bonjour Jeans to do children's wear, needed a designer, a merchandiser. I took the subway from 34th Street up to the interview.

Goldstein lived in a glamorous new building at Central Park West and 68th Street, with a uniformed doorman and tall ceilings in the mirrored lobby. I was a bit nervous, but fear has never really prevented me from pursuing my goals. As we spoke, I outlined my experience and said, "I can do it. Very simple. I can do it for you."

After a little more conversation he said, "Okay, I'll hire you, let's give it a try."

The day was cold and rainy, and I had used my last 50 cents on the subway fare. As I was saying goodbye, I said, "Do you think I could borrow a couple of dollars for the subway to get back? I didn't bring my wallet." Goldstein opened his billfold and gave me a crisp twenty. After I'd made all that money in the early seventies and lived like a king, my only thought now was, "Oh my God, we can eat tonight." I repaid Mr. Goldstein out of my first paycheck.

Hartley Goldstein looked like a portly, proper Englishman, but he was a smart, hard-nosed New York businessman. I thought, "I'm going to really learn from this guy." And I did. However, I don't think Mr. Goldstein got along with Bonjour's owners, the Dayan brothers. They were very successful and didn't love listening to outsiders. When he left the company, I lost my champion.

Bonjour was another jeans company that wasn't really looking for a designer. The job I was assigned involved analysis and calculation, answering questions like, "Based on a certain pattern size, how much fabric would go into certain quantities of denim?" I wanted to create incredible styles and market them to the world; I didn't want to sit on my ass in a production department counting size runs. I told the bean counters, "Let me design. I really want to create some product for you!" They were entirely uninterested.

I needed the work, but it was so uninspiring. I kept thinking, "How am I going to get where I want to go?" I was in no position to quit, but they made the decision for me when, only a few months after I'd been hired, they said, "We think it's time for you to start looking for another job." I was out on the street again.

So I went where the jobs were, to the garment center headquarters at 1407 Broadway. There had to have been forty floors in the building. I took the elevator to the top, got off, and knocked on every single door in the hallway, asking people if they needed a designer.

"No."

"No."

"Where'd you go to design school?" (I hadn't.)

"Do you make patterns?" (No.)

"Do you sew?" (No.)

I had vision and a very clear idea of how I wanted clothes to look, but if they were looking for proper schooling, they weren't going to hire me. I lacked credibility. Most design school graduates possess skills in specific categories—pattern making, merchandising, textile design. I wanted to be a creative director even though I didn't have any traditional experience. But I knew I could! I kept pushing and pushing because I just knew at some point I would meet a believer, and then I would prove myself.

I hit every office on all forty floors and got nothing.

————————

knew from the very beginning that I had a unique design sense. After almost ten years in retail, I could instantly sense what was selling and what was strong. I knew that if you build a better mousetrap, you'll take business away from the competition. I knew every brand, and every style within every brand. I was current on every designer and every store. Susie and I would shop Soho on weekends, hitting all the boutiques and then taking the subway uptown to Bloomingdale's, Saks, Macy's, Bergdorf's, Barneys, or Henri Bendel, studying everything that was happening in fashion. I wanted to build a better mousetrap.

I wanted so badly to sell my designs that I couldn't sit still. I had a vision of making cool jeans, so I went to the Gap on 34th Street and spent all the money I had on six simple, clean pairs. This was before they even had the Gap name on the buttons. I bought leather scraps from Libra Leathers on Spring Street, then went home, cut them into thin strips, and placed them in a curved line along the jean pockets. Voilà, fringed jeans! I said, "I'm going to call them Rodeo jeans," evoking both the high-rent clothing scene of Los Angeles's Rodeo Drive and the rough-and-tumble world of the western cowboy. I had a feeling that a cool western look was coming. I also bought plain red and white sweatshirts to fringe.

Our friends Eddie Virgadamo and Patty Young did the sewing; Susie did the riveting. I put my newly created samples in a duffel bag and went knocking on doors at the Gap, Bloomingdale's, Saks Fifth Avenue, looking for orders. Something clicked. Bloomingdale's wanted a hundred pairs! Canadian Fur, a fashion store on 34th Street, was in. Neiman Marcus loved it. Ellen Saltzman, a fashion director of Saks Fifth Avenue, who was like the Diana Vreeland or Anna Wintour of the time because she had so much power with so many designers, gave me the nod and made me feel I was doing the right thing. Now I had to figure out how to get them made.

I was introduced to a guy named Isaac who supposedly had jean factories. I met him at his apartment one Saturday morning; he was walking around in shorts and clogs, with a T-shirt partly covering his fat belly. He carried himself with a fully developed arrogance, but I didn't care because I wanted a factory.

"Yeah," he told me, "I can manufacture these."

I kept trying to pin him down on cost and delivery and how I was going to pay him. I said, "I've got these orders, I'll split the profit with you."

"Don't worry, don't worry, don't worry," he said. I had heard that before. I should have known.

I left the orders with Isaac, and when I followed up at his office on Monday, he wasn't there; his partner said he had flown to Hong Kong. "Great," I figured. "He's getting my stuff made."

I kept asking the partner, "When is he going to be in? When is he going to be in?" Ten days later Isaac returned, and I was waiting for him.

"Are you going to get the stuff made?"

He said, "I can't get this stuff made in thirty days. It's going to take me four months!"

"Give me the orders," I told him. "Forget it."

I went to see David Schulster, whom I had met at a bar and who'd told me about his cousin who owned a factory, in his office at 1407 Broadway. Schulster's cousin, an older man named Leon Calick, did have a factory. I met their well-dressed sales representative, Ronald Gellin, a tall, handsome fellow who looked like a Hollywood star but was a garmento—a man who is culturally attuned to and deeply understands the business—and a good one. I told Leon that I had a lot of design ideas, and also about People's Place and my recent bouts with Jordache and Bonjour, and that I was looking to start my own line. He said, "Yeah, yeah, yeah, I have factories." I was a little dismayed when he showed me what he was making in those factories: polyester pleated skirts, ruffled fake silk blouses, pull-on polyester pants, and cheap-looking dresses that resembled American Airlines stewardess outfits. Godawful stuff.

I said, "I've already gotten orders on my jeans from Bloomingdale's and other places. If I can borrow one of your factories, I can design a line and sell it. I also know a guy in India with a factory who would like to manufacture my stuff." (This was not my Tommy Hill nemesis, but a man named Subash Suri, whom I'd met through my friends Allen and Doreen Gorman and their company, Flowers. I'd also met a Mr. Premi with a factory on Lawrence Road in New Delhi run by his brother, Batra.) "But I have no way to pay for it, to import it."

Leon said, "Yeah, we can do that."

We formed a partnership, dividing ownership into fourths: David, Leon, Ron, and me. I would design, Ron would be in charge of sales, Leon would do manufacturing, and Dave would be responsible for sales and schmoozing.

What were we going to call the company? I felt the time and market were right for military gear—camouflage, surplus-style cargo pants, and jumpsuits. Official-looking survival wear. The actor Walter Matthau's brother Henry had an army-navy surplus store down on Broadway near Canal Street where I used to go for inspiration and ideas. It was 1981: the Iranian hostage crisis had just ended, both President Ronald Reagan and Pope John Paul II had been shot, AIDS was first identified. I said, "Let's call it 20th Century Survival." This name was also fitting since it was a moment in my life, after a series of difficult setbacks, when I was truly looking to survive.

But I wasn't satisfied creating only one look. I also felt the market was ready for pirates, with ruffled blouses, swashbuckler pants, and something I described as a jagged-edge cross between Robin Hood and Peter Pan that involved brocades in richer, deeper colors and sexier fabrics. Henry Lehr, a retailer on Third Avenue, carried the coolest selection of European clothing in New York. He had jumpsuits and jackets by London designer Katharine Hamnett; he had clothing from Jet Set, a company in St. Moritz. He had Taverniti jeans. Susie and I were shopping there when she spotted a Kenzo blouse with huge layers of ruffles. Beautiful but expensive. "You should do a blouse like this," she said. It was a good idea, and I tucked it away.

We had orders, but 20th Century Survival almost didn't live to fill them. Leon's factory, located out in the borough of Queens, was fine with polyester but couldn't manufacture the camo or the jeans.

They had no idea how to get the fringe onto the pants. We had to delay all our orders until we found a facility able to produce my designs. We finally decided to manufacture in India.

I scraped up enough money to go back to India to design complete lines, this time in New Delhi at Mr. Batra's factory. My ticket included a free stopover in London, so I could get off the plane and reboard a few days later. This was London, 1981. I headed straight for Kings Road and asked some cool punk/glam/Boy George–looking young people, "Where is the best place to hear music?" They pointed me toward the Beetroot club in Soho.

When I descended a narrow set of stairs at the Beetroot, the room was pounding with Culture Club and Duran Duran and The Police. The place was packed with young people dressed like swash-bucklers! This was post-punk, post–glam rock, post-disco. It was very romantic. The ruffles in the sleeves had gotten enormous, the leg-of-mutton sleeves had gotten more poofed, and the cuffs had gotten longer and larger. The knickers, the short trousers, had some sort of elastic under the knee and were held up by big, thick cummerbund belts. High socks dominated, and I saw suspenders with paper-bag-waist trousers. This was a whole new look and feel. I didn't carry a camera, but I embedded the scene deep into my mind. I knew immediately, "This is my next thing!"

I had thought of pirates, and here they were! That's what happens in the design world—something is in the air. That's why, during Fashion Week, you'll see Prada doing the same kind of thing as Gucci. Designers might have seen someone look great in a film, or a celebrity in the street wearing something they've never seen before, or something vintage that looks great and hasn't been in fashion in many years, and they say, "Ah, what a great look. I'm going to do a whole line based on that!" Or maybe it's because last season military was strong and this season they want to do the total opposite.

Also, when designers visit the mills where they buy their yarn and cloth, they see tubes of a season's new colors and yarns in early stages, even before they're dyed: plum, mauve, aqua, and mustard. How did Yves St. Laurent get the same colors as Dior? They're at the factories. *It's in the air!*

The next morning on the plane, from the minute I took off from Heathrow to the moment I landed in New Delhi, I sketched all of what I had seen and felt the night before, everything I could remember, and more.

I checked into my hotel, dropped my stuff, and took my sample bag to Mr. Batra's factory. This bag contained my entire design life: surplus-style clothes, items I had purchased in boutiques wherever I traveled, my sketchbook, a collection of fabrics I had amassed, pictures from magazines, color swatches. Ideas. I spread them all out on a table and set to work with a pattern maker and a master tailor.

Most of my sketch work was very simple and flat, and included a broad range of measurements—*32-inch sleeve; from center back to bottom, 27 inches*—and I numbered and named each for reference. I then showed the makers a sample with a stitching technique on it and the type of button I wanted to use. I gave them ten styles, and while they were cutting and sewing those, I searched out fabrics in a maze of little alleyways in old Delhi called Chandni Chowk, where old dealers would sit around in lotus position for hours, drinking tea and smoking Indian bidis, then take their abacuses and add up how much you bought. I found incredible brocade silk velveteen, and rayon fabrics—embroidered, flocked, and damask—in deep rich colors. Barefooted workers wearing pajamas would climb onto the racks and bring down the rolls. The fabric would be wrapped in brown paper, tied with string, and put in the back of my rickshaw for transport back to the factory. In another area of Chandni Chowk they sold thread, buttons, taping, and bindings. I brought all of that stuff back to the sample room and created a swashbuckler look for 20th Century Survival.

As the samples were finished, we put them on people who looked like they might be the right size, and then critiqued and adjusted and fixed, sometimes remaking them entirely, until I was satisfied. During the process I'd think things like, "I should make that with a hood," or "I should make that with a bigger collar," or "I should put a skirt onto the bottom of that blouse and make it into a dress." It was all possible. I was experimenting—trying to develop something I felt no other competitor would have.

I discovered that in India, you can buy white cloth and have it dyed to the color you want overnight. They would take either white or off-white cotton cloth and put it into a big vat with dye and very hot water, stir it with a stick, and then hang it on a clothesline to dry. Or you can leave it white. Rather than create yet another army green or khaki, I created all manner of cool army surplus gear in romantic white: blouses with billowy sleeves, camo bottoms, and other rugged military-style gear. We made jumpsuits inspired by army surplus and the Katharine Hamnett line we had bought at Henry Lehr. We made my interpretation of the Kenzo and other ruffled blouses in white cotton and called it the 008 Poet Blouse: Shakespeare meets Captain Hook. It was a huge success, our best-selling item.

I had a good eye for merchandising the line: creating the right assortment of colors and the right ratio of tops to bottoms and novelty pieces to basic pieces, long sleeves to short sleeves, heavyweight to lightweight, fashionable to more understandable. I would hang every piece against the wall and stare at it for hours, thinking, "What more can I do to this? What less can I do to it? How do I make it more appealing? How do I adjust it, how do I change it?" Finally, having considered everything I could think of, at some point I would say, "Okay, now I'm done."

It was almost like going to a recording studio and making an album. You create your harmonies, you make your beats, you come up with your hook, you put it together, you play it over and over and over—you find a balance. I had a specific theme and a specific focus per line. I was curating and editing on an ongoing basis.

Within a two-week period I had created seventy-five styles.

I did a lot of business with a small factory called Shahi Fashions, owned by the Ahuja family. Mrs. Ahuja, whom we called "Mommy," had two very sweet and loving sons, Harish and Sunil. Daddy was a calm presence but not part of the business. The factory consisted of ten sewing machines and the pattern maker, Mr. Paramjit, in a small sample and sewing shop with a dirt floor, and Mommy made certain each of her workers was fed and well taken care of, not the norm in the Indian factories I had previously visited. Always wearing a white sari, sandals, and simple jewelry, Mommy had a divine presence and a warm heart. I became and remain very close to the family, and today one of India's largest and most sophisticated manufacturing companies is run by Mommy's son Harish.

But not all of my memories from India are so pleasant. I was visiting a factory the morning after I had feasted for three hours on a large tandoori meal at one of my favorite restaurants, the Bukhara at the Maurya Hotel: tandoori chicken, tandoori lamb, tandoori shrimp, naan, lentils, and all sorts of exotic vegetable dishes. Probably I overdid it. When I woke up, my stomach was not great, but that was not unusual because when I was in India, where the food is significantly spicier than my normal diet, my stomach usually wasn't great. I took some Tums and figured I'd get over it.

I was talking to the factory owner about making samples when my gut started acting up. I said, "Do you have a bathroom?"

"We do. Down the hall to the left."

I went down the hall to the left, and in the bathroom found a toilet, a window, and nothing else. No sink, no toilet paper, just a very primitive commode. But I had to go. So I went. And there was no toilet paper. What to do? I couldn't return to work without cleaning myself. I figured, "I'll just use my underwear."

My BVDs performed admirably. Now what? I couldn't flush them down the toilet; I had to get rid of them. I opened the window, saw a rubble-strewn area out back, and thought, "No one will know." I threw my extravagantly soiled underwear out the window.

I was sitting in the guy's office talking about his factory's capabilities and sewing methods when someone knocked on the door. One of his servants entered with my underwear folded neatly in quarters and said, "Are you missing this?" I turned about nine million shades of pink, red, and purple and slid them into my bag.

When I flew home I went straight to my "office." Mark Warman, whose company Foxy Lady was selling dresses at 1407 Broadway, had given me a desk and a telephone in his showroom for $200

a month. That morning, I called for appointments at Macy's, Gim-
bel's, Saks, Bloomingdale's, Bonwit Teller, Henri Bendel, Bergdorf
Goodman, Barneys downtown, and any other specialty stores we
could add into the mix. I didn't know anybody, I had no contacts. All
I had was my product.

Many buyers routinely didn't, and still don't, answer or return
their calls, and in 1981 not everyone had an answering machine, yet
somehow I found a way to show to every buyer. Retailers that weren't
located in New York, such as Neiman Marcus, had New York offices.
There were buying agents who serviced many stores. If someone
refused, which was often, I threw my samples in a duffel bag and
went to that person's office. One day I took the subway to Bloomingdale's and walked around the selling floor asking for the buyer. Fortunately, I was well received.

I was very excited when Angie Kroll, the head buyer for junior
sportswear at Saks Fifth Avenue, bought 850 pieces, an enormous
order for a start-up company. This was an order that signified accep-
tance. Angie had a reputation for being extremely tough, but she was
kind to me. She arranged personal appearances at Saks in New York
and San Francisco. The store placed an ad in the *New York Times* on
a Sunday for a personal appearance the following week. I stood in the
junior sportswear section with two models, met customers, signed a
few autographs, and sold my collection to people one-on-one.

After we got into Saks we began selling to stores like Hudson's
Bay in Canada, Neiman Marcus, and May Company. I was back and
forth to India designing my lines, and they began selling all over the
place—20th Century Survival exploded! The cotton pirate blouses
were selling like crazy. Girls were wearing them with jeans, with the
military pants. Every window in Macy's San Francisco, all the way
around the store, was swashbuckler! All around the country, this
look became so of the moment it was like having a number one hit
on the *Billboard* charts. This wild success gave me a lot of confidence
that what I was doing was right, so I continued evolving the romantic look.

My next idea was to patch things up, which came from my love for seventies fashion. I made patchwork vests and skirts and then took the brocade fabric and made one sleeve in gold and one in burgundy, with a front panel in emerald and another front panel in black, so it looked really poetic and romantic.

As time went on, I created a nautical look, a yachting idea, a calypso look, a dockworker idea, candy stripes, a scout look, an active sporty look, a look for the beach. I did Chinese-inspired dresses and rugged outdoorsy Robinson Crusoe–looking wear. When I had the opportunity to go to Bangalore I met Rajan Gokoldas, who with his brother owned Gokoldas Fashions, and we started developing suits, jackets, knits. I was working hard to feed the industry and expand our lines.

Eventually 20th Century Survival started making money, and we moved to a brand-new showroom at 1466 Broadway. Our partner Ron Gellin, who was a carpenter on the side, built the space. This tall, Hollywood-looking guy actually knew how to use a hammer and a saw! We built levels and platforms, carpeted it all in charcoal gray, and painted the walls a cool gray. It was a chic space. We hired a chef and fed lunch to any buyer who would come see our line. We had an ample bar. Things were rolling!

In addition to all of this romantic stuff, I wanted to create a line of less feminine clothing. I wanted to do more jeanswear, but not using denim. I wanted to be more utilitarian; I felt that vibe coming on. With Susie's artistic help and encouragement, I developed a new division of the company, which we called 54321. The design team of Marithé and François Girbaud had an incredible store named Halles Capone in Paris, and other lines called 11342 and Closed. I liked the idea of naming a line after a number; it sounded very official and regimented and militaristic. Our company name brought to mind "5-4-3-2-1, blastoff!"

While Bonnie Duchon was head of 20th Century Survival sales, we hired Judy Sinnreich, a super salesperson from the garment center, and I developed a militaristic industrial line of jeanswear with snaps and zippers and pockets and clasps, plus accompanying T-shirts and jackets. I designed menswear stripes, Chinese stripes for rugby shirts, baseball looks, printed T-shirts, toweling, and embroidered nautical looks, and expanded it to pants and shorts.

I began traveling to get new ideas. In addition to stopping in London on my way to the factories in India, I would go to Saint-Tropez in July, when it was most beautiful, to get inspired by the shops and the people. Saint-Tropez had a certain romance because of the yachts in the harbor and the French provincial architecture of the buildings in the port. The town had a cool, casual style you wouldn't see in New York, London, or Paris. It was beachy, but with a real fashion vibe. The women dressed sexily, in either very short or very long and flowing skirts, off-the-shoulder blouses, gladiator sandals, and ornate jewelry. The men looked rugged and nautical in Breton stripes, indigo French sailor pants, and berets. Smoking Gauloises in the cafés, they basically looked like the backdrop for every Brigitte Bardot movie.

My brands 20th Century Survival and 54321 were at the very beginning of the casualwear revolution. There were not a lot of other brands doing this in America. Calvin Klein had only recently done a deal with Carl Rosen at Puritan Fashions to license his jeans. I remember reading that Rosen was paying Calvin a fee of $1 for each pair of jeans sold. That was a unique way to do a licensing deal, and a very simple concept for me to understand. Usually a designer got a percentage of sales, the calculation of which could be byzantine, but the fact that Calvin was getting a dollar a pair, which was a lot of money, was quite genius. When Calvin Klein Jeans came out, the whole designer jeans world, which had barely existed before, really started to rock.

But 20th Century Survival was about to implode. We were a design and sales firm; we couldn't manufacture our own products because we didn't have the funds to prepay to have the garments made. We would give specific orders to specific individual manufacturers, who would pay us an advance and then make and ship the merchan-

dise to the buyer. David and Leon would give the orders to two manufacturers and receive two advance checks. Whichever delivered first
got the order; the other would be stuck with the merchandise. It was
hard to trust men who were dishonest with our suppliers and double-
dipping.

As was customary in the fashion industry, the Indians doing our
manufacturing and shipping would then get paid by the stores and
give us a percentage. Despite what Leon was telling me, I felt there
was more money coming in than he was sharing. This was brought
to my attention when one of our Indian makers, Peter Kukreja,
whom I trusted and who I felt believed in me, said, "Why don't you
leave those guys and come with me? Those guys are screwing you."

I was receptive. I didn't understand exactly what Leon and David
were doing, but they were always whispering behind closed doors. I
walked in on them one day and found stacks of $100 bills all over
Leon's desk. "One of the manufacturers just paid us in cash," they
told me. That was weird, I thought. They fumbled and said, "Oh, and
by the way, this amount is yours. We're just trying to divide it up,
because you are owed some and we are owed some." I felt that something was not aboveboard, though I didn't know what exactly. The
fact that they were cousins made it seem even shadier. I think Leon
was the mastermind. I was in my twenties, and Leon was probably
in his late fifties or early sixties. He had had early success in the apparel business and then lost it all, so maybe this was his next or last
chance to get his hands on some money. And when the money
started rolling in, I think he attempted to control it with his own
method of accounting. The whole scene made me feel dirty, like I
needed a shower. I hated that feeling.

In 1981, I had met Anita Gallo, a wonderful woman who was the
fashion director of B. Altman, the department store on Fifth Avenue
and 34th Street. She gave me terrific support, placing a large order
for 20th Century Survival and booking a personal appearance for
me. Edith Drucker, a B. Altman divisional merchandiser, was also
very kind and supportive. It was a measure of our respect for each
other that I confided in Edith about some of my problems at 20th
Century Survival. "If I leave the company, will I be able to replace the

money I have coming in and the ability to do what I'm doing?" I asked. "The setup is working, but the people are questionable—should I stay or should I go?"

Edith sat with me for a long time, giving me good advice and guidance. She told me, "Don't remain in a situation that will be harmful to you. Move on and find something great. You are very talented. Hold your head high." It was like talking to my aunt Annie.

I don't think our fourth partner, Ron Gellin, was dishonest, but he seemed to acquiesce to Leon and David when it came to dividing up the money or overbilling someone for royalties. So I started thinking, "I know I have talent. I know I have the drive. I'm the one dealing with the fashion directors and the store executives, as well as the magazines. I'm doing all of the design. I would really like to get myself into a much more professional situation, with people I can trust."

I felt that the whole company was happening because of me. These were guys who had been struggling along selling polyester blouses and horrible-looking clothes. Now we were one of the most up-and-coming young brands. We were setting trends; we had all the buyers coming in; we were in all the magazines, we were in all the great stores and store windows; we were starting to set up 20th Century Survival shops within department stores. We had everything going for us! As far as I could tell, Dave and Leon, who were supposed to have brought in factories but didn't, were just sitting around counting our money.

My mouth was dry as I prepared to confront them. I am not a naturally contentious person, and I was nervous, but I was also angry and sure that they were wrong and I was right. I felt a surge of anxious strength.

"Look," I told Ron, "I don't think this is fair. I'm doing all the work and I'm splitting the money equally with you guys."

"Well, that's too goddamn bad," he said.

"Really?"

"Yeah. We are equal partners. We are splitting everything equally."

"That's not fair. David isn't working hard. He isn't doing anything. He's not in sales, he's not in marketing, he's not in design, he's not in production. He's hanging out. Leon might be overseeing the business, and you are overseeing sales, but I am really doing all of the work. I am running to India and Hong Kong. I am selling. I'm going to the stores. I'm designing everything, and I'm also doing all the marketing and promotion. I don't think it's fair."

"So what are you going to do about it?" Ron challenged me.

I was angry, shaking, very upset. "Well, I'm going to tell you that if you guys don't—if we can't establish a more fair—I think I am deserving of more . . ." I composed myself. "If we can't establish a better agreement, then I'm leaving."

Ron said, "So leave."

I turned around and walked out.

I was shocked that Ron would be so absolute; I thought he was smarter than that. Now I was even more angry and upset. If they weren't bright enough to be appreciative and grateful, if I couldn't trust them to grow into a more professional and honorable organization, then I was with the wrong people.

That was that. We didn't speak again, and I didn't get paid. They kept my designs and hired my assistant, a young woman named Dina, as head designer. The whole operation went out of business eighteen months later.

# CHAPTER SEVEN

# GROWING PAINS

*Introducing Seasons jeans*

Back in 1978, when I still had People's Place, a noted industry insider named Micki Duchon told me about an excellent brand called Seasons Jeans. I'd called their office and said, "I'd like to place an order."

The man on the other end of the phone seemed about my age and was brusque in the way that the garment industry teaches its salespeople to be brusque. His name was Alex Garfield, and he turned out to be one of the owners of Seasons Jeans.

"What do you want?" he said.

"I have five stores upstate, and I would like a hundred pairs of your three best jeans."

"You want thirty-three and a third of each jean, or do you want a hundred of each?" Okay, so he was a wiseass.

"A hundred of each."

"That's a lot of jeans!"

I laughed. We talked a little about my stores and his company, and I found it unusually easy to tell him some details about my life. He was such a fast talker and seemed to have a good heart. Sometimes you just feel these things. He even sang me the Seasons Jeans ad jingle!

I asked for his three best jeans. Best, not best-selling. He could have sold me anything—inventory he was trying to unload, a style with a larger markup—and how would I have known? Alex probably didn't get a lot of calls like this. I don't think most buyers put themselves at his mercy.

"You're an upstate Irish Catholic boy," he said, "talking to a New York Jewish garmento, and you are trusting me to do this? Do you want to see them?"

"No," I told him. "I hear they're great jeans. I know from the people I talked to in Micki's office and her son Frank." We both laughed. "Come on. Micki told me I can trust you!"

Micki was right. Not only did Alex ship me great jeans that sold well at People's Place, but we became great friends almost immediately. When we finally met in his showroom, he was the same guy in person that he'd been on the phone: funny, outgoing, honest, and charming.

Sometime after Susie and I arrived in New York, Alex and his partners were taking two buyers from the Gap to the Roxy roller-skating rink, and he invited us to join them. Alex paid his clients' way in and offered to buy our tickets as well. The cover might have been $3. I thanked him but declined.

The Roxy was the home of New York roller disco. The floor was bright white and the rink was all lit up. It was chilly, the music was blaring, and there were incredibly cool skaters zipping around in disco duds, skating backward, doing spins and flips, and just outright showing off. I hadn't roller-skated since grammar school, so we were puttering along, and I felt like a fish out of water. But it was fun! And it was fun being with Alex, because he really went out of his way to make us feel welcome. And he was hilarious, always making us laugh.

Later in the evening, we all took a break and Alex went to the concession stand and bought some snacks. He noticed that I didn't join him.

"Why aren't you getting anything?" he asked.

"I don't have any money," I told him.

Alex bought us Cokes and chocolate bars and made no attempt to either embarrass me or use my neediness to his business advantage. I knew I had found a good man.

Three years later, he proved it to me once again. One day at 20th Century Survival, before our abrupt departure, Susie told me she had a horrible stomachache. As she was explaining the symptoms, our salesperson Judy Sinnreich said, "I think you might have an ectopic pregnancy. A friend of mine had one of those—it's a tubal pregnancy—and that sounds like what you've got. If I'm right and you don't take care of this, it could burst and you could die!"

Susie and I were new to New York—we didn't even have a doctor. We had discussed having kids, but we weren't even thinking about it at that time. Judy called her ob-gyn, and we rushed to her office.

Sure enough, Judy was right. "You need to have this operation immediately," the doctor said. Susie and I both went into panic mode. We raced to the nearest hospital, in Chinatown, and Susie was operated on that night by a surgeon we had never met. Thank God we had health insurance. I sat in the waiting room, terrified. The day had begun like any other, and by the end of it Susie could be dead!

The doctor came out of the operating room in his scrubs and approached quickly. I really didn't want to hear bad news.

The operation had been a success, he said; Susie was in the recovery room, I could see her when she woke up. I felt all the blood in my body rush down to my toes and back to my head. I thanked him.

"Are you squeamish?" he asked.

"Not really," I said. "Why?" I thought he was going to describe the procedure. I was fine hearing the gory details of how this doctor had saved my wife.

"Look."

He brought out a little metal pan holding the fetus he had just removed from Susie. It looked like a baby, but it was smaller than a shrimp. I was shocked. I felt sick to my stomach. I have no idea why he did that, and I have never forgotten the sight. *This could have been my child*, I thought. To this day, I still get chills when I think about it.

Susie was sleeping, still drugged, and I needed someone to talk to, so I called Alex Garfield, and we went out for a meal in Chinatown. I tried to describe this bizarre turn of events, but mostly I babbled. I was still in a state of shock, and somehow I knew that Alex would be there when I needed him. So when I went looking for a new business partner, it was clear to me who would be my first call. We were like brothers then, and we are close to this day.

Susie recuperated, and we were happy to learn that neither the ectopic pregnancy nor the operation would affect our having children in the future.

In 1981, I began planning to break out on my own. I was in Puerto Rico, doing a personal appearance and fashion show at a boutique in a mall that sold 20th Century Survival. I was telling the owner, Wilma Stein, about my partners, with whom I was feeling less and less comfortable, and she said, "Why don't I introduce you to my husband, Gabor—maybe he would like to do a business." Gabor Stein was an old-school knitwear expert who had set up factories for companies such as Lacoste and Izod. Gabor said, "Yeah, I would like to do a business, and I've got some other partners in New York, the Delman family. They own Splendor Form Brassiere company, but they would also like to do something other than undergarments."

I explained that I had a great idea for a new company, and that I had a friend in the jeans business, Alex Garfield, who would be an excellent partner and was the best salesman in the world.

My idea was to do a contemporary line with a simple, clean look. Japanese fashion was happening, and brands like Yohji Yamamoto and Comme des Garçons were doing asymmetrical patterns. Some European designers were cleaning up their aesthetics. Calvin Klein, Armani, and designer Ron Shamask, who later became a friend, were all doing lines inspired by the Japanese. I felt a minimalist trend approaching, but with fine fabrics and architectural finishing.

Gabor understood immediately, and we decided to do business.

After my series of bumps in the road I decided to take professional advice from people who had worked in the industry. This time I was going to have a contract. And once again, I would approach a former acquaintance for guidance.

When I was at People's Place trying to fill the shelves of five shops, I had approached Saks Fifth Avenue, because I knew that department stores had a lot of excess fashion goods for purchase. I had no contacts there, so I'd gone to the selling floor and asked around. I was told, "You have to talk to Mr. Moos."

Emil Moos was SFA's executive vice president and general merchandise manager. He was in his early seventies, very serious, and very smart. In his office, I explained that I was only looking for merchandise they were no longer selling, that I had no intention of competing with Saks in any way. He talked to me at length and paced back and forth, mumbling at times in his German accent, then saying, "I don't know how to handle this!" They certainly didn't want me to resell their goods to a competitor or hawk them on tables outside their flagship store on 50th and Fifth. It didn't take long to convince him I was legit.

I had told Mr. Moos that my real dream was to start my own brand. "Do you realize how difficult that is?" he asked. Yes, I told him, I knew it was very hard, but I had a lot of really good ideas and was motivated to act on them regardless of the difficulty.

"What would you do?"

When I'd woken up that morning I truly had not thought I would be discussing my design vision with the executive vice president of Saks, but I was prepared. "I would develop menswear and womenswear, but more classic and modern, like . . ." I rattled off brands with which I was familiar—their names, where they were positioned, the Saks floor on which they could be found at that moment, their price points. I think Mr. Moos was impressed that for a young guy, I knew so much about the business. He told me if I ever needed help, I should just ask. "I've been around the block," he said, "and I know the ins and outs. If you ever need advice or assistance, you let me know."

So when I went back a few months later and told him that I wanted to start my own brand, but that I needed to find somebody to manufacture it and back me, he said, "I'm retiring next year, and I am going to take on a very few clients to consult. Come see me in September."

In early September, I went to Mr. Moos's shoebox of an office at 40 West 39th Street. I laid out my situation in depth and told him that I hadn't been able to get my own Tommy Hill and Rodeo jeans brands off the ground, that I'd had a guy who was going to manufacture for me who let me down at the last minute, that I'd sold my brother-in-law my store and he wasn't paying me. And I owed the government some money. Long story short: no money, debt, a tax problem.

Mr. Moos got right to it. "First things first," he said, "we've got to get this tax situation straightened out. You need a proper accountant. You need to know Angelo Rosato."

Angelo Rosato had worked with Mr. Moos at Saks Fifth Avenue's parent company, BATUS, the British American Tobacco Company. Standing around five foot four and weighing more than two hundred pounds, Angelo was classically Italian American and very, very bright. At our first meeting he told me, "The first thing you have to do is pay off your tax bill. Then you have to pay off your American Express bill and get your credit line straightened out. You also need an attorney. I'm going to introduce you to Tom Curtin."

When I met Tom, I felt as if I had known him all my life. Well dressed, smart, very friendly. Tom was not only a down-to-earth guy but a caring and smart advisor, and he quickly became one of my very best confidants and friends in the world. He worked hand-in-hand with Mr. Moos, Angelo Rosato, and me to build from the bottom up. He introduced me to many fascinating people he was working with, like the basketball player Bill Bradley, the Mara family (owners of the New York Giants), and Jon Tisch of the Loews Hotels company. He took me to the games locally and to Notre Dame, his alma mater, where we met the coaches, players, and the bigwigs of the university. But I was mostly impressed by Tom as a person. He was and is the most honest, decent human being I know.

Now I had a lawyer, an accountant, and a business advisor. I was developing a team.

I was living hand to mouth, so it took a couple of months to wade through and settle my finances. When it came time to strike a deal regarding my new venture with Gabor Stein, I knew I needed help. I asked Mr. Moos to negotiate for me.

I was more than a little anxious that morning. Susie and I were living in the East Village, on the first and second floors of a townhouse on 9th Street. (Mind you, back then a townhouse between First Avenue and Avenue A was not like a townhouse on the Upper East Side!) I took the subway from NYU to the New York Health and Racquet Club at 56th and Sixth Avenue. At the time I was working out fanatically every day and was in perfect shape, not an ounce of fat on my body. When I left the gym I felt a searing pain in my back that

I later figured out was from stress because I was so worried about this meeting.

Gabor Stein lived at the Sovereign, an elegant building on the Upper East Side. Calvin Klein had had an apartment there, which impressed me greatly. I arrived a little bit early and paced up and down First Avenue, waiting for Mr. Moos. He met me in the rather intimidating lobby.

Gabor Stein's apartment was modern and chic. I sat in his living room, thinking, "This guy is so rich, so successful. I hope he invests in me." I outlined my business plan, describing Alex Garfield as a partner and super salesman, the businessman on the ground who knew all the stores, and myself as the creative.

Then Mr. Moos took over. He had been kind and even-tempered in all our conversations, but with Gabor Stein he was tough. In his German accent, he spoke in a way that was almost threatening. "My client, Mr. Hilfiger, will not do anything without an ironclad contract. He is a very talented young man and he needs to be paid in a very substantial way. We will form a contract between us for services rendered. We will not negotiate, because he is worth a lot of money."

I thought for sure Mr. Moos was going to detonate this deal. Here Mr. Stein had been kind enough to offer to partner with me and back us, and Mr. Moos was talking about me as if I were some superstar, a proven entity. I managed to sit there and say nothing. I held my poker face, but I just knew that any moment Stein was going to say, "Forget it."

But Gabor, who is Hungarian and a soft-spoken gentleman, basically said, "No problem. We will work out a contract and we will work out a deal and be very fair. Now let me meet Alex."

Alex met with Gabor's approval, and then we were introduced to Jack Delman, from Splendor Form Brassiere. (As Alex would later joke, "We had a strong foundation and a lot of support.")

Jack Delman was a scary guy. He eyed Gabor and said, "So what are we doing here?"

I thought, "If Mr. Moos gets into a room with these guys, it's all over." But I'd underestimated him again. Angelo, Tom Curtin, and Mr. Moos created a deal for me that was more lucrative than any I had had to date. Tom was the diplomat, Mr. Moos the negotiator, Angelo the mastermind. Plus, my signed contract specifically permitted me to work on other projects. And I'd actually get paid on time.

I was proud to associate myself with these men. It was always my goal to surround myself with white-glove people who were completely professional, honest, intelligent, sophisticated, and transparent. It made me feel like I was going into the big leagues.

We wanted to call the company Checkpoint, but that name was already registered, so we settled on Click Point. I signed the deal on June 15, 1982, three months after leaving 20th Century Survival.

Stein and Delman had another partner, Bob Strompf. He and Gabor manufactured polo shirts, sweaters, and other pieces for Izod, and that business was exploding. As a result, they had deep access to Asian factories. They had opened a buying office in Hong Kong, run by Strompf's son Richard, a very smart guy who actively helped our launch.

In the early 1980s, there was a difference between making clothes in Hong Kong and making them in India. Hong Kong work was clean and slick, while Indian clothes looked almost handcrafted. Hong Kong was new and exciting to me, so I was happy to do some work there.

From Hong Kong, I flew to Tokyo. I wanted to stay in Harajuku, the shopping area, but I couldn't afford the hotels there, so I stayed in Shibuya. I arrived in the afternoon, put my bags in the hotel, and hit the streets.

I can smell my way around a new place. I can almost sense where fashion is. I started walking through Shibuya, Shinjuku, Harajuku. I went into this shopping mall called Laforet, a series of kiosks and small shops, every one of them filled with incredible fashion. I found so many remarkable ideas I almost ran out of breath. I saw printing on fabric. A lot of raw edges. A lot of asymmetry. A lot of unusual construction. And as I browsed and bought, I kept thinking and thinking and thinking about what my new line was going to look like.

I returned to Hong Kong to actually design it, and was very

happy with what I developed. When I returned to the United States and started getting orders from Angie Kroll at Saks Fifth Avenue, from Neiman Marcus, and from Barneys, I knew I had something different.

Click Point differed from 20th Century Survival in that it was modern, cool, and extremely well made. Because of Bob Strompf and Gabor Stein's contacts, we were using some men's factories to produce women's clothes. I was also using fabrics normally associated with men's clothing—like interlock knit fabric with an almost spongy feel, which is used in golf shirts and polo shirts—in women's skirts, dresses, and tops. We also did what we called an overlocked edge: we didn't hem the edges but stitched them, and they would curl nicely.

I fixated on the smallest details. I created a baby overlock—a raw-edge-type stitch, except tiny. Normally an overlock stitch is about a quarter of an inch wide; I did them a thirty-second or a sixteenth of an inch wide, so it almost looked as if the edges were cut and had curled on their own. I started doing label pieces, printing a label on a separate piece of cloth and attaching it to the inside of the garment.

Alex and I would sell in the showroom, but he was really the master salesman. He succeeded mightily by turning on his charm with the ladies from Bendel's and Bergdorf and Saks. Very quickly we started selling and shipping and selling and shipping and selling and shipping.

Susie wanted to design as well, so when I was approached at this time by two Indian businessmen, Ruby and Roger, to create a line, I said, "I can't, but my wife Susie is very talented and has been very instrumental in inspiring me and working with me, and wants to do something on her own." They saw her work and agreed. Mr. Moos, Angelo, and Tom helped Susie negotiate her contract; I wanted to be certain she was protected. Then she went off to India and developed her line, O'Tokyo.

It was phenomenal! Washed silk, crinkled silk—it had a very cool, chic Japanese look. She was in the windows at Bergdorf, Barneys, and Saks! The following year, during Fashion Week, we rented

Mr. and Mrs. Hilfiger

My grandmother
Dorothy Hilfiger Grega

The Hilfiger family

Mr. and Mrs. Hilfiger

With Billy and Andy Hilfiger

Mrs. Virginia Hilfiger

Hilfiger family home
in Elmira, NY

The Pennsylvania Railroad Company

POLICE DEPARTMENT

Notice of Violation
TRESPASS LAW   Nº   3791

Name Thomas Hilfiger
Address 921 Laurel St.Elmira N.Y.

Age 7     Time 2;45 PM Date 1-3-59
Location Walking Main Track South
Kendall Tower.
Officer G.W.Ruger.

Your cooperation is solicited to stop trespassing
railroad property and prevent personal injury.

My aunt Annie

Billy and Michael Fredo in 1992

Ginny and Bobby

My brother Billy and me

Bobby Hilfiger at
family home

My mother,
Virginia Hilfiger

My mother, Aunt Annie,
Dee Dee, and her kids in 2001

Susie Hilfiger

My mother and sister Kathy

My mother and sister Betsy

Bobby and Joanne's wedding

With my mother
in Mustique

With my mother

Ginny, Dee Dee, and Betsy

Julian, Alex, Ally,
Elizabeth, Kathleen,
and Sebastian Hilfiger

With my mother
and sister Betsy

Larry Stemerman (from left), Tom Hilfiger and John Allen, owners of The People's Place.

*Bell Bottom Business Booming*

# 'Mod, Mod World' for 3 Youths

By DICK MITCHELL

"To the old, anything new is bad news."

This is the philosophy of these "mod" youths—Larry Stemerman of 86 Greenridge Drive, Thomas Hilfiger of 506 W. Clinton St. and John Allen of 400 Carroll Road, all seniors at Elmira Free Academy.

They parlayed a $150 investment into a thriving downtown business known as the People's Place.

People claim their profit making venture the long-haired, mod dressed youth say they have not joined "the establishment"—nor are they fighting it.

Stemerman said that at first the three youths aren't conforming to the established procedures of business.

"What business would hire youths with long hair?" he asked. "We've put whole collar conservatives."

Other youths describe the People's Place as more of an experience than a chore—a seat with the odor of incense, leather and suede and sounds of the latest records.

Discussing this environment

Hilfiger commented, "The members of the establishment are committed to their generation and we're servants to ours."

"I'm my own boss," added Allen. "I don't have the hassles older, established store workers and bosses have, because of my age."

Long-haired mods sometimes are harassed by the older generation, the three agree, "because they think this makes us degenerates."

Stemerman recalled that he and Hilfiger recently sat at a coffee shop next to two women.

"Do you have jobs?" one of the women asked the two boys.

The other woman laughed and commented "Who would love them with hair like that?"

Hilfiger recalls that at this point they told the two women they owned their own business. "It really blew their minds," he said with a chuckle.

He said it will be necessary for his generation to suffer disrespect and humiliation

from older persons until they discover that "some youths really have something going for them."

The three plan college educations but will wait until they consider themselves mature enough for the experience.

"Kids are pushed into college when they are not mature enough to understand the responsibility of a college education," Stemerman contends.

Who would buy a pair of striped bell bottoms, Peter Fonda glasses, white lace body shirts, flutes or strobe candles?

Quite a few people would. For example, since they opened Dec. 1, they have sold more than 160 pairs of bell bottoms and more than 10 body shirts.

They say that the entire stock has been sold three times and their investment has grown to $1000.

During the Christmas season they averaged $100 a day in sales.

They are doing so well, they have enlarged the store to twice its original size.

People's Place,
Elmira, NY

With Larry Stemerman

Andy and Billy Hilfiger
and Michael Houghton

With Larry Stemerman

NOW IT'S OPEN

DEC. 1, 1969

the

PEOPLE'S-PLACE

ELMIRA'S ONLY BASEMENT BOUTIQUE

ON THE CORNER OF MAIN & GRAY STS.

ENTRANCE ON THE MIDTOWN PLAZA IN BACK

Bells    Jewelry
Jackets  Blankets    Suedes
Incense  Leather     Posters
         &           Shampoo
      much, much
         more.

People's Place

PROPRIETORS: L. STEGERMAN, T. HIPPO, J. BLABBERMOUTH

People's Place,
Elmira, NY

further adventures ltd

Promotion company
for concerts

itchhiking to see
onehenge

Further Adventures Ltd. presents

B. B. King

with Special Guest

ESTUS

FRIDAY MAY 11 AT 8:00 P.M.

AT ELMIRA COLLEGE DOMES

ickets — Advance $4.00
         At Door $4.50    N⁰  470

...physical...fitness...is...a...good...feeling...

people's
place

.....is a great store for
College Students

We know that Elmira College's
Athletic Education Center
will be it's greatest attribute!

Shop... people's
place

• No. 1 MIDTOWN PLAZA
  ELMIRA, N.Y.
• 27 W. MARKET ST.
  CORNING, N.Y.

people's
place

HAS THE BEST
"BOTTOMS"
by

Nina

DOWNTOWN ELMIRA AND CORNING STORES

people's
place

Red Fox
FOR
YOUR
Foxy
Lady
$270⁰⁰

No. 1 MIDTOWN PLAZA • DOWNTOWN ELMIRA

People's Place

20th Century Survival

**TOMMY HILL**

**20th CENTURY SURVIVAL**

Factory in India

Tina Bateman at People's Place

With Susie Hilfiger

★ O T O K Y O ★

usie's line

全日本暴猫連合なめ

**CLICK POINT**

*by Tommy Hilfiger*

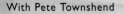

# THE 4 GREAT AMERICAN DESIGNERS FOR MEN ARE:

R A L p h  L A u r e n
P e r r y  E L L I S
C A L v i N  K L e i N
T o m m y  H i L F i G e r

THIS IS THE
LOGO OF THE
LEAST KNOWN OF
THE FOUR

In most households, the first three names
are household words. Get ready
to add another. His first name (hint) is Tommy.
The second name is not so easy.
But in a few short months everybody
in America will know there's a new look
in town and a new name at the top. Tommy's clothes
are easy-going without being too casual,
classic without being predictable.
He calls them classics with a twist.
The other three designers call them competition.

282 Columbus Avenue
at 73rd Street
New York, New York 10023
(212) 877-1270

© 1985 MURJANI

*Hangman* campaign

Coca-Cola clothing

*Hangman* campaign
billboard in Times Square

An *American Classic* campaign

Tommy and the T-Bird!

The bad, bad boy of Seventh Avenue.

Tommy Hilfiger presents An An Evening with Pete Townshend

Joe Fredo and Shannon

Naomi Campbell

Photo: Douglas Keeve

**Boxers in *Tartan* campaign**

T O M M Y

Tommy Hilfiger Men's
Sportswear campaign

HILFIGER

T O M M Y

Ethan Browne for
Tommy Hilfiger Men's
Sportswear campaign

HILFIGE

VH1 Vogue Fashion Awards

Tommy Jeans campaign with Simon Ramone

Britney Spears's . . . Baby One More Time Tour presented by Tommy

np Tommy

TOMMY JEANS

Tommy Jeans
1999 campaign

With Naomi Campbell

Campaign with
Jason Lewis and
Ethan Browne

the FIT auditorium and put on a show together. I presented my new products, and then the lights went out and her show hit. Her line got all the applause and accolades! It was very creative and amazing, while mine was more commercial. That was fine with me. I was very happy for her, and she was pleased for herself.

Life was good. I was traveling back and forth between Hong Kong and Japan and Taiwan and the Philippines, making about $100,000 a year designing and manufacturing the Click Point line. It was 1982, and we had a really great vibe going on.

The one downside to our operation was that we had Jack Delman's son Richard as our babysitter. Jack, Gabor, and Bob wanted to watch their investment, so from the start Richard Delman nickel-and-dimed us like crazy. We tried to explain that the business might not be profitable for a few years, but when it was, it would skyrocket. This did not fly. As a direct result of this penny-pinching, we couldn't buy the amount of inventory we needed, and therefore we couldn't expand the line. We were being held back. I wanted to be with someone who would say, "Let's do it the right way. Let's invest. Let's set it up professionally and go after the big boys!" The dream was alive in my head, but once again, I was not in a position to chase it.

At 1407 Broadway one day, I ran into my old friends Allen and Doreen Gorman, whose clothes I used to sell at People's Place. They told me about Tattoo of California, a Los Angeles company that made young women's California-inspired sportswear, headed by a fellow named Richard Mirkin, that was in search of a designer and a design team. Doreen was going to work there but wanted a partner—was I interested? My contract with Click Point made it very clear that I could pursue other opportunities; that clause had been important to me. I said yes.

But I was concerned about how Alex would react. "Look," I told him, "I'll continue to do Click Point, but I want to make more money, and I want more opportunity, and I want to do this Tattoo thing. I'm going to do both. Please support me." He was not very happy, but he did.

I went to Jack Delman and Gabor Stein, two men of considerable wealth, and said, "I want to be like you guys. I want to make a lot of money, and I can't do that at Click Point because of all the restrictions on our budget. I want you to know that I'm going to work with Tattoo. I'm not going to compete with our company, I'm going to continue to do my work here, but I just want you to know that I intend to take this opportunity." They hemmed and hawed, but ultimately did not get in my way.

By now, Click Point was making money. Alex was working on commission, and a few months in he went to the Delmans and said, "I think you owe me fifty thousand dollars." Jack Delman told him, "Fuck you. At your age, I was making twenty-seven bucks a week." Alex walked. He was a super salesman, he knew his value, and he refused to be messed with. I stayed another month. I was on salary, so they treated me differently, but I wasn't happy. I wanted to spread my wings.

# CHAPTER EIGHT

# NO ONE IS AN INVENTOR IN THE FASHION BUSINESS

Remember

Coca Cola jeans?

My dream team negotiated a Tattoo contract that paid me $100,000 a year. Combined with my Click Point income, I would be making $200,000. I felt like a multimillionaire!

For the first time, I paid close attention to the details of my deal. I learned that there are clauses that can either lock a contract in or keep it open-ended. I became aware of time frames, guarantees, legalities if disputes go to arbitration. I was taught by my representatives and picked up insights by myself, all the while doing the creative for both Click Point and Tattoo and juggling relationships between Gabor Stein, Alex, the Delmans, and Richard Mirkin.

I started commuting between L.A. and New York for a week or even a month at a time. I worked seven days a week—when you love what you do, it's not work—and I loved the challenges. Susie wasn't happy about me being away so often, and though I invited her to come with me, she didn't love the prospect of traveling back and forth to California herself, so she stayed put. The minute I landed there, I'd go to Fred Segal, a shop on Melrose Avenue that at the time was still being run by Fred himself and had the hippest, coolest stuff in town. (Now sometimes they do, sometimes they don't.) I shopped in Maxfield and all over L.A., and breathed in a whole different fashion sensibility. Where New York was dressed up and corporate, L.A. was casual, beachy, and surf-inspired.

Plus, having grown up in the cold and control of Elmira, I absolutely loved the weather and the whole Beverly Hills/Hollywood vibe. It was artsy, it was rock and roll, it was chic. It was extremely easy on the eyes! Driving through Rodeo Drive, driving past the Beverly Hills Hotel on Sunset, was beautiful. I liked the manicured lawns, I liked the restaurants, the shopping, the ocean. In some ways, L.A. was an escape.

Still, all the major fashion players were back in New York. Perry Ellis was becoming important. Calvin Klein, Ralph Lauren, Halston, and Bill Blass were huge. Those were the designers I had my eye on; they were building designer brands. I thought, "Click Point is never going to be that. Tattoo of California will never be that." In order to get into the big game you had to have a designer profile, a designer name, and a designer behind the brand who produced something unique that could become relevant in the marketplace.

So I was in L.A., designing for Tattoo of California, but my mind was going somewhere else.

One day in 1983, while I was working in L.A., my friend Midge Fraser, a buyer from the Broadway Department Stores, called and said, "Have you ever been to a psychic?" I told her I hadn't.

"Would you like to visit one?"

Sure, why not? I was a skeptic, but it sounded like it might be fun.

We drove to Palm Springs to the home of Zvia Holmes, an Israeli woman, who sat me down at her kitchen table and made me a Turkish coffee. "Drink this and then turn the cup upside down," she told me. I did as she ordered. Zvia had a pretty deep accent. She looked at me and said, "Is something wrong with your left leg?"

"No," I told her. My leg was fine.

"Something must be wrong with your left leg," she said. "I am thinking something is wrong with your left leg."

"No."

But she was right! When I was seven years old, my mother had taken a piece of glass from a broken coffee table down into the basement and put it near the trash before putting it out that night. I was down there running around playing cowboys and Indians, and I ran into this jagged edge and sliced my leg open. Big tears. My mom wrapped the cut in a cloth diaper—there was always a baby in the house—and took me to the hospital where she worked. When they took off the cloth, my leg was split like a log. I remember a big pool of blood and getting fifty stitches. From then on, my left and right legs had not been equal. Despite the fact that I had a big scar, I hadn't thought about it in years. Somehow Zvia knew.

She said, "You are married, aren't you?"

"I am."

She asked, "Is your wife Indian?"

I said, "No." But this was spooky, because Susie was in India at that moment, designing her own line.

"Okay, well, I felt something like that. . . . You're from a large family, aren't you?"

"Yes."

"Your mother's small?"

"Yes."

"You don't get along very well with your father, do you?"

Now I was starting to believe. Midge didn't know anything about my family.

"I see you doing something with clothes and fashion."

Midge must have told her, I thought at the time. Later Midge swore she hadn't.

Zvia said, "I see you becoming very, very successful." Well, I enjoyed hearing that because I felt it myself.

She said, "I see there's some connection between you and another of my clients, but I can't figure out what it is. Her name is Rosen. Her husband is the man behind Calvin Klein jeans. I also see a lot of papers. I see lots of papers in your life."

This was definitely spooky.

I flew back to New York the next day and got a call from a headhunter, Vivian Darrow, who said, "I know you have a couple of design projects going on, but I'm looking for a designer for the Calvin Klein brand."

"*What?*"

"They need a person to design all the casual and all the jeanswear."

"That's me. For sure!"

I interviewed with Bob Suslow, who had been president of Saks Fifth Avenue before becoming president of Calvin Klein, and with Calvin himself. I was excited to meet him; he was in the midst of becoming perhaps the most important American designer at that time. He was polite, but he was certainly not interested in getting into any deep conversations about my philosophies or my design experience. I could tell even from the few words we exchanged that the jeans/casualwear part of his business was not his priority. He was much more interested in the more sophisticated elements, like his collection and the marketing of his fragrances. I think he just wanted to put a name with a face, which was okay with me. Bob and I spent quite some time talking about the business, and I was introduced to the design director, Chester Weinberg, with whom I hit it off immediately.

So I was thrilled when they called up and said, "You're hired." All I could come up with was, "Fantastic!"

"The first thing you have to do is go to Hong Kong next week," they told me. "We're designing a whole line and we need someone to navigate it." I was so excited!

I called Zvia to tell her the news, and her response threw me. I don't know what I expected. She could have been smug, she could have been cosmic, she could have been calm and pleased with her foresight. Instead she said, "Not so fast."

"What do you mean?" I thought maybe she had called or told her other client, who then told her husband about me, and this had somehow had an influence. But no.

"There's something better coming along."

Now I knew she was officially crazy. How could anything better come along? I would be working for one of my heroes, learning from him before I started my own business. I was tired of rinky-dink operations; I wanted to go big and I wanted to go strong. And I wanted to prove to Calvin Klein and everyone else that I really did know what was going on. Plus, it was a large salary.

"What are you talking about?"

"I don't know. I see a lot of papers. Don't take this job."

Clearly she was nuts. I said, "I did already."

There was starting to be a little buzz around Susie and me. The New York department store Abraham & Straus honored me with the American Design Spirit Award for being one of the best up-and-coming American designers. At the ceremony Susie looked incredible in Chanel, with a sailor hat and Chanel jewelry, and I wore a tux. Our photographs appeared in the *New York Post* and *Women's Wear Daily*. Tom Curtin and Mr. Moos were finalizing the contract with Calvin. I would drop Click Point and Tattoo and be paid over $200,000 a year!

Then, in 1984, I met Mohan Murjani. In 1982, while in Hong Kong for Click Point, I had met an Indian family in the clothing business, the Harilelas. David Harilela introduced me to Bina and Depu Murjani, who were also in the business. The Murjani Group was huge. They owned Gloria Vanderbilt Jeans, at the time one of the best-selling jeanswear businesses in the world. Bina and Depu kept insisting I meet their brother Mohan.

Mohan was about five foot nine, in his early forties, a trim, good-looking, mustachioed man with a nice way about him. We hit it off immediately. He said, "I've been hearing a lot about you." He asked what I wanted to do, and I told him my dream was to eventually do my own line. "What are you doing nowadays?" he asked.

"I just took a job at Calvin Klein."

"Oh, really? When did you take it?"

"Well, I actually haven't taken it yet," I told him. "I'm starting on Monday."

He said, "Don't do that." Mohan Murjani was very decisive. "Why don't we do Tommy Hilfiger?"

Was he saying I should have my own designer line? "Sounds good to me!" I replied. I pushed forward immediately, as if we had agreed in principle and the deal was already done. "But do you think people would really want a line called Tommy Hilfiger? Do you think anyone will be able to pronounce it?" I did not want this opportunity to go away, so I presented the question as if we were already in business and now all we had to do was name the company.

Mohan was not deterred. "Do you think anyone really knows how to pronounce Yves St. Laurent?" he said. "People can't say my name, either. So, what would you do?" he asked.

"I would design a whole line for myself," I told him. "I would start with menswear and design a line that is classic but modern." I had been hanging out in California, designing for Tattoo, wearing a lot of very casual, relaxed clothes, but in the back of my mind I still had the concept of reimagined preppy. So I blended the two. I told him, "It's got to be classic—with a twist."

I was wearing a navy blue double-breasted shawl-collared sweater with a blue-and-white-striped shirt and Girbaud khaki pants with white K-Swiss sneakers. Murjani asked, "Where did you get that sweater?"

"Adrienne Vittadini."

"You should do a look like that." I liked him already. "When can you start?"

I called Tom, Angelo, and Mr. Moos immediately, then went back and told the Calvin Klein people I wasn't coming. I never in my life thought I would do that—Calvin Klein offers me a job and I turn it down?—but Murjani was offering me the opportunity to fulfill my dreams, and I had to pursue it.

Angelo and Tom represented me, and the Murjanis' in-house attorney, Freema Gluck, negotiated for Murjani. The negotiation was deep. Murjani wanted exclusive use of my name forever. But I didn't want to give it up. For a moment things came to a standstill.

After much discussion, we created a hybrid of a licensing partnership. I would license my name to Murjani in return for a percentage of sales, and also get paid for the design work—a $250,000 advance against 5 percent royalties, plus a car of my choice equivalent to an S-class Mercedes, and first-class travel. Other name designers might have had real ownership in their company and had a salary plus equity in the ownership or profits, but because of my financial situation, I traded the use of my name for free cash flow and the opportunity to do what I needed to do. I thought I was in the big leagues.

Susie and I moved from 9th Street in Alphabet City—a bit of a dangerous neighborhood, but still fun—to a rental loft in the bourgeois heart of Soho, between Prince and Spring Street. I was preparing to go to Hong Kong, shopping around our new neighborhood, looking at different ideas. I felt exhilarated. I was about to start the Tommy Hilfiger line, the first time I was being given the opportunity to set my mind totally free.

---

On June 30, Mohan—we were so comfortable with each other that I almost immediately began calling him by his first name—invited me to his office and said, "I want to introduce you to Joel Horowitz." Horowitz was the president of Gloria Vanderbilt, Murjani's major company. "Joel will be the one watching over your business."

Joel knew absolutely nothing about me before we met, but that day, when Murjani and his company's president, Alan Gilman, walked me into his office and told him, "Here, he's yours," we became the best of friends. Forever.

We talked for two hours, and it was quickly apparent that Joel and I were brothers. Our experiences, personalities, outlooks on the industry, and visions of what my business would be were on the same wavelength. I learned a life-changing lesson that day: in the search for a person to work with closely, like-mindedness is the key.

Joel grew up in Lakeview, Long Island—a "census-designated place" (not even a town!) next to Rockville Centre. His parents' best friends turned out to be best friends with Ralph Lauren's wife, Ricky. Ralph Lauren started in business selling ties and wanted an employee who knew how to make ties and whom he could trust. Joel's father ran a tie factory in Manhattan, and they had met socially on a few occasions, so Joel's father became Ralph Lauren's first employee.

Joel was at college—Miami of Ohio, the "Cradle of Coaches"—at the time. He entered in 1969, intending to study business administration, but all he really wanted to do was learn music and save enough money to hitchhike around Europe for a year. The best way to do that, Joel thought, would be to get a job and live at home. The best-paying job he could find was as a mailman. He got a super-high score on the civil service exam and was assigned a route right in his neighborhood, making $250 a week. As far as he was concerned, this was perfect.

The day he was supposed to report to work, his parents got down on their hands and knees and said, "Our son can't be a mailman, our son can't be a mailman!" His mom said, "Just try working with your father. They need help. Just try it!"

Joel arrived for his first day at the Ralph Lauren office in his bar mitzvah suit, with a mustache and hair down to his shoulders. Ralph pulled him aside and said, "Cut your hair, shave your mustache, and here are a few suits for you. Let's see if they fit." It turned out that Joel was a perfect model size. He went home transformed. He was Ralph's fifth or sixth employee. It was a very small organization.

Joel started at Ralph Lauren Polo in 1969 and worked there off and on through the seventies. He got married and had a son, Dustin; got divorced and got married again; had a daughter, Leigh; and found himself at the point in life where he needed to earn money to support his family. His search for creatively fulfilling work proved unrewarding, and ultimately he decided, "I'm just going to take the highest-paying job I can find." It turned out to be head of merchandising and sourcing at Murjani. He had no particular desire to be there. If a better-paying job came along, he would take it—maybe it would be more exciting.

And then I dropped into his office. It was June 30, 1984.

I sat down with Joel and said, "Look, I don't want to sit here and sketch ideas or come up with creations. The only way I can put this line together is to go to Hong Kong, search for the right fabric, get it dyed in the right colors, get all the accessories, the buttons, the zippers, et cetera, et cetera, then wait while it's put together, and be available for the factories and the sample makers to answer questions, to do the fittings, to make adjustments."

Joel agreed completely. But there were complications. First there was the issue of the company's name. I thought it had been settled: Tommy Hilfiger. Apparently it had not. Within the Murjani Group there was disagreement as to whether it was, indeed, too difficult to launch. Would the public think it was Hillfigure? Hilfinger? "Maybe we should alter it. Maybe it should be . . . Tommy Hill?"

But I was adamant. I felt strongly that Mohan's original reasoning made sense. I wanted to use my real name. And we did. (We also ended up buying the name Tommy Hill from Muna Baig to protect the Tommy Hilfiger brand.)

Men's Market, the week-long trade show where buyers place orders for the following season, was in August. This was June 30. Typically, even with established brands, it takes around six months to put a line together. Here, though, not only were we creating product, but we were launching a brand from scratch! We needed an entire range of specific items to sell to buyers, plus we had to create a vision, a definition, an understandable aesthetic, and a concrete definition of who we were.

I left for Hong Kong the next day and stayed there for the month of July.

From the moment I signed the contract with Murjani, I kept racking my brain, wondering what we could do, what *I* could do, that would be different, noticeable, interesting, fun, creative. I sketched for hours on the plane. By now, after having traveled to makers across the globe, I had a design routine. I had pictures, swatches, colors, samples, suitcases full of stuff. At the Murjanis' offices in Hong Kong, I laid it all out. We went through the shirts, then the trousers, then the sweaters. I knew how to develop a line. But did I have a line to develop? It was time to produce. In my mind, I knew what I wanted to achieve.

I concentrated on two themes: nautical and safari.

I've always loved the look and feel of yachting and sailing and being on the sea. It conjures places in the world infused with wealth, warmth, romance, excitement, inspiration, and aspiration: Newport, Nantucket, Portofino, Saint-Tropez. Just as in my dreams as a boy, being on the water is all about escapism. It embodies class. I think of Jack and Jackie Kennedy. The good life is something everyone wants.

As for military-inspired safari, I just thought it was cool. Close your eyes and picture shades of khaki, olive, ivory—all great colors in different variations of fabrics. You get it, you know what it is. I thought, "Let's give people that, but somehow fresh and new."

Also, both looks were wearable. That was of utmost importance. I wanted my line to be cool and different, but I also wanted it to be affordable, attainable. I had learned from my glam-rock infatuation, for instance, that I needed to approach Tommy Hilfiger the brand not as a niche that would appeal to a tiny audience but as a line that could appeal to large numbers of people. My key elements from the start were quality, fit, shape, fabric, detail, attitude, cool factor, and youthfulness.

I felt this strongly then, and I feel it equally strongly now: when a person picks up a shirt, he or she has to see something special in it, otherwise the shirt is a shirt is a shirt. So I made a mental check-list: Is it classic? *Check.* Is it fresh? *Check.* Is it new? *Check.* Is it fun? *Check.* Is it cool? *Check.* Does it fit? *Check.* Does it have function? *Check.* Is it going to appeal to a fashion customer? *Check.* Is it going to appeal to a regular customer, a normal everyday person? *Check.* Is it different from anything else in its realm? *Check.* Does it look more expensive than it is? *Check.* Does it have unique detail to differenti-ate it from others? *Check.* Is it made very well? *Check.* Is it on trend? *Check.* Is it of the moment? *Check.* Is it not too far ahead? *Check.* Is it not too far behind? *Check.* Every aspect of every garment had to go through that checklist.

Most of all, the collection could not look like any other. That was my main motive. Like I said, it had to be classic, but it had to have a twist.

I hired an incredibly helpful assistant, Lindy Donnelly, to sketch and do the technical drawings and a lot of the detail work, leaving me to concentrate on design. So I would look at a sample shirt and pontificate: "The color shouldn't be that way; it should be this way. Let's make the pocket much larger. Let's make the sleeve much shorter." Lindy took notes as she sketched.

I thought out every centimeter of every item. I innovated. I cre-ated a contrast lining in the neck of a button-down. It had never been done before. It wasn't your basic white shirt anymore—except it was! Buttoned at the collar, it was virtually indistinguishable from its more expensive brothers; only the person who wore it knew how cool he was. Unbuttoned, the coolness was there for all to see. I fash-ioned the piece with less interlining to make it softer and more com-fortable on the neck.

I developed a V-shaped label piece for the inside of the shirt. I thought of this one while I was in the air between New York and

Hong Kong. That space behind the neck had never been used, and instead of accepting the classic placement of the label, I created a frame for it—a V piece that was stitched and visible from behind. My brand and logo would be recognizable without even being seen.

Initially I put a green buttonhole on every shirt; then I put a contrast buttonhole on the cuff and a contrast color in the cuff itself. I developed a contrast lining inside the sleeves, so when a guy rolled them up, he showed not only some forearm but also some imagination and style. It was all about making a shirt that was special. I wanted all of my clothes to be special.

My pants were comfortably unusual, with all sorts of different details. We offered a vibrant combination of pattern, color, fabric, and the right wash, the right twist, the right buttons. The waistband was a contrast fabric. Deep pockets, button-through flap on the back pocket. Belt loops strategically placed. The fit was ever so important.

We knew we needed ties, so we started talking to Herb Aronson, the head of Manhattan Industries, a neckwear company, who said, "Who's Tommy Hilfiger?" He sat in his desk chair and kept smacking a baseball into a Rawlings catcher's mitt—*smack, smack, smack*. He seemed like an older guy who really wouldn't understand what we did anyway, so I wasn't surprised when he passed. About a year later, Tommy Hilfiger had become a sufficiently significant brand that they decided it would be a good idea to have our name on a neckwear line. We reconvened with Manhattan Industries, and they decided to do the license.

Como, Italy, was the neckwear, scarf, and cravat capital of the world—printed silks, beautiful. I had never been there, so I went with Aronson. On Lake Como, there are artist studios in family-run businesses like Ratti and Montero in a succession of beautiful villas. We visited the home of manufacturer Romano Botta, ate pasta, and picked out the ties' foulards, or fabrics. But I didn't want them to design my ties; I wanted to design the neckwear myself. I knew exactly what I wanted: regimental stripes, tartan plaids, solids with embroidered crests on them, all in my own color choices. I wanted them to be different.

I had a very specific idea in mind. I wanted the front to look like a regular tie, but I wanted the back to have a tail that was in contrast. This had never been done, and at first the makers said they couldn't do it. But I wasn't taking no for an answer. When I have an idea and I want to do it, no is not an option. The most confrontational I've ever been has been with product people who say they can't do something that I know they can. At that point I become almost fanatical, because I can see it in my mind.

I saw this tie. Mr. Aronson gave me a thousand excuses, but I said, "Why don't you just take the back of a solid tie and sew it onto the front of the tie?"

"Well, that's very expensive."

I kept pushing, and finally we figured it out. We created a unique signature in neckwear. Now, when a guy puts on a Tommy Hilfiger tie, it has a little contrast, just a little detail that doesn't frighten the customer away but basically sets our neckwear apart from anything else that might be in the store.

We switched licensees from Herb Aronson's Manhattan Industries to Superba Neckwear, a company owned by Mervyn Mendelbaum. Mervyn and I went to Lake Como together. Rather than being a no-can-do guy, Mervyn was a man who figured out how to get things done. As a result, our neckwear line exploded. It's still selling today, twenty-six years later. People copy it, people do their version of it, but it's ours. It's iconic. And that, to me, is exhilarating.

I was very retail savvy, as a result of having had my own stores, and I knew that if you put your clothes in a department store, you are in a sea of other people's clothes, and if your clothes look like everyone else's, they're not going to sell. It's no different from the music business. If you create a song that sounds like twenty other songs, it's not going to stand out. If it's familiar but has a certain something that sets it apart, you've got a hit. That's always been my philosophy. The Eagles made a career out of taking phrases that were already in people's vocabulary—"One of These Nights," "New Kid in Town," "The Long Run"—changing them slightly to make them their own, and then producing beautifully crafted, illuminating music. They sold a billion records that way.

There is always the possibility that a designer will go over the line, from classics with a twist to classics with a *crank*, and we've gone over the line many times, sometimes on purpose, but mostly not. Subtlety is crucial when putting detail into a garment. It's almost like being a chef. How much spice do you add to your dish? If it's too spicy, your diners can't digest the meal you have so meticulously prepared for them. If it's not spicy enough, the flavor is bland and diners are unsatisfied.

I learned early on that most people, men especially, do not want to be frightened. They do not want to stand out too much or be too fashion forward. I often feel as if I'm walking a tightrope: lean too far to the right or left, and you fall into the canyon. You have to maintain balance at all times. We have been out of balance many times, but we are right more than we are wrong, and when we are balanced, we are *rocking*!

If you set trends, great. But it's very, very risky. My People's Place misadventure with glam rock proved this to me. I would rather follow trends than lead them. But when following, I want to create my own version and make a new trend out of an existing one.

This is one of my core beliefs: *No one is an inventor in the fashion business.* No one creates the pant, no one creates the shirt or the sweater or the jacket. Designers *re-create* fashion. We take something that exists and make it newer. It is the re-creators, the ones who do it really well, who are the moneymakers.

The real asset in any brand is in the logo. An effective logo does not simply say to a customer, "Here's a nice-looking shirt." There are a lot of nice-looking shirts. It says, "This is what you ought to be wearing." It is a signal of confidence and intent. Think of Rolex with its crown, Mercedes-Benz with its star. Think of Chanel, Gucci, Mont Blanc, Louis Vuitton, Bentley, Rolls-Royce. Look at the Rolling Stones' tongue. Look at the Converse star, the Nike swoosh, the Penguin penguin, the Apple apple. When I see brands without a logo, I think the company is not smart. I think whoever is creating that brand is missing something. Look at Kellogg's cereal versus no-brand. What are you going to buy? You are going to buy Kellogg's, because it has history and cachet, and Tony the Tiger says it's "grrrrreat!"

When I began thinking about my logo, I thought about Lacoste, with its alligator-logo polo shirt, which had been in existence since 1933. Polo Ralph Lauren had its horse. Nike's swoosh was coming on strong, Adidas had its triple stripe, Puma had its puma. Today we live in a logoed, status-oriented society. Back then, it was just beginning to seriously trend.

Mohan Murjani introduced me to the people at Landor, a graphics company in California. I told them I loved flags—countries, yachts, important buildings, and official vehicles all have flags—and that I liked red, white, and blue. I thought it would be really cool to have my own flag. I wanted to put my stake in the ground.

When I told them I wanted it to be nautical and regal, Landor went to a semaphore alphabet—a nautical alphabet. The perfect metaphor! The designers took my initials, the *T* and *J* and *H*, and combined them into a tight rectangle, then placed *Tommy Hilfiger* in the navy bars top and bottom. I took one look and said, "That's it!"

It was my dream to become so successful that we could take the name off altogether and people would still know what it stood for, like Nike with its swoosh. I wanted my flag to become an American icon.

I also thought it would be cool to have something akin to a presidential seal or crest, to introduce heritage into my brand. I kept thinking, "My Swiss and German relatives probably had crests." So I created my own—a lion with a sword and some laurels around it—that I adapted from a figure I saw on a cigar band. I placed my flag label on the back of my garments and my crest on the front.

Just as important as my logo was my use of red, white, and blue to create an overall point of view. Hermes has orange, Tiffany has light blue. My colors connote the nautical and Americana.

I felt the competition around me was beginning to look a little boring. With an interesting detail and a great logo on our shirts, all of a sudden we had snap, crackle, and pop. It was just what we needed to make it cool and right for the time. Between the logo, the crest, and the design, everyone who bought my clothes became a billboard for the company. I wanted people to say, "Oh, that's a Tommy Hilfiger shirt!" And then go out and buy some.

When I returned from my design trip to Hong Kong for my first collection, Joel and I spent endless hours together building Tommy Hilfiger the brand. Our partnership was magical. Joel was strategic, thoughtful, and diligent. He would take risks at the exact right moment. He always knew when to step on the gas and when to let up.

The distinction between me and the brand was negligible. I knew from the beginning that the two things were one and the same. The only time I part with the brand is at home with my family, where I'm Dad or Tommy.

We sold the Tommy Hilfiger spring 1985 collection—the first under my own name, what a thrill!—from a clothing rack out of Joel's office. The retailers loved it. But there was a problem with the order.

So many things can go wrong in the production of a fashion line: they make a mistake in the sewing; they use the wrong color; they're going to be late; shipments are delayed because of monsoon rains in India, or because the factory didn't get the money, or because the workers were on strike, or because of a holiday such as Chinese New Year or Diwali. This time, it was fabric issues and fit. We were garment-dying some styles and found irregularities in the color shading.

Because the design, buying, and manufacturing were all so rushed, the product came from Hong Kong poorly made and poorly finished. We were launching my new collection, and there were threads hanging from the garments, which were wrinkled and unpressed. When you open a container full of problems, it's devastating. We didn't have time to send the shipment back for repair or remanufacturing; we would have gotten massive cancellations. So instead we hustled, assembling temporary workers to cut the threads, press, and repair. Joel's entire business background prior to this disaster was founded on organization, systematization, developing a calendar, and getting everything done as precisely as possible. Thank

God. Through a combination of hard work, long hours, and inspired panic, we managed to salvage the line.

Joel helped me mold and shape the collection. His first contribution was an informed critique of its price. When we showed the line, he gauged retailers' reaction and determined that our clothes were too expensive.

He said, "Tommy, the stores think seventy-five dollars on that shirt is too much. Let's lower it to fifty." I was not averse to this. I was happy to defer to Joel on business decisions. My goal was to make money. However, if we cut back the margin, we would not make up for it in volume; we would simply make less money. Joel made the excellent point that we needed to establish ourselves as a brand first and increase our volume as we increased our visibility. We basically went back and took a haircut. We decided to charge $25 less per shirt. After a lot of discussion, we realized that the magic price point was $49.50.

Of course, we tried to mitigate some of that loss. We went back to the factories, fabric suppliers, and button suppliers and said, "How can we get this quality at this price?" The button manufacturer would say, "If you do a button that is pearlized but not mother-of-pearl, you can save money." Makers told us, "If you wash the garment for sixty seconds instead of twenty minutes, you'll save money." "If you ship it by boat rather than by air, it'll be less." "If you cut down on consumption, you can economize—do you really need three and a half yards per shirt?" "If you buy a million labels upfront . . ."

We learned as we went, and after a while, we asked the right questions. I would go to a factory and say, "I want this design, but we can only pay thirty dollars for it. What do we have to do? Oh, you can't use that thread? We have to buy the fabric in Taiwan rather than Italy?" We found that we could make pieces in China rather than Hong Kong: same sewing machines, same needles, same everything, but lower price. We could make something using printed rather than yarn-dyed fabric. There were all kinds of tricks to decreasing the price.

However, there was a level of quality I insisted we maintain. Just as a chef would never use oleo instead of butter, I would never use the coarse cotton jersey used for clothes sold at Kmart and Walmart. I liked to use the finer-combed 80s or 120 two-ply. I would never use inferior piqué. I would never use a type of yarn that doesn't have a memory—I want it to snap back when you stretch it. I would never use a lesser grade of denim. Pocketing, zippers, buttons, and other small details are never too small.

We were on the money. The retailers loved it, the Tommy Hilfiger brand name started to be known, and we began getting orders from a range of store groups.

Our big supporter at the time was Burdine's department store in Miami, run by Howard Socol. We staged our first fashion show under a tent in the parking lot, and Don Johnson and Philip Michael Thomas, co-stars of that moment's hit TV show *Miami Vice*, attended. Afterward, I went into the Tommy Hilfiger shop inside the store to meet customers and promote the brand.

It was not a smashing success. There I was, in a sea of clothing racks, with quite a bit of traffic walking up and down the aisle, and no one was paying any attention to me at all. After such a big buildup, I felt defeated. But Joel consoled me: "You're in the trenches. Don't worry. Pretty soon we'll go to the next level." Deep down in my heart I felt that it would work eventually, but I was impatient. It was not immediately obvious to me that he was right.

In the beginning, we had fit problems. The pants were too baggy in the thighs. They didn't fit properly around the waist; they were a little too tight in the butt. It turned out that this was not a manufacturing error, but part of the design. We tried to fix it, but on our second shipment, it was still an issue. This was a big lesson at the beginning of my journey: you can have the best-looking clothes in the world, with a great label, great advertising, the right price point, and the right style, but if the clothes don't fit perfectly, you might as well hang it up.

So we made the clothes fit.

We hired a fit specialist, Siran Tarzy, an Armenian pattern maker who was a perfectionist. She was very disciplined and hard on me and the design team to get it right, to do the fittings, to look at every centimeter. One of the reasons that Tommy Hilfiger has sold so well for so many years is that we finally figured it out. While all bodies are different, we made sure that the sizes we put into stores could accommodate a wide variety of bodies. A man with a 36-inch waist could be six foot four or five foot eleven, and our pants fit both to perfection. Our trick was always to leave a little room in the hip and thigh.

As we became comfortable with the business, we established a design protocol. First I would come up with an idea. Then I would show a sample I had purchased in a vintage store or in Europe, a picture, or a rough sketch. One of my design assistants would perfect the sketch, which we would send to one of the factories in Asia, often in Hong Kong, where they would make a prototype in any fabric and send it back. Then we would fit it on Joe Pilewski.

Joe was a model who looked like Brad Pitt. He was from Toledo, Ohio, a real football fan and outdoorsman, a ladies' man. Also a loyal, patient guy with the perfect normal body: six feet tall, 170 pounds, 32-inch waist. Joe would stand for hours while we studied a pair of pants on him and picked it apart: "This is too big, that's too small, the butt should be bigger, the belt loops should be higher, the pockets should be lower." In turn, Joe would sit, crouch, wear the pant like a customer. He'd tell us, "I can't get this over my ankle," or "Every time I sit down it's pulling in the crotch," or "The pockets are too deep." We learned a valuable lesson: fitting on mannequins is not as successful as fitting on live models who actually move around. Siran would take notes, re-pin, and sometimes cut a new pattern.

We made four different versions of each sample: one a little bigger, one a little smaller, one way bigger, one way smaller. Kind of like Goldilocks. We would wash and shrink the garment. We would go through multiple renditions of everything. We would remake a shirt collar ten or fifteen times to get it right. We would make a jean in several weights of fabric, because a 14.5-ounce jean will fit differently and hang differently than one at 10 ounces. The pockets had to be perfect. We wanted them deep enough to be useful but shallow enough that you didn't have to dive for your change. It was imperative that after the pant or jean was washed, the pocketing didn't completely shrink up.

Thickness counted. The pocketing and interlining in the waistband had to be thick enough, but not too thick. We wanted a felled (folded, then stitched) seam in the interior, maybe a double-needle seam at thirty-two stitches per inch. We would make sure that we had the optimal size of thread and that the zipper was the perfect weight and size. We would see that the shoulder on the shirt would drop an inch and a half from the top of the shoulder and that the yoke would fall in the exact correct place. The shirt would be loose enough yet trim enough, and the size of the armhole would fit everyone perfectly.

Joel focused on the overall road map and strategy of growth. He said, "We need a core of basics." If we could create and sell men's clothing necessities, if we could be the place men went for all of their basics, if we could give them what they wanted and do it with style, not only would we be filling a need, but we would own a very large share of the market.

So what did men need? Chinos—we called ours the Public pant. A pair of shorts—ours was the Officer short. A polo shirt, which we named the Newport polo. A sweater, which we called the Prep crew. A jacket, our Ivy jacket. Jeans—we called ours the Canyon jean. Our shirt was the Harvard shirt, and we offered it in oxford shirting, checks, chambray, and denim. This was our Core Basic line.

I named everything in the beginning because I was a control freak. I wanted everything to be done in my very specific way. The five-pocket Canyon jean was like a Western jean that cowboys would wear. The Ivy jacket was our Baracuta jacket, the kind of lightweight, zip-up jacket you'd see on a college campus. The Newport polo represented yachting, Newport Harbor, and New England preppy. The

Public pant fit the public—it looked good on everyone. The Officer short was military, with box pleats. The Prep crew was very preppy—I wanted it on every cool kid in the world. I considered these names very carefully. The more I could steep each item in aspirational, New England, Ivy League imagery, the more I felt I was enhancing the entire brand. I wanted to own that category of fashion.

Then we opened it up. We took all the Core Basic items and colored them for the season, or added stripes and checks and other patterns. We called this Core Plus.

We built a business pyramid. Core Basic was designed to be at least 50 percent of the business. We wanted Core Plus to be 40 percent of the business. And then Fashion, which would be the themes created seasonally—nautical, cricket team, calypso—would make up the remaining 10 percent. Respectively, those three parts of the pyramid would make money day in and day out, make money seasonally, and lead the charge. Because we relied so heavily upon our formula, we had to make sure that every item fit perfectly, and that every item was priced properly and would actually make money.

The beauty of Core Basic was that it would sell continually and never get marked down. We updated the details as fashions changed over the years, but Basic truly became the core of the business. It also freed us to experiment and take risks in other parts of the line. Early on, when we had a Fashion group that didn't sell, we felt a collective "Uh-oh." It was a little scary. But with Core Basic solidifying our base, if we did have a Fashion group that wasn't great and wasn't making its numbers, it wasn't the end of the world.

Joel was always looking to the future. He would ask, "Where are we going? What are the goals we have to put in place? Who do we need and what do we need and how do we get there?" He believed in the concept of risk as a means of moving forward, but at the same time, he was controlled and disciplined in his outlook. He completely understood what I was doing and helped me evolve and improve on a daily basis. He would consistently come in with a slightly different point of view. I was happy when he would say, "Tommy, have you tried this?" He was strategic in everything we did, whether it was advertising, marketing, or distribution. He had the background and expertise to talk to lawyers and accountants as well as designers. Better than anyone, Joel could look at the merchandising of the line and tell us which price points we should be at. Retailers had tremendous respect for him because they knew that he knew what he was talking about. If we were the Rolling Stones, Joel was Charlie Watts. He kept the backbeat.

In late 1985, as the Tommy Hilfiger business was just starting, Mohan came to me and Joel and said, "I am signing a license with Coca-Cola for clothes, and I think it is going to be huge—what do you guys think about it?"

I thought, "Coca-Cola clothes? Who's going to wear that? What are they going to be, red-and-white T-shirts?" It didn't seem too exciting or cool to me, not the kind of upscale wear I wanted to be involved with.

But, seeing that we were getting some traction with Tommy Hilfiger, Mohan had faith that we as a team knew what we were doing. He said, "I really would like your help in designing and marketing this." We didn't know whether he was threatening to decrease his support of Tommy Hilfiger if we didn't agree to participate, but the unspoken message was clearly that one hand washes the other: he would continue to back Tommy Hilfiger if we would do Coca-Cola for him. After some discussion, Joel and I agreed to it.

Joel set a March 1 deadline. I tapped some of the talent on my team and said, "Let's lay out what it should be." We would give nothing but our best.

I came up with the idea that I should take everything that I would want to wear and put a Coca-Cola label on it. I began shopping in stores, from boutiques to big boxes. What would Coca-Cola clothes look like in those establishments? I began imagining a Coca-Cola label on everything, and what had started as an accommodation to a boss began to resonate and come together.

At that time, Benetton was a global fashion brand, based in Italy, known for its use of vibrant colors and youth-based merchandise. It had taken America by storm—in the 1980s, there was a Benetton on every street corner. Since we were living in Soho, Susie and I walked into the one on West Broadway. We were both struck immediately by their rugby shirt. The Benetton logo was printed on a piece of muslin and sewn onto the front, similar to how authentic rugby shirts may have been made in the early days, when a number was printed on a piece of cloth and sewn onto a knit jersey. It embodied authenticity and cool. Susie and I said almost simultaneously, "Wouldn't that be incredible as a Coca-Cola rugby shirt?" I bought one, took it to the office, and inspected and critiqued and redesigned it, as I had done with so many garments in India and Hong Kong. We had something here.

We made the Coca-Cola rugby shirt in red and white, as one would expect, but also in blue and white, yellow and white, and orange and white. That was the basis for the line.

I went to Europe that spring and found that many jeanswear companies in St. Germain, Les Halles, and other neighborhoods around Paris had begun printing on fleece—washed fleece, hooded fleece, and more complicated fleece pieces. When I got back to the States I started looking at various techniques being used by makers who were printing T-shirts, and said to them, "Show me something different. Instead of just printing with ink on a shirt, is there something with some texture?" I discovered felt printing and various types of raised printing, and I stumbled upon a technique in which the lettering looked rubberized and spongy. This was what I wanted!

Using that spongy look, we printed COCA-COLA onto sweatshirts and rugbys and polo shirts. I created a natural twill tape with a running printed line of COCA-COLA COCA-COLA COCA-COLA and used that on the placket. I put it on everything to create a common thread; I wanted every detail to become important on every garment. The twill tape was used under the collar and on top of the seams. I developed an embossed Coca-Cola snap for the top button of the jersey, and then a hidden placket with rubber buttons like a real rugby, and printed COCA-COLA on muslin and sewed the muslin on the stripe, and then rolled that out in color. I did the same thing on the sweatshirt. I did a whole range of T-shirts using sponge printing. Jeans, shorts, polos, fleece. I incorporated incredible logo presence into all of the garments. The stores were buying it—and it exploded!

I spent half my day in the Coca-Cola design studio directing a team headed by the incredibly talented Krissy Blakeway. When we expanded Tommy Hilfiger in 1987, Krissy, an Englishwoman with great design tenacity, became our first womenswear designer. I kept feeding her ideas, which she would take and run wonderfully wild with. We built a young, hip group and traveled to Hong Kong every other week to continue the momentum—making new samples, composing new ideas, creating new techniques. In a very short period of time, we created a phenomenon.

Krissy would design for hours on end, tirelessly covering every detail by hand. I would bark directions—"Let's do it longer, let's do it shorter, let's do it this way, let's do it that way"—and she was like a machine, pushing the work through. The stores were buying it, and people were loving it. The women's line was beginning to take hold. Not like the menswear, but there was traction.

In 1986, we had opened a 400-square-foot Tommy Hilfiger store on Columbus Avenue between 73rd and 74th Streets, very compact but very cool, and a bit later a women's store right next door. A corner space at 73rd and Columbus became available, and Mohan asked, "Should we open a Coca-Cola store?" I said, "Yes, but let's make it really modern, really different." I knew he'd like that; Mohan embraced innovation and creativity. He had many out-of-the-box breakthrough ideas himself, which is what I loved about him. He was quite a fashion visionary. I said, "What if we set up the store like a cafeteria? You get a tray and you walk through this line as if you are filling it up with food, but you load up your tray with a T-shirt, a rugby, a sweatshirt, a baseball cap, a backpack, a fanny pack, socks, sneakers, anything!

"And wouldn't it be really cool," I continued, "if when the store's closed there's a vending machine out front, like a Coke machine at a late-night filling station, and someone could come, put a credit card in, pick out what they want on a screen, and have it just fall down the slot like they're buying a bottle of Coke? We could sell twenty-four hours a day!"

He said, "What a great idea!"

The Coca-Cola clothing store was a big, instant PR hit. We produced a TV commercial like the video for Michael Jackson's "Thriller," with dancers in Coca-Cola clothes and crazy, wild, incredible stuff. As for the vending machine, the idea was great, but the execution, not so much. The machine was always broken; we could never get it to work.

The Coca-Cola line was bustling. After the second year, gross sales were around $250 million. Every once in a while in the fashion business, something comes out of left field and hits, and you never really know why. I do think that a lot of customers were tourists from outside the United States who thought it was cool to buy something very American with a sense of humor. That's precisely why I was never afraid that I would cannibalize my own line while designing for Coca-Cola. Coke was very commercial, and I wanted Tommy Hilfiger to be more sophisticated. We may have even been under the radar because of the Coca-Cola success, but Tommy Hilfiger was starting to gain momentum.

# CHAPTER NINE

# HANGMAN

## THE 4 GREAT AMERICAN DESIGNERS FOR MEN ARE:

R_ _ _ _ _ L_ _ _ _ _

P_ _ _ _ _ E_ _ _ _ _

C_ _ _ _ _ _ K_ _ _ _ _

T_ _ _ _ _ H_ _ _ _ _ _ _

THIS IS THE
LOGO OF THE
LEAST KNOWN OF
THE FOUR

In most households, the first three names
are household words. Get ready
to add another. His first name (hint) is Tommy.
The second name is not so easy.
But in a few short months everybody
in America will know there's a new look
in town and a new name at the top. Tommy's clothes
are easy-going without being too casual,
classic without being predictable.
He calls them classics with a twist.
The other three designers call them competition.

282 Columbus Avenue
at 73rd Street
New York, New York 10023
(212) 877-1270

© 1985 MURJANI

*The Genius Vision of George Lois*

W e were making good clothes. In order to sell them, we needed to be recognized. In late 1985, Mohan called me and Joel into his office and said, "I met this guy, George Lois, an advertising genius, and I'd like you guys to talk to him because maybe he can come up with an idea for us." While the line was selling, we were still having quality and shipment problems and were not becoming the success I had hoped. We needed help.

A tall, strong, confident man, Lois was the *Esquire* magazine art director who had put Muhammad Ali on the cover with arrows through him like the martyr St. Sebastian, the agency head who had come up with "When You Got It, Flaunt It" for Braniff Airlines, and both "I Want My Maypo" and "I Want My MTV." I knew his work, but I didn't know who George Lois was. He had never heard of me, either. He called me "kid."

I had thought about our advertising campaign, and I told him, "Maybe we can photograph a great-looking model on the beach, in the clothes, untucked shirt, a little nonchalant . . ."

He said, "Kid, you'll never make it. You're going to have to spend millions of dollars, and you're going to look like everybody else." If there was one thing I didn't want to do, it was look like everybody else.

Lois had brought ad boards from every other big-deal designer, minus their names and logos. This was when Bruce Weber was shooting Calvin Klein and Ralph Lauren, and they both had horses in their ads, and they looked very similar to each other and to Armani and every other brand. He said, "Identify who's who." I prided myself on knowing every aspect of the fashion world, but I couldn't.

"What would you do?" I asked. He said he had an idea.

A few days later he put this in front of us. It was like the kid's game Hangman:

THE 4 GREAT AMERICAN DESIGNERS FOR MEN ARE:
R_ _ _ _ L_ _ _ _ _
P_ _ _ _ E_ _ _ _
C_ _ _ _ _ K_ _ _ _
T_ _ _ _ H_ _ _ _ _ _

THIS IS THE LOGO OF THE LEAST KNOWN OF THE FOUR

In most households, the first three names are household words. Get ready to add another. His first name (hint) is Tommy. The second name is not so easy. But in a few short months everybody in America will know there's a new look in town and a new name at the top. Tommy's clothes are easy-going without being too casual, classic without being predictable. He calls them classics with a twist. The other three designers call them competition.

Then he put a second version in front of us, using pictures of Ralph Lauren, Perry Ellis, Calvin Klein, and me.

I said, "Is that even legal? Can you do that?"

George, in his genius way, was very sure of himself. "Of course you can," he said. "What are they going to do?"

After I caught my breath, Mohan and Joel said, "It's an amazing idea."

George said, "You're going to be known overnight. It will take you twenty years and two hundred million dollars the other way."

I was actively apprehensive. In fact, I was afraid. I thought people were going to see this ad and say, "Who does he think he is?" and laugh at me. I thought people would find me arrogant, full of braggadocio; a fake doing work that wasn't innovative, couture, or high fashion, just redesigned classics. And worse, people wouldn't buy the clothes.

I looked up to those three designers, and I didn't want to get blacklisted. I had interviewed with Calvin a year prior, and had accepted a job and then gone back and told him I wasn't taking it. So he must have thought I was a complete lunatic anyway. I had the highest respect and regard for Ralph Lauren, even though I had never met the man. He was and is one of the most successful designers in the world. He has maintained a consistent image and has created a perception around his brand that is like no other. What's more, he has remained true to his beliefs all this time. Perry's business was starting to catch fire. He had great taste, had had major fashion shows and advertising, and radiated a cool vibe. I had met Perry—he was soft-spoken with a slightly southern accent, had longish hair, was sort of preppy, and always wore chinos. I looked up to him, too.

This ad made me look as if I believed I was in their league. I did not belong there at all.

But at the same time, on some level, I knew George was right. This was a wildly audacious opportunity to jump the line.

Many times in my life I've said, "Okay, what do I have to lose? Do I start from scratch again? I've been there before, I can dig my way out." But this time I had everything to lose.

I went home and talked it over with Susie. By now, we lived on the Upper West Side, at 68th Street between Columbus Avenue and Central Park West, right near our stores. I had just turned thirty-four, and we had a new baby, Alexandria (Ally), who was not yet a year old. We had begun to do well—were we willing to risk it all? I pondered and contemplated and went back and forth, which was not my usual nature. Joel said he felt okay about it, and I had such trust in him and Mohan that I was inclined to go for it.

I was glad when Susie agreed. She thought the idea was a little ballsy, but that it might work, might get my name out there. We decided to do it.

The ad appeared in magazines and on an outdoor billboard in Times Square, "blatantly placed across the street from the offices of the schmatte kings," George Lois said. As they say, go big or go home!

The phone started to ring.

Sure enough, people were talking. We heard everything from

"Who the hell does he think he is?" to "He's not a designer!" (Apparently that title was off-limits to me because I hadn't gone to design school. But Ralph and Perry never went to design school, and they were doing quite well without the degree.) The *New York Post*, the *New York Times, New York* magazine—all the newspapers and magazines were basically saying that Ralph, Calvin, and Perry were established designers, and how dare I mention myself in the same breath. Or on the same two-story billboard! If I had been Ralph, Calvin, or Perry, I would have wondered who this upstart was and not been too worried about him. But apparently they were up in arms.

Almost immediately we noticed an uptick in brand awareness at our Columbus Avenue store. Momentum had begun to build before the ad, but this definitely jet-propelled it, which annoyed some people in the fashion industry even more.

Mohan doubled down by having George do a ten-second television ad in which a deep baritone voice said, "First there was Geoffrey Beene, Bill Blass, and Stanley Blacker. Then Calvin Klein, Perry Ellis, and Ralph Lauren. Today, it's Tommy." This would be either the icing on the cake or the final nail in the coffin.

Early on, members of the fashion press put their noses in the air. Carrie Donovan said in the *New York Times*, "I don't think anyone takes him seriously as a creative force." They may have found my line wanting, but I also think they were worried about pissing off the masters. Calvin and Ralph were the Beatles and the Stones—maybe I was the Byrds? They were, after all, touted as "the American Beatles." But I think reporters and editors were concerned that if they supported me, the big two would not react kindly.

I went to designer functions, and not one designer would look at me or want to be seen talking to me. (The exception was Oscar de la Renta, who was a true gentleman, always very cordial.) In 1986, under the headline "Tommy Who-figer?" *New York* magazine wrote, "Fashion-world feathers are clearly ruffled by what they see as a relative nobody trying to be somebody by comparing himself to the incomparables." Jack Hyde, the consulting head of menswear and fashion marketing at FIT, told the magazine, "It's like when Pia Zadora put herself in the same league as Barbra Streisand and Liza

Minnelli. . . . Tommy Hilfiger is not a designer, he's a creation. In my forty years in this business, I have never seen an advertising campaign so arrogant and tasteless. There is nothing wrong with his product. Everyone else has done well with those looks, so why shouldn't he? But why not just come out and say we're marketing a successful line? Why all this song and dance about a great new designer? In the fashion world, it's not you or your publicity agent saying you're great that makes you great. It's *Women's Wear Daily, GQ* and the *Daily News Record* and merchants." But even *New York* had to admit we were selling. "Of those," they wrote, "the last are far the more enthusiastic Hilfiger fans."

Reading the article, I was devastated. I thought, "I'm a laughing-stock. I should consider doing something else, because I'm not going to make it. I had the opportunity and I ruined it. I crossed a line, and I no longer stand a chance. Oh my God, what have I done?"

Soon after, Hyde asked me to speak to a class at FIT. I accepted, but it turned out the invitation was only so he could compound my embarrassment. He basically buried me. "Who the hell do you think you are? You can't even call yourself a designer. You are not even close to being in their class."

I ducked my head, thinking, "Everyone in the fashion business thinks I'm an egotistical person with serious delusions." And then I felt, "Wow, you know something? He's probably right. He's an established professor, he has been in the business a long time. Should I hang it up? This is going to crash and burn if I don't roll up my sleeves and make sure my stuff sells." I could not wait to get out of that classroom. I felt like I was back in math class.

But in time, George Lois was proven correct. The name Tommy Hilfiger became widely known overnight, and people became curious and went to look at the clothes. A certain percentage of those people decided to buy the clothes. Ultimately, the media couldn't help but recognize me, because I was creating a new niche in the market. My line was focused toward a younger crowd, and they were eating it up. I've always found it much more interesting to focus on the young, because they embrace trends first and make fashion exciting and ever-changing. A new casual revolution was taking place, and my clothes weren't starched or pressed or uptight. We were building a better mousetrap! We became an alternative to Ralph Lauren and Calvin Klein. We had our Columbus Avenue store, we were in Bloomingdale's and Saks and Neiman Marcus. Now we had to make it work.

Many people in the fashion industry look down on designers who are blatantly commercial. They think, "My work is artistic and creative, expensive, and museum-worthy. Yours is inexpensive and for the masses." Okay, well, my clothes fit people and sell to millions of people all over the world, and we make a lot of money and we have fun doing it. And, by the way, it's also creative. In $400-a-yard cashmere, the simplest, most *un*designed garment is beautiful because of the luxurious nature of the cloth. By the same token, there is great artistry in taking an inexpensive cloth in an everyday style and making it special. That's what I tell my assistants and design team: "Let's keep it affordable, but do something that makes a person say, 'Wow, I need that!'"

Many fashion people in the late 1980s and grunge-fueled early 1990s favored a deeply serious, elitist demeanor and celebrated heroin chic, with unsmiling, anorexic models staring blankly. I, on the other hand, was happy. Tommy Hilfiger clothing was fun, humorous, carefree, spirited, healthy, wholesome, all-American! We were upbeat and positive—the total opposite of what the competition stood for.

And that was the lesson I took from the entire experience of this Hangman-style advertising campaign: that my time would be better served working hard and nurturing my brand, as opposed to putting my energy into worrying about what the industry was saying about me. I have to give a lot of credit to Joel Horowitz for helping me get there, because there were days where I would sit with him for hours at a time and say, "What do you think? Do people really believe what the media are saying?"

And Joel would tell me, "Stop worrying about what people think. Let's just worry about the next collection. Let's worry about getting the new shops open, or getting the fits and prices right."

Joel was absolutely correct: at the end of the day, it really doesn't matter what they say. If you have great product, consistent and cohesive marketing, the right positioning, the right people around you, the right locations, stores, and flow of product—if you have *uniqueness*—you have a shot at staying in and growing your business. There have been times when I have had six out of eight of those elements, or seven out of eight, but it is hard to go eight for eight all the time. That's okay. I know perfection does not exist. As long as I can be more right than wrong in this industry, I'm doing fine.

# CHAPTER TEN

# PUTTING THE BAND TOGETHER

The Fab Four of Fashion

Though the Tommy Hilfiger business was beginning to take off, we soon found ourselves in a precarious position. The advertising campaign had just run and we had endured a lot of criticism. We hadn't perfected the distribution or gotten the quality quite where we needed to, and Murjani was having problems. Gloria Vanderbilt Jeans had already hit its peak by 1985, and the Coca-Cola clothing line was in trouble.

In 1987, Mohan Murjani got a call from his PR people. "Factories, schools, and institutions in the South are taking Coca-Cola machines out of their workplaces because Coca-Cola clothes are being made in Asia!"

Apparel manufacturing, one of the South's leading industries, had been deeply damaged by jobs being taken overseas. Coca-Cola was an iconic American brand based in Atlanta, and when people in the South found out that their favorite son was making clothes in Asia, they went crazy. Murjani flew to Atlanta to meet with corporate and found the Coca-Cola people up in arms. He asked the Coca-Cola Company to fund the building of factories in America to keep the jobs here.

Keeping Coca-Cola products American-made was so important to the corporation, and the idea that Coke machines would be removed from *anywhere* so intolerable, that they agreed. However, while Murjani was in the process of developing profitable manufacturing for Coca-Cola clothing in the United States, he also sped up production in Asia to continue the brand's momentum. It was a classic case of oversupplying the demand, and when stores became overstocked and began returning merchandise, the business started crumbling. I knew from experience how this would turn out.

With the simultaneous demise of his two giant lines, Murjani could no longer support my brand. Tommy Hilfiger was this little gem of a business in desperate need of products it couldn't pay for.

Our name had become well known, and people were curious as to what our brand was all about, but we were having trouble shipping to stores and fulfilling the orders.

Larry's sister, by then married and working as Lynn Stemerman Surry, was a resourceful public relations professional. Murjani wanted to use the company's in-house PR team but I didn't feel they were paying enough attention to me, so I reached out for help and she was there for me. I'll always be grateful. Unfortunately, when money got tight we had to pare down and no longer had the budget for her and others.

Once again, I was convinced we'd go out of business. Joel and I brainstormed. What if we bought the license to Tommy Hilfiger back from Murjani? Our company was somewhat solid, the line had potential for growth, and we were developing a public awareness of the brand and the name. We would repay him whatever he had invested in the company and start over. He certainly needed the dollars.

The one stumbling block was that neither of us had that kind of money. Who did we know who did?

Our first thought was to approach banks. We went to Wall Street and met with Goldman Sachs, Merrill Lynch, and others. Nobody wanted to hear about a fashion business. "Too risky, we don't invest in that." "It's not the right game plan for us." "How much cash do you have? What are your assets? What is your inventory?"

Joel and I visited the French bank Crédit Agricole and told their representative our story. After the meeting, as he walked us to the elevator bank, the man asked Joel, "Are you Jewish?"

"Yes," Joel told him.

Tall and French, the banker turned to me and said with pinched Gallic certainty, "You know, in this business you need a Jew."

Was this outrageous anti-Semitism? A helpful hint? Both? Joel and I looked at each other and broke out laughing. This was our response to bigotry: laughter. As one of the rare non-Jews in the business, I said, "Joel, thank God I have a Jew!" To this day, Joel and I say to each other in French accents, *"You need a Jew!"* and start giggling.

But after that meeting we looked at each other and said, "This guy is not going to loan us money."

We were not an easy sell.

By now, Susie and I had moved to Greenwich, Connecticut. Peter Seaman, my next-door neighbor, was a Harvard Business School graduate and a pretty smart guy. Over the weekend, I mentioned our predicament, and he said he would help us figure things out and raise money to buy the company from Murjani. He also said we could partner going forward.

"First," he said, "we need a business plan to show to potential investors." Peter introduced us to Dave Tobin, a strategic numbers cruncher who had previously worked for Warnaco, who told us what we needed to show: How many stores were we in? What were our price points? How much were we going to sell per store? "If we do this business plan, it will be no problem getting money from anyone. You just have to show profit."

Meanwhile, Joel and I were sweating because we had to ship the next season and promise stores they would receive our merchandise, but we couldn't get the goods out of the factories because Murjani wasn't paying for them.

While they were working up the business plan on a spreadsheet, Peter said, "Look, I'm not going to do this for free. I have to be paid." How much? He had said we'd be partners down the road. "Yeah," he said, "but I've got an office to run." He needed a retainer of $25,000 up front and $25,000 a month. I paid the retainer out of my pocket, which was tough with a new baby and a mortgage.

Joel and I flew to Hong Kong to finesse the makers. We stayed at the Holiday Inn in Tsim Sha Tsui, sharing a truly disgusting room with rust-colored shag carpeting, dirty-looking brown bedspreads, and twin beds. It was dark and dreary and we paid by credit card, hoping it would go through.

We visited the manufacturers, all of whom wanted either direct payment or letters of credit before they would ship. At the sweater maker South Ocean Knitters, I met Silas Chou. I had heard he had shopped at our Beverly Hills store on Rodeo Drive, bought some clothes, and wanted to meet me. I was happy to oblige.

Silas Chou was the third generation of a textile family. His grandfather had started the business, and his father now ran it. Silas had finished high school and been in a hurry to learn the ropes, so he did not go to college, which was unheard of among his contemporaries. Instead he started out in the stockroom, sweeping floors and arranging the stock. On his first day his father said, "Son, all of your life you have to remember: you never want to keep stock, you want the stock to be liquidated. Every single yarn, every piece of cloth, has to be utilized, not stay here and take up space."

At twenty Silas told his father, "Daddy, I'm going to make this the biggest factory in the world." (He succeeded. As I write this, South Ocean is the biggest sweater maker in the world.) I hadn't gone to college, and Joel had lasted little more than a year. We were all collegeless and had worked our way up. We felt the kinship of strivers.

Silas recognized that designer labels were trendy. As his wealth increased, he didn't buy stocks. He bought equity, the companies themselves. He approached Pierre Cardin, but the company would only license a limited number of products, so Silas bought the master license of Ted Lapidus, a Cardin contemporary. He licensed that name to a variety of products, made that business huge, and sold it. That became his business model.

Silas had a partner named Lawrence Stroll, whose father was a licensee of Pierre Cardin in Canada. Lawrence hadn't gone to college, either. When Stroll took Ralph Lauren's children's wear license in Canada, he came to Hong Kong to make sweaters and met Silas. They became good friends. A few years later, when Lawrence had the opportunity to take the Ralph Lauren license for Europe, Silas told him to go for it. Two years later, he joined him in ownership. Ralph Lauren Europe became extremely successful. They were multimillionaires the day Joel and I knocked on Silas's door and said we couldn't pay our bill.

"What's the problem?" he asked.

We told him the whole story. Then I said, "If you release the goods and let me ship to my customers, I promise I'll pay you. Murjani has difficulties—he doesn't have the money. We have orders from Bloomingdale's and Saks and Neiman Marcus and Macy's. You should become partners with me."

Silas, who, like me, was in his late thirties, slammed his hand on the table. "Let's do it! Get Murjani on the phone!"

Mohan and Silas discussed whether Joel and I would partner with Silas or whether he would invest. I was excited and hopeful but deeply anxious. There were a lot of balls in the air, and the situation was difficult and confusing. Remember, Peter Seaman was simultaneously talking to Murjani about raising money so we could keep the business intact. The clock was ticking—if we didn't get the merchandise into stores, we had no business to go home to. I wasn't sleeping, my stomach was in an uproar, I was a wreck.

A few days later, Silas told us, "Look, I'm only going to do this if my partner Lawrence Stroll can be partners with us. But you must go meet him in Paris."

I would have done anything to keep my company afloat, so I telephoned him and said, "Hi, Lawrence, Tommy Hilfiger. Silas said that we should meet."

"Yeah, yeah, yeah, I'm very busy right now," he said, and hung up.

After that brush-off, Silas called him, apparently waking him up. "Look," Silas said, "we're going to buy Tommy Hilfiger."

"Tommy what? Who?" He didn't know what Tommy Hilfiger was. But Lawrence reluctantly agreed to see us the next day in Paris.

Joel and I flew from Hong Kong that night. Again, we stayed in some crappy little Sofitel outside of Paris, and traveled to the Polo Ralph Lauren offices on Place de la Madeleine for our 10:00 a.m. meeting. We were jet-lagged and nervous and concerned that this was yet another wild-goose chase. We had had so many meetings, and so many people had said, "We are interested, but come back in a couple of years" or "We are interested, but we don't invest in fashion brands."

Lawrence is a big man who changes the energy of a room when he walks in. That day he clumped in and said, "I need some tea. Get me a tea right away!" His assistant scurried to serve him. Lawrence was smoking a du Maurier. Very tall and handsome, he was expensively and tastefully dressed and I could tell from his bearing that he was used to getting his way. He was just twenty-seven.

"Hey, so what's going on?"

Joel and I gave a brief description, after which he said, "Okay, I'm going to be in New York in a couple of weeks. I'll come and see." This was barely a commitment, but he did ask several intelligent questions, and I could hear that behind the bravado he was a smart man. And, hey, he ran Polo Europe! He had to know what he was doing.

Lawrence invited me and Joel to his home on Millionaire's Row in Neuilly-sur-Seine that night, a very modern and expensively decorated apartment in an elegant and highly secure building. We hit it off over lots of wine and talk. It quickly became apparent that Lawrence took his business very seriously but was all fun in social settings.

He did come see us in New York. He leafed through our samples as if they were all shit and said, "What is this stuff?"

I said, "Let's go to Bloomingdale's and Macy's. You'll be able to see the whole collection." This was not going as well as I'd hoped.

We took his big black limo, accompanied by Lawrence's father, Leo Stroll, born Strulovitch, who was a consummate gentleman, the very definition of the word *distinguished*, and the nicest guy you would ever want to meet.

Tommy Hilfiger did not have individual shops in Macy's and Bloomingdale's, and it was clear that Lawrence was not impressed. I didn't think this deal was going to happen. I got back to the office and called Silas.

"We're going to figure out how to do this," he told me. The negotiations continued.

We thought Silas saw the potential of the Tommy Hilfiger brand, but we did not know he had been conducting consumer research in his own home! Silas's wife was Jewish. For their son Luis's bar mitzvah, Silas wanted his thirteen-year-old dressed in Ralph Lauren, but Luis had refused. "No, Daddy, it's too tight, it's too stiff. I want to wear a T-shirt—oversized—and baggy pants!" Silas would not go that far, but he noticed that the Ralph Lauren consumer in his own household was looking elsewhere. As the owner of South Ocean Knitters, Silas saw that the sweaters he was making for us used 20 percent more material than other designers because we wanted them oversized. He was also aware that our price point was lower than Ralph Lauren's, and he found high quality and low price to be a good formula. His son didn't want to wear Ralph things; he wanted to wear Tommy things!

As the talks progressed, Joel and I began to beg Mohan to let Silas and Lawrence buy back the license. I kept telling them, "We've got to give Mohan something, be fair with him, so he doesn't feel like you're trying to steal the business. I feel that we owe him, and I don't want to ever feel that we took something and didn't give him anything in return." After much talk, Silas came up with the idea to give Mohan the eternal rights to Tommy Hilfiger in India. Silas felt the Indian business was a very long way off but could eventually, if the company succeeded, be of value. (The Indian rights did ultimately develop into a phenomenal business, and when Mohan sold them to Phillips–Van Heusen a few years ago and made a lot of money, I felt very good.)

Our deal took three months to finalize, during which time we managed to stumble along. As the culmination approached, Silas told me, "Tommy, when the license comes back from Murjani, you have to donate your name to the new company."

This was news to me, and I cannot say I was enthusiastic about it. In the normal course of the fashion business, a designer leases his or her name to an investor but retains actual ownership.

Silas told me, "Tommy, do you really want to be successful?" I did. "Do you really want to be rich and build a big brand?" I did! "Okay," he said, "you have to understand that for a partnership to be successful we have to be in the same boat and rowing in the same direction. Even then, the success comes from God's wish. If you don't focus, if you don't have all interests aligned together, the boat will go nowhere.

"Most license businesses never succeed," he went on, "because the interests in the end are not aligned. In a license relationship, the licensor [in this case, me] is more interested in building long-term brand equity," for sale of the company down the line, "while the licensee's [Silas's] focus is on the short term, immediate sales and profit. They are pulling in opposite directions. That's why the licensor-licensee agreement is rarely a long-term business or the most successful model. Of course there are exceptions, when both sides are aligned."

He made a lot of sense.

Silas always telephoned me at home, either late at night or in the morning. Susie would usually answer, and Silas and Susie struck up a good relationship, speaking often by long distance. One day she said to me, "Whoever you are talking to every day and night on the phone, I have a feeling he is good for you. Go for whatever he wants to do." That made a difference.

Instead of earning 3 or 5 percent on the sales, I was offered 15 percent in equity. Silas and Lawrence would own 65 percent—32.5 percent each—because it was their money fueling the business. Mohan would keep 15 percent, and Joel would own a 5 percent share option, which he earned out. Just before closing, Silas came to Joel and me and said, "This is your last chance to negotiate additional equity, but it has to come from Murjani. So if you want it, go for it now." We did and got 5 percent more. Joel and I split it. So I wound up with 17.5 percent and Joel with 7.5 percent. Silas told Joel, "This is going to make a big difference in your life. The extra two and a half percent, you have to have." He was proved right tens of millions of times over.

The deal was finalized on March 20, 1989. Within a year, when the company needed more capital to keep it afloat and Mohan was not capable of contributing, Silas and Lawrence bought his remaining 10 percent. They kept 5 percent—2.5 percent each—and in a great gesture of generosity gave me another 5 percent. "This makes our group even more coherent," Silas said, "and everybody is rowing the boat in the same direction."

In all, I owned 22.5 percent of Tommy Hilfiger, and Joel owned 7.5 percent. Silas had asked me, "Do you want to own a big part of a pea, or a small part of an elephant?" I had said, "The elephant." I no longer owned my name, but I had a piece of the elephant.

# CHAPTER ELEVEN

# BIGGER AND BETTER

Photo: Douglas Keeve

*Bigger is not always Better!*

n the fashion business, four areas are of parallel importance: design, marketing, manufacturing, and execution. As designer, my job was to anticipate what the market needed. Silas, with his background first at South Ocean Knitwear and then at Ralph Lauren Europe, provided strong expertise in cost control of the manufacturing and sourcing. He was the financial strategist, constantly investigating ways to build the company's profitability. He changed our home domicile from Hong Kong to Barbados to the British Virgin Islands. He knew how to deal with the bankers to make the most of our credit lines. He set up our own Hong Kong buying office and turned it into a major profit center. He established separate subsidiaries and divisions for licensing and operating and manufacturing. He created a European operation. When we wanted to go into the denim business, he spearheaded the purchase of Pepe Jeans in London and used that as the vehicle for the license for Tommy Jeans, which we built and ultimately sold for a significant sum. Silas was a financial engineering genius.

Lawrence Stroll taught us how to think big. He was fearless about making life-changing decisions. He determined when and how to expand into Europe, expand our footprint in American department stores, and expand the entire line of clothes. Lawrence also taught us how to live well. We all lived well, but Lawrence lived well on another level. He ate only the finest food and drank only the best wine. He had the most extraordinary private jet and private yacht, and one of the world's largest collections of Ferraris. He owned helicopters. His many homes and properties were incredible in scope, design, and expense. He had his own Grand Prix race track! He had amazing taste, and never accepted second-best. When I was a boy dreaming about being rich, I'd never thought about it on that level; I'd never even understood what that level was until I teamed up with Lawrence!

When we were considering expansion into Europe, Lawrence and Silas brought in a European all-star team who had previously worked for him at Polo Ralph Lauren, headed by Fred Gehring. He insisted that we select the very best retail locations, so in London we opened a sumptuous store across from Harvey Nichols, which began the trend of luxury designer shopping on Sloane Street in Knightsbridge. We followed this with a beautiful store on Bond Street. Next, we established high-visibility presences in Munich, Amsterdam, Berlin, and Düsseldorf.

When we began the Tommy Hilfiger expansion in American department stores, we were initially placed in men's clothing areas, surrounded by competing lines. Lawrence walked in and said, "We need full-blown shops!" When we started dreaming about what those shops should look like, our dreams were never grand enough; Lawrence wanted more beautiful mahogany, thicker columns, better flooring, better lighting. Always more of the best. Because of my history, I was afraid of spending grand amounts of money, but Lawrence would say, "No, no, no, no, no. We need bigger and better. *Bigger and better!*" And he was right. Thanks to Lawrence's persistent grandness, the perception of our brand in the outside world also became bigger and better.

Our sweet spot in the market was "affordable luxury." For a time we defined ourselves as designer sportswear and our goods as accessible, aspirational, relatively inexpensive. But "affordable luxury" captured the essence in a phrase, and we stuck with that. All my partners were on board. We would be a status brand for a very broad audience. Even in 2008, at the depth of the financial crisis, we did well—in fact, we had our best year ever—because we were *affordable* luxury.

As CEO, Joel Horowitz was the day-to-day keeper of the flame. He set the business strategy with a team of people he hired judiciously, and dug into the logistics of the business, imposing discipline, stability, and order. Under his system, we lived by a master calendar. He established specific deadlines for design, editing, pricing, and delivery, year in and year out. Under his leadership, the Tommy Hilfiger engine hummed.

Silas, Lawrence, Joel, and I were in touch with each other constantly. We ate together, talked together, traveled together. We gathered in Hong Kong at the Regent Hotel on a regular basis. Silas, who was living in Hong Kong at the time, would come over and join us in Lawrence's penthouse suite, room 1100, the best in the hotel and the only one he would accept. We'd sit and strategize and talk about what we should do, how we should do it, whom we should hire, whom we should fire, what the next move would be.

My models were Ralph Lauren and Calvin Klein. I looked at those guys as the Rolls-Royce and Mercedes-Benz of the design world, and me as the Audi. I thought, "If I continue to expand the product line, get it in the right stores, improve the design, fit, and quality, I'm going to move up to being a Porsche."

Having spent my late teens and twenties at People's Place, I could walk in and eyeball a store and know what was selling, what was not selling, what was good, what was bad. I understood merchandising, and at the end of the day, fashion retail is all about merchandising. So I became a student of the stores. I studied the competition's product line, positioning, pricing, colors.

It was clear to me that Ralph Lauren was the best. Ralph created a lifestyle, inspired by British aristocracy. He believed in the best quality, the best store design, the best imagery. I viewed and still view him as the ultimate perfectionist, and I had him in my sights at all times. I like the classics, and he did classic better than anyone else.

Ralph wasn't as innovative. His clothes were beautiful, but not exciting or unique. They were similar to Brooks Brothers', but with a better product and advertising environment. What made him an overwhelming success was that the flavor, quality, and atmosphere he infused in his work were the best. He set the bar.

Many times, my assistant design team would respond to the success of Ralph Lauren or Brooks Brothers by copying them exactly. I would respond, "No, we need something different. We have to create a product that doesn't exist." With an edge. With a cool factor. Whether it was a shirt or a pant or a jacket, I wanted mine to be unique. In order for the consumer to really love Tommy Hilfiger, I was determined to overdeliver on quality for the price, and provide a garment that made a statement and had its own personality!

This also meant that we would deliver new product every thirty days—twelve lines per year—and they all had to be different. We needed to tweak a certain number of basics and add a certain number of fashion pieces and a certain amount that would meet everyone's needs. We had to be right on trend, not too far ahead or too far behind. And we had to hit the bull's-eye every single time. My inspiration came from my love for Americana, the outdoors, New England, Hollywood, Aspen, Miami, Malibu, sports, music, pop culture, travel, film, and what was going on in the streets. Always has, always will.

In January, we would deliver an early spring line: classics, but in a lighter, brighter, spring-like color range. Not too spring-like, though, because it was early in the season and still cold out in most states. In February, we would deliver a group with appropriate weights of fabric, all around a given theme—maybe it would be travel, or bush jackets, or military-looking gear.

Going into April, we might do something more Caribbean reggae cool, with fuchsia and orange and lime green and floral prints. In June, we would begin to transition, so that might be time for "Out of Africa"—madras plaids and khakis and olives, appropriate for the season but friendly for fall, too.

In July we would begin to deliver fall goods. Fall has always been my favorite season, because with the weather cooling, you use wool and tweeds and corduroy and heavier fabrics with some richness to them. I might start out the July delivery with a collegiate line, very Ivy League. Navy and burgundy and gold and off-white and forest green. We would put crest prints into the line, and regimental stripes, and tartan plaids, and show melton varsity jackets and duffel coats and tasteful, preppy, all-American sportswear. But always with a sense of humor and a wink.

What kind of a wink? Maybe you would open up a toggle coat and find a funky surprise print of college emblems in the lining. Or the toggle itself might be one you've never seen on a traditional garment. Or maybe it's a tartan toggle coat, or one with a regimental stripe. Where classic design houses would do them in navy, black, and gray flannel, maybe we would do them in tomato red and forest green and mustard. Striking, unexpected, cool! Imagine making a splash on campus in a mustard toggle coat! I wanted it to be fresh *and* familiar.

August was the beginning of back-to-school season, when students and their parents are shopping to make an impression in high school or in preparation for going away to college. The collegiate Ivy League line would still be on the selling floor, but we would deliver, say, *Field & Stream*, what you would wear hiking or apple picking or going out fly-fishing in hip boots. Country weekends in Vermont in the fall.

In October and November, we would start to convert to something slightly dressier, the black or navy velvet jacket you'd wear to a Christmas party, with a pleated tuxedo shirt and tuxedo-type trousers. Maybe something with a little bit of shine in it, as a party favor, so to speak. In another shipment, we would convert to a lighter weight, which we would call holiday resort, for people to buy and take on a trip someplace warm. Maybe floral prints and swimwear, something you might wear on a yacht or on the beach.

In addition, four times annually we would deliver all our Core Basic items: polo shirts, turtlenecks, wool sweaters, cotton sweaters, chinos, trousers, jeans, jackets. These drove the business. No store would ever be out of those things, and they keep the register ringing continually. We didn't mark them down; we just added color.

Lawrence took Core Basic to the next level. When he reviewed my designs he said, "Don't have ten colors, have twenty colors! Don't have six colors in corduroys, have twelve! This fabric is shit; let's use a much better fabric. And if you want to, have pinwale *and* wide wale, and throw in a velvet pant!" There he was, thinking bigger. He pushed us to raise the level of quality in every part of the line. I loved it!

Was there a downside? Well, you know you're never going to sell all twenty colors; there will be some dogs. But Lawrence understood that the presentation on the selling floor is overwhelmingly powerful when you have color rollout, overcoming any individual color shortfall. Lawrence's philosophy: if it appears that we, the designers and manufacturers, believe in our product enough to put it out in multiples, the customer will believe in it as well. The large selection of color gives the consumer a lot of confidence, and they won't buy just one, they'll buy four.

We carved out a merchandising concept that was the turbo-powered engine behind the brand. We surveyed the competition and found the pricing sweet spot; we surveyed manufacturers and found the best margins.

Designers and manufacturers know that every company importing clothes from Asia needs a buying agent, a person or firm in the region who acts as a liaison between the brand and the factories. Buying agents speak the language, check the quality, and communicate daily with the factories on details, pricing, changes, anything that comes up. John Doe can't just walk into a factory; you need someone who knows all the operators. We had been using the Murjani buying office, but as soon as our new group got organized, Silas said, "Why don't we set up our own Tommy Hilfiger buying office?"

The team leader of a buying office is a crucial hire. You need someone who fully understands how to make, deliver, and price a garment, as well as how to deal with all the factories, fabric suppliers, and accessory suppliers and—most important—bring all the pieces together. It takes a huge amount of time and a gargantuan effort. Sometimes the fabric will come from Italy, the zippers from Taiwan, the buttons from England, and the lining from China—but it's being sewn in Singapore. This was a world rife with potential disasters, and someone had to coordinate it smoothly.

We hired a lady of Indian descent named Bubbles Bott. Bubbles spoke five languages, had been with Yves St. Laurent, and really knew the business. I had met her in 1986 at a store appearance, and we had hit it off immediately. She was striking, with a huge bright white smile, big brown eyes, incredible jewelry, and an American accent. We needed someone to head production and product development, and Joel thought she would be perfect as well.

Bubbles was probably the best and most important hire we ever made. She became my partner in all things, from shopping to planning to simply getting everything done. When I said, "Let's take a foulard print and overdye it to give it a lived-in look," either she knew how to do it or she figured it out. She was responsible for delivering prototypes, samples, production, and perfection for all of my ideas. She dealt with factories all over the world and helped devise systems for the flow of goods. Bubbles was one of the reasons we became so successful in casual sportswear: we invented it together in a way that had never existed before.

Bubbles put everything on spreadsheets and pretty much lived on airplanes, flying between Asia and New York, all while raising a family. As manufacturing production head, she spent endless hours with me, going over how each individual piece should be manufactured, whether it should be in cotton or cotton cashmere, whether it should be 14-gauge with twenty-two stitches per inch. We're talking about thousands of different designs per year. And best of all, she understood me and loved what we were doing.

Craig Reynolds was the head of merchandising. He directed the buys and curated the collection. Craig, a Burdine's department store grad, knew pricing and what assortments we needed in each retail space. He was a fastidious man with great vision and impeccable taste.

I assembled a design team consisting of superstars: knitwear sweater expert Voula Solonos; knit polo shirt and golf shirt designer Susan Williams; Michael Sondag, our creative director for sportswear; Christopher Cox, Aidan Cassidy, Charles Teti, Kyle McDonald, Sara Hand, Alice Flynn, Mike Mombello, Lois Theisen, Ubi Simpson, Malcolm Crews, Rogan Gregory, Dustin Horowitz, and Lloyd Boston. Reed Krakoff, who left us to become the mastermind behind Coach, was one of the best creative directors I ever had. He was followed by Susie's cousin, the super-organized and creative Stephen Cirona. My brother Andy did marketing; my sister Ginny came into the design team and headed up Tommy Jeans when we started it, then moved over to womenswear. We had a magical group with genius ideas flowing out of our studio on a daily basis. The joke was,

"My wish is Bubbles's command." I would work with my assistants, we would create something wonderful, and Bubbles would get it made.

I've always tried to select the right people to be around, people who can fill in the gaps in my knowledge and expertise. I also look for employees with integrity and strong ethics, because I never want to do anything that is even slightly questionable in terms of being legal, moral, or just. And I never want to burn a bridge. This is pretty uncommon in the fashion industry—same for the movie business, the music business, a lot of businesses. But I was brought up to believe that how you feel about yourself when you look in the mirror is more important than besting other people. Maybe that sounds corny. I can't help it.

My challenge was to effectively communicate my vision to my team so they could execute my ideas. We began the season doing storyboards, maybe pictures of the U.S. Navy or a beautiful vessel; you're cruising the Mediterranean on a wonderful yacht, so what would you wear? I would dream on a continual basis, conjure ideas, and distill them down into individual products. And in January we would start all over again, following the same pattern but with different themes.

To present our lines to buyers, we filled our showroom with dynamic displays. One season, a section would look like the deck of a yacht, complete with a ship's wheel and mannequins dressed in our samples. We'd pipe in music or even host a band to bring the story to life. We'd serve drinks out of cups festooned with anchors and immerse the buyers from Bloomingdale's or Saks or Macy's in our world. We gave them several worlds to choose from: *Field & Stream* to the right, Ivy League straight ahead, rock and roll to your left. And then we would have a section devoted entirely to Core Basic, rolled out Lawrence's way, in twenty colors.

I wanted to build Tommy Hilfiger into a mega-brand, which meant we needed to logo just about every product. And how else could we distinguish ourselves? I loved emblems, I loved numbers, I loved anything sporty or athletic. I loved authenticity. I loved the flag—the American flag! I grew up in touch with American iconography. I had none of the sixties cynicism that affected so many. My feeling, then and now, was, "We are America, and we are very spirited and fun-loving and cool." I collected books on flags, on American history, on George Washington, Abraham Lincoln, Thomas Jefferson, the Declaration of Independence, the Liberty Bell—and thought, "How do I make clothes out of all of this?"

I began with the red, white, and blue. The lining in the neck of my shirts became mini stars; the lining in the waistband of my pants was stripes. Some shirts were printed with flags all over. Abbie Hoffman had been pilloried for wearing an American flag shirt on *The Merv Griffin Show*, but he could've picked (or stolen!) one of ours off the rack. The times had changed, and I was celebrating the country, not criticizing it. We wanted our clothes to look old, like Old Glory, so we tea-stained them. When we wanted clothes looking newer and fresher, we dyed them in brighter colors. I had Voula, our sweater designer, create a selection of sweaters featuring hand-knit flags, flags going up the sleeves, and the words *TH, USA,* and *Tommy Hilfiger America.*

The sweaters worked out so well that I thought, "What would I do if this were all fabric?" I made one shirt with all stars on one sleeve, another with all stripes. I started patching and piecing. I used the stars and stripes because I wanted to own America! I wanted to be *the* American designer, and I wanted my clothes to resonate with every American. It worked. We had a lineup of heavy hitters and best-sellers, and we sold many millions of dollars' worth of American flag clothes.

We were on a roll. One season I looked at monuments; another, Norman Rockwell prints; next, Martha's Vineyard; next, Nantucket. Frontier dishes, jewelry, bedspreads, quilts—I converted Americana into clothing. And then jeans with patches of flags, and red-white-and-blue, and stars and stripes. Those became very hip because people like Bruce Springsteen would wear a jean jacket with a flag lining.

Buyers purchased from every group and staggered the deliveries, one for January, one for February, one for March. Six months later, they shopped the next set of themes, ordering five thousand pieces of this, ten thousand pieces of this, twenty-five thousand pieces of that. Now it was up to us. The clothes had to end up in their stores six months later looking the same as the samples. Or better!

I added swimwear, and then athletic wear. It was exhilarating to come up with a new idea, a new theme, season after season after season. I knew we were setting trends, and I knew the whole market was following us and trying to keep up. An article in the menswear newspaper *Daily News Record* described the demise of the WASP. I told them, "There's not a lot of difference between preppy and WASP, except that preppy has a sense of humor." They called me "The New Killer Bee." We were selling a lot of clothing and making a lot of money.

Years later, Silas would share his perspective on our success— one I had not considered at the time. He felt that in the late 1980s and early 1990s, American society changed from the industrial age into the information age. Now it's obvious, he says; in those days it wasn't. The personal computer ascended—Microsoft, Apple, the Internet—and that ushered in the era of casual wear.

Why? The industrial age was a command economy: the boss commands you through all of the hierarchies, and you do what the boss tells you. In the industrial age, people were uniformed, blue-collar or white-collar. A tie. Why wear a white shirt? Because the boss says you wear a white shirt. In the information age, you are less likely to have a boss; you are more independent, you are freethink-ing. Microsoft was one of the first to develop the campus office; it was the pioneer in casual dressing.

Then the casualwear revolution expanded. Even bankers, the very embodiment of the boss-driven hierarchy, began to come to work in something other than pinstripe suits. Casual Friday became an institution. Neither my partners nor I thought this through fully; we weren't consulting opinion polls or sociologists. I just had the gut feeling that Americans were a casual people and wanted looser, less-formal wear. Now it's clear that when we were getting started, society was in the midst of great change.

This is what Silas believes really made Tommy Hilfiger: America entering the information age.

———

Joel Horowitz and I had been out looking for office space when we stumbled across a building at 25 West 39th Street, between Fifth and Sixth Avenues, that housed a racquetball club. Previously, it had been the Engineering Societies Building, a 1907 gift from Andrew Carnegie. When we walked onto the thirteenth floor and found twenty-five-foot ceilings and Palladian windows, we looked at each other and said, "This is it!"

We built multiple showrooms and put a conference room in the back and a design studio on the balcony. When Silas, Lawrence, Joel, and I needed a corporate headquarters, we renovated the penthouse. As our business started to blow up, we rented and refurbished another floor, and another, and another, until we bought the entire building. Twenty-five West 39th Street became our ancestral home. Sixteen floors of Tommy Hilfiger showrooms. Menswear, womenswear, children's wear, licensed products. The building also housed a tremendous New York City bonanza: a parking garage! We hosted fashion shows and parties there, presented openings. We had so much cool stuff going on in that building, the energy and vibe were just incredible!

With our business bursting at the seams, we began renting space at 485 Fifth Avenue, a short walk away and directly across from the stunning New York Public Library. Again we rented and renovated one floor after another, and again we eventually bought the building—another excellent real estate investment. We moved the design and production departments and were continually walking back and forth between two workplaces practically vibrating with creativity.

Department store real estate is a world unto itself, one in which we had not made great inroads. To sell properly, we needed premium adjacencies, which is to say that we needed to sit right next to Ralph Lauren and Calvin Klein.

One Sunday afternoon, Silas, Lawrence, Joel, and I were lying around Lawrence's hotel room at the Regent in Hong Kong. As was our custom, we'd ordered cheeseburgers and fries and Chinese food, and were talking business. Lawrence, in one of his Ascot Chang hand-tailored shirts, chinos, and Tod's, said, "We need to figure out a way to get into the department stores in a bigger way."

"Well, we have to advertise more and expand our product line," I said.

Joel added, "We have some delivery problems. We need more discipline in manufacturing and delivery."

Silas slammed his fist on the table. "We need somebody who knows the business! Who has the best relationships with the department stores? Who's the best salesman in the business?"

"It's Edwin Lewis," said Lawrence. Edwin was the number three guy at Ralph Lauren, beneath the vice chairman, Peter Strom, and Ralph himself. He had a reputation for being tough, he knew the business inside and out, and he'd built big relationships and licensing deals with all the owners, CEOs, and heads of the major department stores in America. Edwin was a legend.

"Edwin is with Polo," said Joel. "He's been with Polo and Ralph Lauren for seventeen, eighteen years, and he's never going to leave."

I agreed. "He would never leave Ralph."

Lawrence echoed me. "He's never going to leave Ralph."

Silas did not like that answer. He said, "Let's try."

"Okay," Lawrence told him, "I'll give him a call, but there's no way he's going to leave Polo."

"He's not going to leave Polo," I said again.

We went back and forth and back and forth until Silas said, "Lawrence, you call him. Call him now."

To everyone's surprise, Edwin agreed to meet.

Silas said, "What's the most that anyone has ever been paid in this business?"

"I don't know," I told them. "Maybe a half a million a year? Edwin probably makes a half a million a year or more. I don't know, he's been there—"

Silas said, "Let's pay him a million."

Joel and I together said, "Pay him a million?"

I continued. "Come on, that's a lot of—"

Lawrence said, "I still don't think he would come."

"Let's offer him a partnership in the business," said Silas, "and let's offer him a million dollars a year."

Not only was I hesitant, I was not in favor. I had already given up a big piece of the business to share with my partners, and I was fine with that, but I didn't want to give any more.

It took a lot of talk, but ultimately I was convinced that, because of his experience and strength, Lewis could move the company significantly forward.

When he met with Silas and Lawrence and learned that we would give him space to do what he needed to do—plus the grand financial incentive—Lewis agreed to sign on. What we didn't know at the time was that although he had built the hell out of Ralph Lauren, he had smacked the ceiling there and was frustrated because he couldn't go beyond it.

We all pitched in so that Edwin would have both equity and a salary. In 1992, after multiple meetings and negotiations, we brought him in as the president of Tommy Hilfiger and handed him the baton. His job was to sell Tommy Hilfiger to the big department stores. Lawrence ceded Edwin the large corner office at 25 West 39th Street, and he went to work.

I tried very hard to like Edwin, but our personalities were very different. He was a brash, arrogant guy who thought he knew it all. And maybe he did; he had, after all, blazed the trail for an American designer lifestyle brand in the largest stores in America, gaining respect from all of the top retailers. He was a genius in that respect, and he let you know it.

I try to be conscious of how I treat people, and to care about their feelings. But Edwin Lewis—not so much. He had a chosen few he worshiped and loved, and everyone else didn't know what the hell they were talking about. He would say things like, "Jesus Christ almighty, that goddamned tie looks like it went out with the Model T Ford." He would scope a woman and say, "Jesus Christ, that is one ugly skirt you are wearing, girl."

Lewis, a well-groomed southern man with a range of expletives, often sat with his feet on his desk. When someone walked in, he would look them up and down and say, "Where the fuck did you get those shoes?"

"In Paris. I just bought them."

"I don't give a shit where you bought them. They are the ugliest goddamn things I have ever seen in my life."

People would come into his office with an idea and say, "I think . . ." and he would say, "I don't give a shit what you think. This is the way we are doing it, and you do it this way or don't come back!" At meetings we would offer suggestions—maybe we should position a shop at the back of a men's department instead of next to the escalator, or outfit a shop in wood grain rather than white lacquer—and he would say, "There's no way we are doing that." Why not? "Because it's just not the way it's done. We're not doing it your way, so forget about it." At times, I felt I was losing control.

Edwin came in, surveyed our product, and said, "The line's not big enough to do the kind of business we need to do." Apparently, we had not expanded enough under Lawrence. "To compete against Polo Ralph Lauren, you don't need one or two plaids," said Edwin, "you need twenty-five plaids!"

We went to work. We hired more designers and better fabric people. We knew that if we followed Edwin's lead and built more and better product, he would get us into bigger and better stores. As soon as we amped up production, it was like we'd sprayed gasoline on a bonfire: the brand exploded. Edwin essentially bullied store executives. "You go tell them motherfuckers if we don't get in that space next to the Polo Ralph Lauren shop in the San Francisco store, they ain't getting Tommy Hilfiger. You hear that? We'll give it to their competition." This guy was out of a movie! He told them, "Tommy Hilfiger is the new Ralph Lauren, and he's going to be the most important designer in the coming years. We want a bigger goddamn shop, better damn positioning, and customers will buy more from you." It worked.

I didn't hate the job Edwin was doing; he did a lot of good and opened a lot of doors. I just didn't like the way he steamrolled people.

As time went on, many of the people we hired from Polo Ralph Lauren arrived with an arrogant, chest-pounding, we-know-what-we're-doing-and-nobody-else-does attitude. Ralph certainly did cultivate a lot of talent, and some became great team players, but a lot of them had an approach that I found unsettling.

Once we made it clear that he was never going to be totally in charge, Edwin softened somewhat. We were very grateful for his accomplishments; we would not have been able to push our way into all of those stores and all those selling positions if he hadn't been so good.

Now that we were in these stores, we'd better look good. We had been building department store shops using pine stained a mahogany color, a cheap flooring that tried to look expensive, and shelving and lighting that could have come from Home Depot. Lawrence came around and said, "No, no, no, we don't do it that way. We are going to hire Jerry Robertson, who built the Ralph Lauren store on 72nd Street, who built a lot of the Ralph Lauren stores, and has the right taste, the best taste for us." I didn't want to be accused of copying Ralph Lauren, but I was partial to that Old World mahogany ambience; to me it meant wealth and luxury. But Jerry and Edwin convinced me that we should modernize instead.

Jerry was a guy who really didn't work within budgets, but his shops for Tommy Hilfiger were absolutely beautiful. He used the most incredible lacquered wood, robust shelving units, and big signage, and created white Tommy Hilfiger shops with modern edges that were stunning. The cost of his masterpieces blew me away, but when I voiced my concerns—we could shave some dollars here, shave a few there—Lawrence said, "No, we're doing it. We need the best."

Okay, Lawrence!

Then Jerry built our offices and showrooms.

Was it worth the expense? I think so. Our presentation—our presence—made us look serious and strong as a brand. It made people view us as a company that was putting stakes in the ground.

In 1992 and 1993, Ralph probably wasn't very happy with us. My intent was never to copy him. I wanted to be newer and fresher and younger and hipper and cooler. But we all liked Ralph's business model: the basics, classics, and fashion delivered on a regular basis; the in-store shops, the stand-alone shops; the advertising; the lifestyle image.

I particularly admired his company's replenishment operation in department stores, which we adopted. After the sale of a single chino trouser in, let's say, a 32-inch waist, another one is delivered the next day or as soon as it can be supplied. It is an electronic data interchange (EDI) system, computerized so that when the clerk rings up an item, the information is transmitted to us automatically, activating the release of more merchandise into the stores. The stores like it because we are carrying the inventory instead of them, and we like it because we are entirely confident that because we can get more inventory on the shelves quickly our business will turn over even faster.

On the creative side, we held what we called adoption meetings. All our designers would bring their ideas to the table in the form of boards, swatches, sketches, and samples, and we would critique and collaborate on every piece.

"Why don't we take the collar from that one and put it on this one?"

"Let's take a hockey jersey and a rugby shirt and marry the two."

"Let's take skiwear and jeanswear and marry the two. Could you imagine jeanswear with nylon stripes on it?"

I would direct the vision, and these young, smart, and talented people, from age nineteen into their late thirties (I was the oldest person in the room), would add to it, implementing themes of the whole season and expanding the Core Basic and Core Plus lines. Initially the meetings consisted of three to five people, but as we grew, they went from ten to twelve to twenty, and then became way too big.

Our adoption meetings were like a train. The creative meeting was the engine, followed by the merchandising, execution, pricing, technical fit, and delivery meetings, and finally the marketing meeting. We were really hauling freight!

Creative was a lot of fun because it was new, fresh, experimental. We had a shirt team, a sweater team, a knit team, a jeans team, a pants team, a jacket team. And I would walk among them and say, for example, "Why don't we get behind hoods this season? Why don't we line the hoods?" The shirt team would come up with something outstanding, and I would say, "Why don't we take this idea and put it into sweaters, too?" I might see ideas coming out of the knitwear team and say, "Why don't we put this into shirts?" or "Why don't we take this trim to the jackets?" We were always cross-pollinating.

After that, we had to turn our attention to the reality of the business: "Okay, how much of this can we really sell? What is it going to cost? Where are we going to make it? How fast can we deliver it? How much is the business going to grow next year?" The sales force would be working on getting additional floor space in the department stores, and I might be working with an architect in the next room on what the shops should look like.

Then I would go to a public relations meeting: "How are we going to present this to the magazines and the press?" Then to a meeting to figure out what the advertising would look like. Then to another to figure out what everything was going to cost and how many people we needed to hire to take it to the next level: "How many cities are we in? How many stores are we selling in? How many Bloomingdale's? How many Macy's? How much inventory do we have? How many stores of our own are we opening? What are we spending on advertising?"

At the same time, I started building an archive of samples—pieces from my travels and one-off pieces that we sampled but never manufactured. In the early 1990s, we installed an automatic rack for them (like the ones dry cleaners use) so that the designers, assistants, and merchandisers could push a button and instantly see a specific item. We now have twenty-five of those racks in the archives, holding thousands of samples from all over the world. If we are designing a collection and we want to look at motorcycle jackets, we can flick on the jacket rack and see motorcycle jackets that would blow your mind. One looks like Dennis Hopper's, one like Peter Fonda's, one like James Dean's, one like Justin Bieber's. The archive is one of our most valuable assets.

The best part of those creative meetings was our spirited exchanges. We would sit for hours with Lawrence and the whole team. Lawrence, of course, would zoom in on details and make his opinions known. "Make the collar another quarter inch longer, that's too short," he'd say. And he would be right. I would turn to the team and say, "Let's make it another quarter of an inch. As a matter of fact, why don't we make one a quarter of an inch, one an eighth of an inch, and one a sixteenth? We'll try them all on and see which is the best. And while we're at it, why don't we make a couple a bit bigger?"

I'd show a new sample. "What do you think of this, Lawrence?"

"I would never wear that. You wouldn't fucking get me to wear that!" Eventually, he would look at us and say, "I've got to get out of here. I can't sit here any longer. I need a martini!" Lawrence had a bar set up in his office, and at five forty-five, his assistant, Amy, would make the martinis. We also had a special cigar room and our own chef.

Lawrence had his stretch limo sitting outside, and we would go to Mr. Chow's or Cipriani or the Four Seasons and eat and talk business and just talk and talk and talk and talk. "Do we want to expand to Mexico or go to South America first? Or Brazil rather than Venezuela first? What about England? Should we go to England first or France?" Everyone contributed beautifully. It felt like we were the Beatles. And boy, did we have fun!

Lawrence was strategizing how to be bigger and better. Silas was figuring out how to financially steer the company so we would always become more profitable, pay fewer taxes, get better terms from the banks, and build new profit centers. Joel was executing and strategizing with the executive team, and Edwin was out opening doors for us. I was running a creative machine—new ideas, good product, what's the next, the newest, the freshest? Always keeping the DNA of the brand intact.

By the early '90s, we were taking market share from everyone and had the youth market eating out of our hand.

# CHAPTER TWELVE

# THE KIDS ARE ALRIGHT

Being a father
is the greatest
joy in my life

Back in May 1984, when Susie and I were living in Soho, we found out we were going to have a baby. We had been married for five years and were thrilled. Susie was working with Ruby and Roger on her line O'Tokyo, but she was extremely stressed. They weren't paying her on time, they weren't delivering on time, and the sampling had become more difficult. Her work was giving her a lot of anxiety, and I thought it would be best for her to take it easy, enjoy the pregnancy, have the baby, and then someday, if she felt like it, go back to work.

It was early enough in Susie's pregnancy that I could go to Hong Kong in July to design my first line for Tommy Hilfiger. The lease on our West Broadway apartment was up, and when I came back we started looking for a new place to live. We thought, with a baby coming, that an uptown neighborhood near Central Park seemed safer and more stable than Soho, which at the time was party central. I suppose we could have walked the stroller in Washington Square Park, but it was the '80s, and that piece of the Village was full of drug dealers.

We found an apartment in a doorman building at 25 West 68th Street, on a nice block between Columbus Avenue and Central Park West. We had already checked out the neighborhood when we were planning to open the Tommy Hilfiger store on Columbus Avenue. John Lennon had lived not far away, at the Dakota. Perry Ellis owned a place nearby. There were good restaurants and cool shopping. Charivari, an excellent clothing store, was up on 81st. We were half a block from the park.

We painted the apartment in forest green with off-white trim, and bought a French country dining set at Pierre Deux on Bleecker Street. The ultrasound told us we were having a girl, so the nursery was white with pink accents, the furniture upholstered in pink-and-white ticking stripe from a children's store, Au Chat Botté, on Madison Avenue. We were ready to go.

In January 1985, I was designing the next collection and starting the Coca-Cola line at the Murjani offices when Susie called to say she felt contractions. Her water had broken. By the time the subway got me to our apartment, she was more than ready to go. I looked around, thinking, "I don't know when we're going to be back here," so I quickly cleaned out the refrigerator because I didn't want any vegetables to rot.

"What are you doing?" Susie said.

"Cleaning out the refrigerator."

"What are you, nuts?"

It made perfect sense to me at the time, but in retrospect it does seem kind of strange. It's now part of Hilfiger family lore.

We jumped in a cab for the hospital. The driver was crossing the park and heading downtown on Second Avenue, and I was worrying that he was going to hit a pothole and the baby was going to come out. I kept telling the guy to slow down, slow down. Susie was cool with it; she just wanted to get there.

We arrived at NYU Medical Center around eleven in the morning, and by 5:20 that afternoon, we had a baby girl. When the doctor handed her to me I couldn't believe it. I felt this little thing snuggled in my arms, and I broke down crying.

Alexandria Susan—Ally. Oh, she used to giggle and laugh. She had very dark hair, like Susie's. Big brown eyes, a Hilfiger mouth and nose. She was cuddly and full of spirit and love, and I would look into her eyes and know we had a deep connection.

Susie was so exhausted from having the baby that she slept like a rock. I think I was more nervous than she was. The first night we brought Ally home, we put her in a bassinet at the foot of our bed, and every few hours I woke up and put my finger under her nose to make sure she was breathing.

Susie's father visited the next day. So did Susie's cousin Stephen Cirona. He was always super-fashionable and had the latest, coolest stuff. That day, he showed up in a black-and-white houndstooth

Kenzo jacket—don't ask me why I remember this! Larry Stemerman came over. And Joel, with his wife, Ann. The Murjanis arrived. We had a steady stream of visitors. Susie finally said, "I just can't have any more guests." I took everyone out to dinner, and when I got back, Susie and Ally were sleeping. Once again I put my finger under my daughter's nose just to make sure this perfect being was still in this world.

We had an Irish nanny, Maggie Mangan, but I was as hands-on as I could be. I changed diapers, and Susie and I would tussle over who was going to give Ally a bath.

"It's my turn," I'd say.

"No, it's my turn to give her a bath!"

"No, let me!"

Just touching this little bundle was such a thrill. I was so full of love, and Susie was floating on cloud nine! It was a new chapter in life; another dream had come true. We were building a family, we were financially secure, and my dream of building my business was beginning.

That summer, we rented a weekend house in Bridgehampton. Ally was just a wee little thing, and I would take her in the swimming pool and hold her close to me—the best part of my day. My childhood friend Michael French and his wife, Virginia, came out, and we ate bran muffins for breakfast as I held Ally, giggling with joy the way we had in school when we made mischief together. My sister Betsy and my mother came. We went to the beach, the farmer's market, out with friends—it was just a wonderful time.

My father showed up and turned into someone I had never seen before. Very sweet, very nice. Not critical. I think my father saw me maturing, starting a family, and building my brand, and thought, "Hey, my son has made it."

I certainly was determined to be a different father than he was. First, I would never ever consider hitting my children. I wanted to be connected and involved, and to let my children—however many I ended up having—know that I would be supportive of them regardless of what profession or life they chose.

That fall, we started thinking it would be nice to live in the country. The city is great, but after a summer at the beach, in a house with a yard, having more space seemed emotionally important. There was something very calming about raising a baby with space around.

We looked in New Jersey but didn't love it. And we definitely didn't want to live in upstate New York again; we had made it out, we weren't going back. So Connecticut was our target. We drove around Greenwich, eyeballing houses. We drove to New Canaan, to Westport, all over the area.

One day we stopped in a Friendly's ice cream shop for lunch, and the lady sitting next to me was reading through a book of real estate listings. I asked whether she was an agent. She was, and introduced herself: Janet Milligan. We browsed the book together and found a beautiful white colonial on Round Hill Road that Susie and I fell in love with. The property cost $750,000, which was a real stretch. Fortunately, Angelo Rosato helped me get a bank loan, and also loaned me money of his own. Tom Curtin helped me with the paperwork. My guys.

Having Ally was like receiving a gift from God. When we moved to Connecticut, we played out in the woods; I would hide behind trees and pop out and make her laugh and giggle. We set up a playroom with a pretend grocery store, where she would pick out little plastic apples and carrots and tomatoes, and we would add it all up and put them in a bag. We did that for hours. She loved all my classic rock music. I would rush home from the city so I could read to her and rock her before she went to bed. Even as a baby, Ally was an old soul. I almost felt as if I'd had a past life with her that neither of us could remember.

Susie and I were excited about moving to Connecticut. We had had wonderful times at our schoolhouse in the woods in Elmira, so it was a little like bringing it all back home. But I was working long hours, and commuting in and out of New York City was not fun. Still, I got used to it. I liked living where there were trees.

After Ally started pre-kindergarten, Susie wanted to work again. I took a bank loan so she and our friend Nancy Seaman could rent a small space on Putnam Avenue where they opened a fabulous little children's shop called Beauchamp Place, after the street in London.

They had the floors painted black and white and the cabinetry a deep royal blue, and made it very English, very posh, selling clothes from Europe and from various children's companies. It was absolutely charming.

However, both Nancy and Susie were busy with children, and the store eventually became a burden, so after a few years, they decided to close it. Some years later, Susie got the fever again, and with partners Pamela Farr and Ellen Keogh, she bought The Children's Shop in downtown Greenwich. Susie was obsessed with Best & Co., an old-world Fifth Avenue children's clothing chain that had operated from 1879 to 1971 next to St. Patrick's Cathedral. After months of investigation, she found that the name was defunct, and that she could register and take ownership of it.

This was undoubtedly the most amazing children's boutique department store anywhere. Beautiful goods, wonderful ambience, a great place for suburban parents to outfit their children. She opened a larger store in Greenwich, then a shop in Bergdorf's, and then set out to manufacture her own designs. She was finally going to design again!

The business eventually sold to FAO Schwarz, which retained her as creative director and promised to roll out an expansion. Unfortunately, that never happened, and she decided to leave Best & Co. altogether. It closed soon after.

We were vacationing on the beach in Nantucket with Nancy and Peter on July 4, 1989, when Nancy said to me, "Congratulations, Tommy! It's incredible that Susie's pregnant!"

"What?"

Nancy drew back. "Oh, you don't know?"

I turned to Susie. "Are you pregnant?"

"Yes." Apparently my wife had told her friend and former business partner before me.

"Why didn't you tell me?"

"Well, I wasn't sure, so I shared it with Nancy, and I did finally take a test, and I am."

"Oh," I said. "Okay. Great." This was very peculiar. I felt Susie was trying to withhold something from me, but I couldn't imagine why. I still don't have an answer, and I don't know if she ever realized how much that hurt me.

My father had a pain in his back and thought it was a pulled muscle. It didn't seem to heal, so he went in for X-rays. He was stunned when they revealed a cancerous tumor in his right lung. My dad had been a lifelong smoker. They operated almost immediately to remove part of his lung, but the cancer spread. Radiation treatments followed, and emphysema. Within a year he had become sick and weak, in constant need of his oxygen tank. His heart started to give out. We all knew he was not long for this life.

Fortunately, before my dad became ill I had wanted to do things for my parents that they had never experienced. I sent them on a cruise, I sent them on an excurision to Italy, I rented them a house in the Hamptons. I found joy in seeing them have fun in life after working so hard. I had not seen my dad much since I left Elmira, but now the whole family spent as much time as possible with him. My mom was strong but hurting. In the last months of his life, we were basically waiting for him to die.

At the end of his life he was attached to an oxygen mask, and all my sisters and brothers gathered in his room. He was incoherent and was making breathing noises you don't want to hear coming out of anyone, particularly a parent. My sisters and mother were all crying, and my brothers were very upset. The nurse said, "He's going to go very soon." The family walked into the hallway as I sat with him. My dad opened his blue eyes very wide, his pupils like pinheads, and looked at me. He said, "I'm sorry about the way I treated you." His speech was labored and difficult. "Please take care of your mother and my mother and the family."

I felt pummeled, almost physically weak. I had hated him when I was young, and even though he occasionally tried in later years to be nice to me, I still couldn't understand or accept the way he had treated me. We never talked about it; he wasn't the kind of man with whom I could even bring up that conversation. He was bigger and stronger than I was, and even as a grown man I never stopped being afraid he would get mad and physically do something to me. He passed away that night, December 21, 1989, four days before Christmas. I was afraid of my father until the day he died.

And yet finally I felt at peace with my dad and understood him. As a father now I realize he only wanted me to be the best I could be.

By some terrible coincidence, my dad's brother Robert had died the day before. I called my grandmother. Even though she had been miserable to me, how terrible for Nana to have two sons die before her over the course of two days. I visited her in Jacksonville. She was bedbound and had a couple of caregivers rotating. I said, "Nana, my dad asked me to take care of you, so I'm going to."

As I walked down the hall to the bathroom I heard her tell her nurse, "You know my grandson Tommy, he's a millionaire, and he's going to take good care of me!"

I thought, "Now that I'm successful, now you want to be nice?" But I said nothing.

When I got hold of Nana's expenses, I found that she was running out of money. I thought, "She's senile; she just lost her two sons. I'm not going to give it a lot of thought. I'm just going to take care of her." I supported my grandmother until she died seven years later.

In March 1990, just as we were going to sleep, Susie felt something and called the ob-gyn, who said, "Come in." We headed for Greenwich Hospital. This time I wasn't in the delivery room. The doctor came out and said, "It's a boy. And he's a big one!"

I named my son Richard, after my father. We knew we were having a boy, and when my father was ill we'd sat with him on the couch in his house in Elmira and told him, "Dad, we're going to name our son after you!" Despite the way he had treated me, he was in such miserable shape that I wanted to do something to make him feel good. Then I had to be as good as my word.

From the moment I first held him and felt what was radiating between us, Richard and I have had a bond of love that exists beyond words. I know, it sounds sappy.

Much as we loved the Connecticut life, we decided to move back to New York so I could see my family and not lose hours of work time commuting. We sold the Connecticut home on Round Hill Road and rented a five-story townhouse at 123 East 80th Street, which Susie and Cindy Rinfret decorated beautifully, even though it was a rental.

Ally was shaking when she walked into the Convent of the Sacred Heart on East 91st Street on her first day of kindergarten. She didn't want to let go of me, but a nun convinced her everything was going to be okay. I watched as she walked down the hall in her little gingham jumper and thought, "This is the beginning of her growing up," and there were tears in my eyes to see her in such discomfort. It didn't take long for her to acclimate, though, which eased my own anxiety.

Every morning, Susie and I would wake up at six for a run around the Central Park reservoir. We would get cappuccinos at E.A.T. on Madison and 80th Street and then jog home, where I'd spend time with Richard. He would sit in his little blue-and-white-striped pajamas and watch cartoons while I showered and dressed, and we would talk while his breakfast was being made. Three mornings out of five, when it was time for me to leave for work, Richard would start crying, "Daddy, don't go, don't go!" I was his buddy, and the last thing I wanted to do was leave him. Anyone who has closed the door with his child in tears will know that tortured feeling.

I was happiest when I came home in time for us to play together: army, G.I. Joe, Power Rangers, cars and trucks. He dressed up in football gear when I took him to Giants games, and in cool little hockey sweaters when we went to Rangers games. When we rented a summer house in Greenwich, we would go hiking in the woods and build forts. Having a son made our family complete—it was as if Richard was our missing link. I said to Susie, "The size of this family is perfect." There was peace at the dinner table, not the chaos I had known at family meals growing up. The Hilfigers were balanced and happy.

# THE HIGH LIFE

What an experience!

Advertising has been one of the key elements in the creation of the Tommy Hilfiger success. In 1986, when we were still with Murjani, I had been thrilled and honored when Francesco Scavullo, who was renowned for shooting great *Cosmopolitan* covers, accepted our assignment to shoot me for a series of ads we were calling "Tommy Hilfiger by Francesco Scavullo." This was another attempt to raise our profile and place us in the company of greatness.

I went to Scavullo's Upper East Side townhouse studio thinking, "Wow, he's photographed Diana Ross and Sylvester Stallone and Elizabeth Taylor and Grace Kelly . . . this should be exciting!" His partner, Sean Burns, made me feel entirely comfortable. Francesco was very short, wearing a Greek fisherman's cap and glasses with very thick lenses. He seemed almost humble and meek, but also interesting and eccentric. And focused. We ate a healthy lunch, as I recall, perhaps a lentil and kale salad and sparkling water, and I thought, "This is the way I want to eat in life." I was impressed with his home, which was decorated with chic restraint and featured wooden floors and a lot of streaming light, and I couldn't help but stare at the photographs of all the notable people he had shot.

I stood in front of a white screen in a white oxford shirt, the Canyon jeans, a Movado chronograph with a leather strap that I'd inherited from my father, and Alden loafers with no socks, and he got into a pit and started shooting. I hadn't been photographed like this before. I had been to shoots where the photographer had stood in front of me, but never where someone popped up and down from a pit. It was like the Antonioni movie *Blow-Up*, except in real life!

Scavullo shot and shot and shot and shot. "Stand up . . . okay, good, good, good. Let's see that arm again, put it to the side . . . okay, turn toward me. Look at the camera . . . now look away . . . now look up at the sky and then glance toward me." I am by no means a professional model, and at that point I was not extremely comfortable in front of a camera, but Scavullo got me far enough out of myself that I felt comfortable.

Scavullo delivered a silkscreened set of the photographs. I said, "Wow, it looks like Warhol!"

Scavullo said, "I taught Andy how to silkscreen." He described taking Warhol to a studio in Pennsylvania to teach him the technique. I didn't question him. I knew Andy and certainly did not want to get in the middle of any dispute about who had done what when. The campaign was a pleasure to do, but in terms of driving the business, it didn't move the needle.

I knew that I had to stand for something, both as a company and as a person. To me, Ralph Lauren was western on one hand and British on the other. Calvin Klein was a minimalist. Donna Karan was a designer for women with her signature Seven Easy Pieces. Oscar de la Renta was chic and Latin. Carolina Herrera was chic and Latin. Bill Blass was American good taste, Halston was minimalist. So I started thinking, "What do I want to be?"

I wanted to be American classic preppy with a twist—that never changed—but I also wanted to be *cool*. To guide us, I made up an acronym, F.A.M.E.—fashion, art, music, entertainment—which is essentially what pop culture is. I wanted to bake pop culture into everything we did.

George Lois's billboard had put me on the map in 1985, and three years later his idea was to have me photographed next to two American classics: a vintage Harley and a 1957 T-Bird. At the shoot George said, "Okay, kid—stand in front of the T-Bird, just lean against it, act casual." I styled the shoot myself, leaning on the T-Bird in a pair of Public pants, a mock turtleneck with my sleeves pushed up, an Hermès watch, and Alden loafers. For the Harley shot, I wore the same shirt, our Springsteen jean jacket, Canyon jeans, and a pair of Alden shoes with no socks. To enhance the cool factor, I draped a Tommy Hilfiger duffel bag where the Harley's saddlebags usually hang. We called the campaign "Tommy Hilfiger: An American Classic."

The reaction was very similar to what hit us in the earlier

campaign—"Who does he think he is?" but this time with an addition, "Here he is again." People thought I was an egomaniac, but by now I'd learned to roll with the criticism. Every well-known person has an ego; you can't be in this business without one. I never wanted my ego to take over, but I figured, "Okay, I'm going to put my balls on the line and be in the ads, so that I, and by extension my company, will be considered an American classic." That campaign helped lay the building blocks for more success.

In 1992, we began preparing to take the company public. We were expanding, and in order to compete in the big leagues, we needed capital.

No designer brand of my era, other than Liz Claiborne, had ever listed a company on the stock exchange, so we were breaking new ground. Joel and Silas and everyone worked feverishly with the bankers to prepare. When the time came, we all went on the road show.

We sold a growth story unlike any other. We had the core of the Tommy Hilfiger business doing nearly $100 million annually. We had a team of experts. We had fragrance and underwear licenses. We had excellent positioning in all the important stores. We were going into tailored men's clothing, belts, and leather goods. Silas, Joel, and Lawrence worked on the numbers every day, and we showed a whole pyramid of opportunity for growth.

The process took more than a year and a half, and in the end we rattled the market. In September 1992, Tommy Hilfiger Corporation (TOM) went out at $14 a share and shot up to $40. We reinvested significantly in the business, opening shops and stores and advertising. And all of a sudden I had a lot of money.

This had been my goal for as long as I could remember—even before the day my sister Kathy had said, "This is where the rich people live!" as we drove past the biggest homes in the Strathmont area of Elmira. From the paper route to People's Place to pieces of each company I had worked for, my goal had been to amass enough money to live in one of the houses in Strathmont. Now I could.

I had more money than I'd ever thought possible, and I wanted to handle it the right way. I wanted to be prudent and wise in my investments. I wanted to make sure that everything was set up properly from a tax point of view, and that I had no debt—not credit debt, not mortgages. And I wanted to buy real estate, which I felt was a safe move. Susie and I had never had a cushion of cash, and I wanted both the security and the freedom that came with it. I also wanted to make sure that my contract was sound, with no leaks or holes. With this public company, I wanted to be truly protected. No one had taught me how to handle finances. My father had had no money at the end of the day, and had never even had a conversation with me about it.

Prior to our public offering, we had met for extended periods with my attorney Tom Curtin and his team. One of his young lawyers, Joe Lamastra, was our point person. He was in the heat of the deals on my behalf, working on the contracts and documents.

Joe Lamastra was a middle-class New Jersey kid almost exactly ten years my junior. He had gone to public school, majored in finance at Villanova, earned his law degree at Seton Hall, and had started his career at Deloitte Touche. Joe had spent five years at Tom's firm, working on the Donald Trump empire until the all-nighters began to wear on him. He had been thinking of moving to Wall Street when Tom assigned him my pre-IPO tax work. As with many of the people I work with, he and I clicked right away. I asked him questions about investing, and he helped me get organized, interviewing money managers and keeping track of the details. I asked whether he would consider working for me full-time.

Joe was smart. He told me, "I want to be your partner, not an employee. I'm already a partner in a firm, and I have an entrepreneurial element to my bloodstream. If we can figure out a way to do things together, that would be great."

I agreed completely. It was the Silas Chou school of incentivization. "That's better for me," I said. "I want you to participate, because then you will really care."

Joe had vision, and he took care of everything brilliantly. With his help, I invested in triple-A real estate and triple-A art, two things that only increase in value. Plus, I find it absolutely wonderful to live in beautiful places surrounded by inspiring things.

In the mid-1980s, Susie and I vacationed in St. Bart's. We loved it, but as word got out about how cool the island was, it started to get very busy and very New York. We couldn't get into restaurants anymore. We couldn't get a house because all the good ones were rented. It was too much of a scene. We tried Bermuda and the Bahamas, but they weren't exotic or bohemian enough. They were built-up and glitzy and shiny, with casinos and golf courses and high-rises. I didn't want any of that.

We went to St. Maarten and the Virgin Islands but didn't fall in love. Then I read about Mustique, a much less-traveled destination without a lot of nightlife. I called our travel agent, who happened to be Joel Horowitz's aunt, Selma Kon.

She said, "No, dear, I have never been there, and I don't know anything about it, but let me find out."

A short while later, she called back. "There's a house available with its own cook, and it's on the water. I can book it for you. But there is no direct flight—you have to fly to Barbados and then . . ."

We took the puddle jumper to Mustique. The little bamboo airport was empty, very green, and almost primitive. We followed Jeannette Cadet, the house rentals manager, in a little Kawasaki Mule. We had no idea what we were getting into.

The very British colonial house stood at Point Lookout between two bodies of water, L'Ansecoy Bay and the Atlantic Ocean. All stone. The gardener was working on the lawn with a rake, the cook was in the kitchen, and the housekeeper was standing in the front door. We put our suitcases in the bedroom and found a big mosquito net draped over the bed. I had never slept under a mosquito net. The interior of the house was nondescript, but perfect for a one-year-old because there wasn't a lot to break or bump into. There was one beach bar downtown, called Basil's, and one small hotel with fewer than fifteen rooms. That week, we snorkeled, relaxed, did nothing. Heaven.

Next door to our house stood a little yellow beach cottage, and next to that was a construction site. Our gardener worked out in the front quite a bit, often chatting with the gardener next door. I asked, "Is somebody building a house over there?"

"Yes," he said in his Caribbean accent, "this is Nick Yagor's house."

"Who?"

"Nick Yagor."

When I called Selma to arrange the next year's accommodations, she said, "Would you like to rent Mick Jagger's house?"

I said, "Yeah. Is it built?"

Yes, she said. "But he wants to know who's going to rent it, and you have to be vetted by him." Jagger and I had never met, and I was kind of hoping for a phone call, but that never came. A few days later Selma said, "Okay, he'll accept you."

Mick's home was a low-slung Balinese/Indonesian/Thai/Japanese beach house, beautifully decorated, with a master bedroom, game room, bedroom here, bedroom there. Six pavilions connected by elevated walkways. We would end up renting it for several years because it was set up for his children, who were close in age as ours. At that time, Mick Jagger and Jerry Hall had two kids, Elizabeth and James.

We became friendly with Rodney and Lady Touche, the extraordinarily sweet and charming elderly couple who lived down the beach. A few years later, after we'd finally moved into our own beach cottage, they invited us to dinner at their oceanfront home, Pelican House, where they introduced us to Mick and Jerry. The six of us sat around a small table, laughing and talking about everything from children to mosquitoes to music to scuba diving. The Touches had quite a clever sense of humor. My first impression of Mick was that he was very laid-back, and Jerry was giggly and funny and fun. It was not like meeting some mega-superstar backstage before a concert or in a crowded nightspot. It was an easy, relaxed evening in a small beach cottage with my former landlord.

Susie was pregnant with Richard, and we talked about babies and children. They were concerned about the kids getting too much exposure that day, because the Mustique sun could be scorching, especially on pale skin. So, yes, we talked to Mick Jagger about suntan lotion. I also remember asking him about Burma, which he was very interested in visiting and knew a lot about. We ate curry, and when the conversation came around to India he was interested to hear Susie's and my stories about Juhu Beach and our early travels.

Years after that, my stepson Alex, about thirteen years old at the time, came to visit. We dropped our stuff, put on bathing suits, and went out to the pool and the beach. Alex loves dogs, and he chased Mick's dog Star all the way down the white sand. Hours later he came back.

"Alex, where have you been? You didn't tell us where you were going."

He said, "I went to that guy's house."

"Where?"

"The broken down house next door." Mick was doing work on his property and the primitive scaffolding was made of bamboo. Alex must have seen that as a sign of decay, and because he lived with his father in Italy at the time, he had no idea who Mick was. Over dinner that night Mick had a good laugh at his supposed poverty.

After dinner that night, we all went to my library to watch Pete Townshend's movie *Quadrophenia*, and after a long day of dog chasing, Alex plunked himself in the corner of the couch near Mick and began to nod off, quickly stretching himself right across Mick and falling dead asleep. We whispered Alex's name, trying to get him to move, but he just grunted and turned over. Mick, being a father, laughed and let him lie there.

When we decided to buy a home in Mustique in 1990, we found that the house next to Jagger's was for sale, a beachfront fixer-upper called Pamplemousse, which means "grapefruit" in French. I invited a local architect, Arne Hasselqvist, to take a look. He walked up, put his finger right through the wood siding, and said in his Swedish accent, "Yeah, you can't have a house like this here. You have to use mahogany or stone."

"You mean I can't just fix this?"

By now we had bought two properties in Connecticut and renovated them to a fine polish. But this was another league altogether.

"The best thing to do is to tear it down and build a new house," Mr. Hasselqvist told me.

"What would that cost," I asked, "and what would that look like?" He said, "I have plans here. What would you like?"

"I would like an Oliver Messel design," I told him. Oliver Messel was a flamboyant London stage set decorator whose nephew, Antony Armstrong-Jones, had married Great Britain's Princess Margaret. Messel had designed their fabulous Mustique home and retired to Barbados, where he built his own British colonial home and many others.

It turned out that the same Mr. Hasselqvist who put his finger through the wall of my home had worked with Oliver Messel on building all those houses. What a coincidence! And more extraordinarily, he had one Oliver Messel design that had never been built. When he showed it to me, I had one change: "I really like it, but I want my house to be symmetrical." I like balance. So I bought the plans, and Susie and I redesigned them with him.

The work took four years. Originally we were going to build one house with four bedrooms and a master for us, but as the work progressed, we decided to add a beach cottage, so my family could visit, and then another beach cottage for more guests. Then the house on the other side came up for sale. Tommy Hilfiger was taking off, and we had the money, so we bought it and tore it down to build a guest house to match the main house. Ultimately, we created a compound—a private paradise.

David Bowie also had a house in Mustique. In 1990, he invited us to a seventies-themed New Year's Eve party. Susie didn't feel like going, so I went alone. Bowie was wearing platform shoes and a shag wig, and Iman looked not dissimilar. The crowd was fun and diverse. Everyone was drinking and dancing. Diane von Furstenberg was there. I saw Calvin and Kelly Klein, Barry Diller, David Geffen, and Fran Leibowitz. They were all sitting on benches, observing but not really partying.

David and I became somewhat friendly, and when I chartered a plane to take me to the island a few months later, I asked if he wanted a ride. We talked for four and a half hours. Bowie was an art connois-

seur and was as fanatical about collecting as I, and we discussed
Charles Saatchi's very impressive collection. He told me that he
didn't remember much about the 1970s, but that when he lived in
New York, he basically locked himself in an apartment for long
stretches of time and worked on art projects. He said he didn't go
outside, which made sense: David Bowie on the streets of New York
in the mid-seventies would have caused as much pandemonium as
Michael Jackson taking a stroll in L.A. a few decades later.

His dream, he said, was to gather incredible musicians and create music that they had never rehearsed, read, or even seen before—
they'd simply go into a studio and play something for the first time
and record it in that raw state. I found the idea thrilling.

I knew his given name was David Jones, and he told me how
he'd named himself David Bowie. In the early seventies, he said, the
London newspapers were calling Mick Jagger "Jagger Dagger." He
liked the idea of knives and sharpness and Americana. So he decided to be David Bowie.

I was so very, very sad when Bowie died in early 2016. The news
made me cry. He was such an influence on style and music in my
life. Breaking rules all the time. Pioneering new beginnings. Such
an inspiration. It was the first time I'd cried since my mom's death.

Lawrence called me from a two-hundred-foot yacht in St. Bart's
and asked, "What's this Mustique place all about?"

I said, "Come visit!"

"How long is it going to take to get there?"

"I don't know. Ask your captain—it can't take more than a day
and a half."

Two days later he called and said, "This fucking place better be
good, because the seas are rough and my family is bouncing around
on this fucking boat and everybody is getting sick!"

I told him, "Lawrence, turn around, don't come. Please go back.
If you don't like it, I don't want you to be upset with me. It's not a
flashy place. It's a primitive island, it's—"

"I'm already halfway there, I'm not turning around."

"Damn," I thought, "Lawrence is going to hate it. There's no shopping, there's one beach bar and an okay-at-best restaurant in the hotel. Oh God, what am I going to do?"

I called him back several times, but there was no answer, no answer, no answer. I said to Susie, "You are going to watch Lawrence freak out and he's going to be so pissed at me, but what can I do?" My house was being built; it was a hole in the ground with construction equipment lying around—a real pit. I was renting probably the worst house in Mustique. I loved the island, but I was sure he was going to hate it.

Lawrence pulled into the port, which really isn't even a port; you just anchor near Basil's Bar. He called and said, "I'm here, come see me." I went down to the dock, and he said, "Show me around." I put him in my little Mule and started driving.

"This is Basil's," the bamboo beach bar built on stilts in the water. "This is the Cotton House," a small hotel with fewer than fifteen rooms. "This is the purple boutique," which sold suntan lotion and bathing suits. "This is the pink boutique," selling straw hats and gifts. We'd been driving for ten minutes when I said, "That's about it. This is a house"—there were only about fifty houses on the entire island. He said, "Show me where you're staying." I took him to our rental, and I could tell by the look on his face that he wasn't impressed. He said, "Let's have dinner on my boat tonight. Invite some people."

So we did: Mick Jagger and Jerry Hall; the managing director of the island, Brian Alexander, and his wife, Joannah; and a few others. We had cocktails and dinner with Lawrence and his wife, Claire Anne. The boat, of course, was spectacular. At the end of the night, Lawrence said, "I'm going to look at houses tomorrow with Brian."

"So you like it here?"

Lawrence said, "It's okay. I just want to see the houses."

He ended up putting down a substantial deposit on the huge, beautiful, $20-million-plus Villa Rosa dei Venti, which sat on a cliff overlooking the Atlantic. He sent his guys to inspect. They ticked off the long list of necessary repairs, and in the meantime Lawrence rented the Great House. This was the true gem of the island, one of the original homes, a replica of the Taj Mahal built by the founder of Mustique. A short time later, Lawrence bought the Great House for an undisclosed amount of money and left his deposit for the Villa Rosa Dei Venti on the table.

Lawrence does everything in a big way, so of course he would buy the Great House; it was the biggest and the best. Lawrence hired the descendants of the craftsmen who had built the original Taj Mahal to come over from Agra and spruce the place up—classic Lawrence! I had to hand it to him: in the end, the place was exquisite.

# CHAPTER FOURTEEN

# SONS AND DAUGHTERS

*the Next Generation*

Susie, the kids, and I spent five years in the 80th Street townhouse as the business was building. We threw dinner parties for friends, had editors over for drinks, and did a lot of entertaining with fashion people. In the summer of 1992, we rented a home in Connecticut and loved it so much that when Susie became pregnant again that year, we decided to move back full-time. We found a Tudor home on majestic Mayfair Lane in Greenwich.

I was doing a personal appearance in a Woodward & Lothrop store in Washington, D.C., when I got the call: "Susie is on her way to the hospital." I hustled out, jumped on a private jet, flew into the White Plains airport, and got to the Greenwich hospital just in time for my daughter Elizabeth to be born in May 1993.

Elizabeth was an interesting little character. She would giggle and smile all the time. Susie used to read her the nursery rhyme "Little Bunny Foo Foo, hopping through the forest," and every time Susie said "Foo Foo," Elizabeth would break out in a belly laugh. So of course we started saying "Foo Foo" just to hear her laugh. A child's belly laugh is just so wonderful! We started calling her Foo Foo, and she has been Foo Foo ever since.

As she grew up, whatever conversation we were having, wherever we were having it, Foo Foo would always pipe up with her opinion. Her observations were irreverent, brilliant, and funny, making everyone laugh. She was so bossy and so very smart that Susie started calling her "the little CEO." And yet she followed her big brother around like a fan. Richard would say, "Foo Foo, go get my toys," and she would run and get them. "Foo Foo, get me some water." She would run and get it. Always a bit of a tomboy, Foo Foo was part of the pack and head of the peanut gallery. She commented on everything and everyone, and was usually right on target.

In 1994, a realtor knocked on our door in Greenwich and told us that somebody was interested in buying our house. We had bought it for $3 million three years prior, so I said, "Well, it's going to have to be $5 million." Within a couple of days, the guy came back and said, "I want it." Time to find another house.

Susie quickly found Denbigh Farm up on Riversville Road in Greenwich, a beautiful, historic twenty-two-acre horse farm owned by Joseph Verner Reed, Jr., George H. W. Bush's former chief of protocol and a direct Mayflower descendant. The house needed extensive renovation, and once again we were moving while Susie was pregnant, this time with our daughter Kathleen.

We had vacationed on Nantucket in the late 1980s and fallen in love with the place. In 1996, we found an extraordinary property there, Point of View, at 9 Lincoln Avenue. Now we had two construction/design projects going on at once and the house in Mustique, plus our fourth child was only a year old! It was quite a handful, but what an exciting time.

Kathleen was born in June 1995, when the Connecticut house wasn't quite finished. We moved in when the paint was still wet, which gave us some concerns about the effect on the baby. Even so, I could not believe my good fortune. My life was actually exceeding my dreams.

My travel schedule was chaotic. I would come home from work on Friday and tell Susie, "I've got to leave for Hong Kong on Monday."

"Again?" she would say.

I tried very hard to balance my itinerary and be around as often as possible. "I'm going to go do what I have to do and come right back," I'd tell her. "I'm only going to stay three days this time," whereas I used to stay three weeks. But three weeks later I'd say, "I've got to go to Europe for a week. And when I come back I've got to do personal appearances in Texas and California, but I'll try to do Texas as a day trip."

Susie's patience was wearing thin. She'd ask, "Can't someone go in your place?" And as the team became stronger, they did travel more than I. But Susie felt my absence, and let me know that she was upset.

Sometime around Kathleen's first birthday, we noticed she

wasn't moving her body like other babies. She was very limp and always uncomfortable. She wasn't trying to hoist herself up or crawl. She cried for long periods of time, did not sleep well, and did not respond when we talked to her or tried to get her attention. She would just stare blankly, not giggle or laugh. We didn't know what was wrong or what we could do to help her.

We took her to specialists, who came to no conclusions. One measured the circumference of her head and told us that her brain might not be developing like a normal child's. She didn't pass hearing tests, so the doctor suggested an operation that basically put a hole into the eardrum. We were very anxious about having our baby undergo anesthesia and about the procedure itself, but the doctors convinced us it was the right thing to do.

We were told Kathleen didn't have true autism, but that she had autistic tendencies. Without a real diagnosis, we constantly wondered what was going to happen next. Would she regress? Maybe we could mix a cocktail of one medication and another and another, but how healthy would that be for her? And what were the side effects? Did she have ADD or ADHD? We tried a variety of medications. One was too strong, and she couldn't sleep at night. Another was so weak as to have no effect at all. We took Kathleen to occupational therapy, speech therapy, and physical therapy, but there was no silver bullet.

Kathleen's difficulties were devastating, and not knowing how to soothe our child was terrifying for us. The stress on everyone was enormous. We kept thinking, "What went wrong? Did the paint fumes in our new house contribute to our daughter's problems? Did we do wrong by moving in before it was finished, and are we therefore responsible?" That question has gone through my mind many times.

Because Kathleen needed to be watched constantly, our other children must have felt slightly abandoned. Ally, Richard, and Foo Foo were wonderful and very supportive of Kathleen, but while we were focusing on their sister, they didn't get the attention they needed, which made me feel even more awful.

When she was three years old we found out that Kathleen had a muscle condition called hypotonia, or "floppy baby syndrome," meaning she had a severe lack of muscle tone. She was classified as developmentally delayed. At four years old, she could hardly walk, and we had to get braces on her legs. Children with special needs often have special issues, and Kathleen was no exception. She bumped into people or things, fell down frequently, or needed something *at that moment* and did not have the awareness or patience to sit back and wait for it.

We thought these problems would continue for the rest of her life, but miraculously, Kathleen grew and developed. At age twenty-one, she is now in a postgraduate program in a school in upstate New York, doing extremely well, working at a day care center, and learning life skills. She loves working with babies and children. We couldn't be more thrilled that she is happy. She is growing up to be quite a young lady.

These trials definitely affected my marriage; they were the main reason Susie was not happy that I was working all the time. I certainly wasn't about to quit or even slow down, but I told Silas, Lawrence, and Joel that I had to do something. Silas said, "Why don't you just helicopter in and out of New York? That will save you a lot of time." It was a good idea. Although I arrived at work a bit later each morning, it was worth it because I got to drive my kids to school and spend time with them. When Richard was around fourteen, he was on the school hockey team, so I would get up at four-thirty in the morning to take him to practice, come home, take the other children to school (between them, our children were in three different schools, which was another trial), then jump in the helicopter and head to the city. I worked into the evening every night and then choppered back to spend as much time with the family as possible.

At a very young age, I had taken on the role of father for my siblings, and as a result, I always felt I could handle any problems that arose. I knew I could handle chaos. If something negative was happening, I thought, "We'll turn it into a positive." So what if I had to get up at four-thirty in the morning and then work until well after seven at night? Juggling the business, Kathleen, the other children, and trying to be present in my marriage at the same time was exhausting. But I really thought I could do it, and I think I ended up balancing pretty well. If I had it to do over again, I don't know that I would have done anything differently.

My work gave me some respite. To promote the brand, we ran what we called a multipronged attack. We didn't just do advertising. We dressed celebrities. We hosted and sponsored events. I did personal appearances in stores and fashion shows, and traveled all over the country and the world meeting customers, signing autographs, and doing newspaper interviews. This was the early 1990s, the beginning of celebrity marketing.

Record companies were using street teams, and we followed that model, the concept being that wherever there were cool people there should be Tommy Hilfiger clothes. My brother Andy and Peter Paul Scott were completely plugged into the music scene and perfect for this job. They would go to a music video shoot, a movie shoot, or a dance party and get our product in the hands of the right people. We were also doing charity events and hosting parties with DJs— promoting all the time.

Early in our business relationship, Silas had asked me about my vision for the company, and I'd told him, "Eventually I'd like to have a separate jeans division." I was thinking back to my roots, where jeans meant youth, but at the same time I saw an opportunity to build the designer jeans business with a different point of view.

In 1994, we bought a company called Pepe Jeans and used it as our infrastructure. We licensed Tommy Jeans to Pepe and asked my sister Ginny, a talented designer who was working alongside sweater expert Voula Solonos, to work there. Of course we didn't want to make jeans like everyone else's, so I said, "Ginny, why don't you take athletic wear and jeanswear and marry the two?" Not long thereafter, she showed me boards that blew me away. She had disassembled those cultural staples and reassembled them in remarkable ways, uniting denim and athletic details in jeans, jackets, and warm-up suits.

Ginny took stripes from athletic jerseys and ran them down the legs. She did pocketing made from nylon and spandex and all sorts of baseball jackets and warm-up suits, mixing them with denim. We put a big red-white-and-blue patch on the back of our basic five-pocket jean. Then we took a carpenter jean, which was baggy, over-sized, and relaxed to begin with, and made it *way* too big, because that was the Tommy Jeans look. Comfort was a factor, but more than that, this was the beginning of American streetwear.

Up until this point, everyone tucked in their shirts. But walking around the streets of New York, I noticed that kids were wearing their shirts out and turning their baseball caps backward. They were wearing Rangers hockey sweaters with Lee carpenter pants and Adidas sneakers. If a kid had a 32-inch waist, he'd buy a 36-inch-waist jean and let it hang low. I took American workwear—carpenter jeans, overalls, painter pants, farmer jackets—and logoed it, enlarged it, and paired it with athletic wear: authentic-looking football jerseys, basketball jerseys, baseball jerseys. I added all the gear to go with it: backpacks, messenger bags inspired by the bicycle messengers who were ubiquitous at the time, baseball caps, bucket caps. That was the look we were beginning to see surfacing in the streets, and not only did I find it fresh-looking, I was very certain it would sell.

Carpenter jeans were a big phenomenon at that time, but ours really took off when we put the Tommy Hilfiger label on the hammer loop just above the knee. When it was combined with our oversized hockey jersey, which came down to the middle of the thigh, you could still see the logo and its splash of color. It got to be a thing. A very big thing. Pretty soon Tommy Jeans was almost dwarfing Tommy Hilfiger. At the same time we reengaged with womenswear, which we'd started, struggled to define, and put on hold in the late 1980s.

Our advertising was evolving, too. I loved George Lois's genius campaigns, but now it was time to create a true all-American lifestyle campaign. We met Mike Toth, who had done a lot of the Ralph Lauren Boys advertising. Toth had an incredible eye and he understood us completely. We gave him Tommy Jeans to work with, as well as sportswear, and we created an all-American campaign. And what was more all-American than Norman Rockwell?

I bought an oversized book of Rockwell paintings and wore down the pages showing it to Mike, Lawrence, Edwin, Joel, and anyone else who would look. This was the advertising I wanted! I loved the minutiae. I loved the small-town flavor. And I especially loved the detail in the clothing he used: the saddle shoes, the tartan skirts, the wool sweaters, the military uniforms, the quilts. I loved his Christmas paintings. I loved the faces of these all-American characters. I thought, "This is really us. We are more Norman Rockwell than any other company. We're very, very Americana."

Mr. Rockwell had passed away, and I thought of getting a painter to render our campaign, almost as an homage. But would we ever be able to replicate Rockwell's detail and coloring? I doubted it. Then Mike said, "I think we can capture it in a photograph."

So we looked for a diverse group of fresh-faced all-American kids. I didn't want all blond-haired, blue-eyed models like my competitors were using; I wanted the melting pot, just like our customer base and just like America. We ended up with one blond white model, one brunette white model, one Latina, and one African American. One of our models was an all-American-looking boy named Ethan Browne. At the shoot someone said, "You know, that's Jackson Browne's son."

I have tremendous respect for Jackson Browne's music, so I started talking to Ethan. "Tell me about your childhood. Your dad was one of my heroes, a real, incredible rock star." It turned out that Ethan had spent most of his childhood on tour with his father, hanging backstage with the band, traveling from city to city, listening to rehearsals and sound checks, being there while great music was being created. His dad had loved him and made him a part of that life. I thought, "Ethan Browne isn't just a good-looking kid, he has music in his blood! Let's find others!"

I couldn't use Rod Stewart, Mick Jagger, Quincy Jones, Goldie Hawn, Keith Richards, or Sting, maybe because they were expensive, maybe because they didn't want to get involved, maybe because they no longer had the Tommy Hilfiger look of youth. But, I thought, I sure would like to use their offspring! That was an exciting idea! They had something other kids didn't have. They had what I love in their blood. Now that I had kids of my own, I was even more into it. So we went out casting for the next generation.

The Jagger children immediately came to mind. Lizzie and James were just considering going into modeling. I gave them their first job.

We traveled all over America. We shot in Florida, Maine, and California, in Nantucket and the Hamptons. We shot Lizzie Jagger in Texas. I assured Jerry that she would be safe, so I assigned one of our public relations assistants to watch over her. Lizzie met a very handsome South African boy with longish blond hair. We photographed her holding on to him on the back of a motorcycle, and they fell in love. Later I asked Mick, "What do you think of Lizzie's new boyfriend?" and he said, "He looks good, but he's a bit boring, isn't he?"

My brother Andy was always introducing me to interesting people from the music world. One day, he said, "Tommy, you have got to meet Kidada."

"Who's Kidada?"

"Kidada Jones, Quincy's daughter."

So Kidada came around and was absolutely adorable. She had perfect skin, big, big eyes, and a beautiful smile, and was just so hip and young. We were setting up to do a Tommy Jeans fashion show, and she said, "You should wear big T-shirts and mix them with . . ." and she rattled off a half-dozen perfect style ideas.

I said, "I will give you a credit card, and you go shopping. Bring me back all the things I should be doing."

Kidada and Andy hit the streets and returned with warm-up pants, basketball jerseys, cool sneakers, and all sorts of stuff I'd have loved if I'd seen it first. Andy said, "Tommy, we should really hire her full-time, because otherwise she is going to go work for somebody else." So we did.

Probably because she grew up with a famous dad, Kidada was not afraid of me. She would tell it like it was. I'd tell her I liked a pair of jeans, and she'd say, "I hate those jeans! You can't put those on the runway! They look so tacky—they look pedestrian, man!"

Then I'd tell her, "Okay, Kidada, just tell me what I should do, because I know you know," and she would enlighten me as to what was going on streetwise. I caught on fast. Between Andy, Kidada, our model and street team member Peter Paul Scott, and people in our design studio like Ubi Simpson and Malcolm Crews and Joel's son, Dustin Horowitz, who graduated from FIT, we developed our own street style.

When Quincy Jones came into New York to do some work at the Hit Factory, Kidada said, "My dad wants to meet you; why don't you come over to the studio?" I was more than pleased to meet the great Quincy Jones.

The first thing he did was hug me and say, "Thank you for giving my daughter this opportunity."

I said, "Well, thank you for allowing us to utilize your daughter's talent." And then another idea dawned on me: "Hold on, we should use her as a model too! Kidada," I told her, "I need you to model for us!"

"Okay," she said, "but only if I can wear what I want to wear!"

"Of course! Take your pick, and tell me what everybody else should be wearing, too."

"And you have to meet my friend Aaliyah."

"Who?"

"Aaliyah. She's an R&B singer, Tommy. She's beautiful and she's really talented."

I did a little research and found out who Aaliyah was. What I didn't know was that Kidada was dating Tupac Shakur and Aaliyah was dating R. Kelly. Hip-hop royalty. We teamed her up with Mark Ronson, who was the stepson of Foreigner's Mick Jones and a young DJ at the time, and they were a perfect match for Tommy Jeans. Later, we became friendly with Mark's sisters Charlotte and Samantha and their mother, Ann Jones. DJ Cassidy Podell worked for us as an intern before he started to deejay for everyone from President Obama to Sean "Puffy" Combs to Leo DiCaprio.

We gathered Rod Stewart's daughter Kimberly, Donald Trump's

daughter Ivanka, Kareem Abdul-Jabbar's son Amir, F. Scott Fitzgerald's grandson Luke, and Goldie Hawn's daughter Kate Hudson before she started acting. I included my daughter Ally and my nephew Michael Fredo; Keith Richards's daughters Theodora and Alexandra; James and Elizabeth Jagger; Kidada's brother Snoopy; Brandon Davis, a really handsome guy who looked like a young Elvis and was the grandson of Marvin Davis and the son of Nancy Davis; Sting's son Jake Sumner; and David Foster's daughter Sara. We dressed them, put them in the ad campaigns, and put them on the runway.

Mike Toth and Dewey Nicks, this cool guy from California at the beginning of his career, photographed these kids, and we'd be blasting the music. Dewey liked Muddy Waters and a lot of blues artists. He had a great eye and really understood surf and music culture.

In 1995, we became the first-ever license of the Estée Lauder family, thanks to Leonard and Evelyn Lauder, who believed in me and the Tommy Hilfiger brand. Mr. Leonard Lauder, the son of Estée Lauder, is one of the smartest businessmen I have ever encountered. He's also one of the nicest people I've met, and I look up to him as a father figure, a mentor, and a consummate gentleman. We developed a fragrance together, asking ourselves, "What is the all-American scent?" I wanted it to be fresh, clean, and outdoorsy, to smell like driftwood on a beach, fresh-cut green grass, apple pie, grapefruit. The smell of fresh rain and the fresh outdoors in a bottle—that's what I said to a fragrance designer at the fragrance house Fermenich, and they developed the scent. Leonard's wife Evelyn, who, I am sad to say, passed away in 2011, was instrumental in selecting the bouquet. We experimented with many renditions, some richer, some deeper, some spicier, but finally Evelyn said, "This is the one." We took her lead.

Leonard and I also worked very closely on the packaging, bottle, and advertising. In a conference room at Estée Lauder, we convened around a table teeming with bottles—some antique, some new, some created by a bottle maker with us in mind. At first I was overwhelmed: I knew the look of the Tommy Hilfiger bottle would say as much about the product as the actual scent did, and this was the moment of decision. We were on a short deadline because we wanted to launch in the spring, only nine months away.

The tag on the first bottle I picked up, a vintage piece from a company called Thatcher Glass, read, "Made in Elmira, New York." I said, "This is the one." I must have turned over almost every other bottle in my hand, trying to get the feel of such an important product, but that's the one we ran with.

What were we going to call it? Leonard said, "What else? Tommy. The all-American fragrance."

We scheduled a launch party and needed someone who would be a magnet for the press. Who could attract the kind of attention our fragrance demanded?

John F. Kennedy, Jr. was the living embodiment of the spirit of the fragrance. The Lauders knew the Kennedys and made the connection.

When we were informed that he was busy on the date we had scheduled for the party, the fourteenth, I told our people, "Change the party date to the sixteenth." Told he would be away until the nineteenth, I asked, "What is he doing earlier in the month?" His secretary said he would be in town. I said, "Change all the dates!" But the restaurant we chose didn't have availability. "Find another restaurant!" I said. Find a way! My question, then as now, was "How do we become not good but great?" Mediocrity was never a solution.

And when we had our party, there was John F. Kennedy, Jr., surrounded by reporters from every newspaper, magazine, and TV network. The coverage was fabulous. That's how you establish a brand.

John and I became friends. He was launching his magazine, *George*, which we were supporting with advertising, and he and I regularly had lunch or dinner or drinks and bounced ideas off each other. A few years later, I invited him to a Thursday night dinner at my home in Connecticut and mentioned I was heading to Nantucket for the weekend. He said, "I love Nantucket—one of my favorite places. I'm not sure if I can come to the dinner, I'm taking my pilot's license exam, but I will let you know." I quickly received a handwritten note that read, "Dear Tommy, thank you for inviting me to dinner at your house. I'm sorry I won't be able to make it, I'm taking my pilot's license exam. Watch out, the skies over Nantucket will never be the same."

We scheduled a transcontinental personal appearance launch tour for the fragrance. I signed every bottle and box at stores in Charlotte, Atlanta, Dallas, Birmingham, and Scottsdale. We were relentless, and Tommy became the number one fragrance in the United States for five years straight, breaking all records. In 1996 we won an unprecedented four Fragrance Association awards, or Fifis, including Best Men's Fragrance, Best Packaging, Best Men's National Print Advertising Campaign, and Best Men's National TV Advertising Campaign. The next year we won Men's Fragrance of the Year—Luxe. We were sitting on top of the world. What more did we need?

A women's fragrance!

I asked Evelyn Lauder what we should call it, and she said, "Tommy Girl. It makes sense." What else could it possibly be called?

We launched Tommy Girl under Leonard's oversight, and it luxuriated in the number one slot for women's fragrances for two years in a row. Our team leader, Pamela Baxter, was extremely well dressed and had great taste—and she was also incredibly hard-driving. She went into meetings with department store heads and came back saying, "They gave us the largest order that they have ever given anyone for a fragrance." When we visited stores, we found the marketing, packaging, and counter displays were all perfect. For the advertising, we hired a guitarist to play "The Star-Spangled Banner" à la Jimi Hendrix at Woodstock, and photographed fresh-faced kids running through the fields of Nantucket and New England carrying American flags. It solidified Tommy Girl as an all-American, youthful brand. Today, Tommy and Tommy Girl are sold in 120 countries and territories.

When I explained the sons and daughters concept for our first Tommy Jeans ad campaign and showed Leonard the photos we were about to run, he said, "That's the fragrance ad. That's it!" Leonard had true vision; he could see it so clearly. And he was right: it was about the attitude of the young people. They weren't supermodels, but together, they looked like the in-crowd, the cool kids' table. The ad said, in essence, "If you are cool and young and American, you should wear these clothes and this fragrance." It was fantastic! The Lauder Group launched it worldwide, paving the road for our international business.

Then Bob and Harvey Weinstein asked if I would be interested in collaborating on a film. What a great opportunity for Tommy Jeans! *The Faculty* was being shot in Austin, Texas, with a cast that included Usher, Josh Hartnett, Elijah Wood, Jordana Brewster, Clea DuVall, and Salma Hayek; the film was directed by Robert Rodriguez. We agreed to dress them and run an ad campaign featuring the cast, but only if they included Kidada to add spark. They loved her, and she was in the film.

We licensed our underwear with Jockey and created a Times Square billboard full of young guys dropping their jeans to show their boxers in tartan plaid, ticking stripes, stars and stripes, and prints. Soon all the cool college and high school kids were in our boxers, and their dads were in our briefs. The underwear business was on fire!

We licensed our tailored clothing with the old-line Chicago manufacturer Hart Schaffner & Marx. President Ken Hoffman and CEO Bert Hand were great partners. We developed three-piece suits with reversible vests, great fabrics and linings, and a new fit. Three-piece suits were back! Ivy League style! What fun!

We were really rolling.

# CHAPTER FIFTEEN

# ROCK STYLE

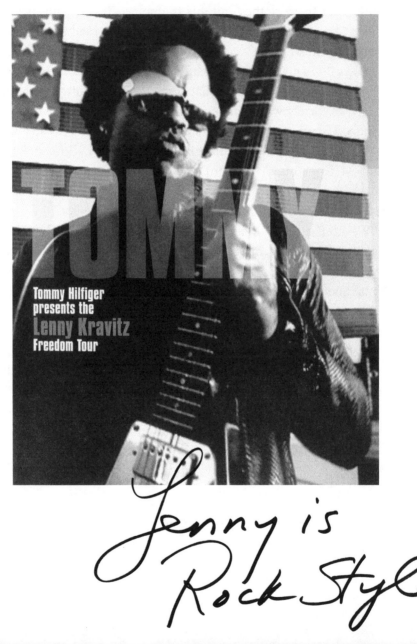

Tommy Hilfiger
presents the
Lenny Kravitz
Freedom Tour

n the mid-1990s, Andy was the Tommy Jeans PR marketing guy, in charge of product placement, when he took a call from entertainment lawyer Larry Rudolph, who said, "I have a new artist who just did a video that hasn't come out yet, but I think it's gonna be really big. We need help—we need five grand. Maybe she can model this or that?" The video arrived, and it was Britney Spears singing ". . . Baby One More Time." Short pleated skirt, bare midriff, cardigan, knee socks, pigtails. Andy watched it and said, "I've got to introduce her to Tommy and see if we can do something."

The next week, as I stepped out the side door of a design meeting, Andy said, "Tommy, this is Britney Spears." The little girl from Louisiana standing in front of me with greasy hair looked nothing like she did in the video. She didn't strike me as beautiful or amazing, but I wasn't looking for beauty at that time, I was looking for cool. After they left I asked Andy, "Are you sure?"

"Tommy," he said, "you gotta see this video! And we should mix up our advertising. This is a new artist, and they want five grand."

Andy knew his music. "You decide," I told him. "I'll trust you."

Andy signed her. The day of our photo shoot, she hit number one. Britney and I were on the cover of *USA Today*, and the press exploded. We sponsored her . . . Baby One More Time tour, and my nephew Michael Fredo—who had been signed by Quincy Jones's Quest Music—opened for her. This was the beginning of celebrity-driven advertising and marketing.

Andy was sitting in his office another time when a deal guy called and said, "Michael Jackson wants to do a clothing line with you guys."

"Okay."

"I want to send you his clothes right now."

"Okay."

An hour later, Michael Jackson shirts showed up. They were festooned with gold buttons, epaulets, and military details, but done in satin, leather, and polyester. Then Andy called and said, "Michael Jackson wants to meet with you."

"Let's go meet him! Could be a fun experience in any case."

The next day we were sitting in the lobby at the Palace Hotel, waiting to be summoned upstairs. Michael Jackson had a whole floor. Finally the guards told us, "Michael's ready for you."

When I shook his hand, he was totally made up with foundation and eye shadow, and had a makeup compact tucked into his white sock.

"I designed all of my own stuff," he told us. "No one has what I have. I'm the most famous person in the world, and I really want to work with you."

We were preparing to go to L.A., where I was sponsoring the Race to Erase MS, an event that Nancy Davis has organized since 1993 to aid the fight against multiple sclerosis. So I said, "Maybe we can meet and keep talking." He agreed.

As we were getting off the plane in Los Angeles, my phone rang. It was Michael Jackson.

"I hear you are in L.A. I heard you landed."

WTF?

The event was that night. The next morning, Michael called. "Are you coming to Neverland?"

Ally was with us and said, "Let's go!"

It was a three-hour drive to his ranch, so we took a helicopter and landed on the Neverland helipad. A choo-choo train, with a conductor and everything, picked us up. We were driving through Neverland, and no one was there. As we passed the Ferris wheel, it started up. Every seat was empty. We saw teacup rides and a racetrack and an amphitheater, all deserted.

We pulled up in front of the house, and a butler came out wearing white gloves. "Hello," he said. "Michael will be coming; he is expecting you." We were standing in front of this massive gingerbread-style house when a giraffe walked by, followed by a string of baby elephants. Ally and Andy were looking at each other, like "This is crazy!"

All of a sudden, a huge white limo pulled up and Michael stepped out, his staff surrounding him with ruffled umbrellas. We walked inside and Michael disappeared. Jackson Five gold records, *Gone with the Wind* memorabilia—all his collections were artfully displayed. There were cherub sculptures, and Disney music was playing in the background.

The butler informed us that Michael would like us to have lunch. His kitchen restaurant was complete with menus. I asked, "Will Michael be joining us?"

"Mr. Jackson would like to meet with Tommy alone," he said, and told Andy, "You and the young lady may go to the game room." Later, Andy told me it was fully loaded—every videogame in the world. The original Pac-Man! Candy of all varieties. And nobody there but them.

When I entered his dark mahogany office, Michael was sitting in an enormous gold-and-burgundy throne and asked me to sit across from him. He apologized for being late and wearing dark glasses, and told me the kids had kept him awake all night and he hadn't had much sleep. He was wearing a red flannel button-down shirt, black pants, and black boots. His face was heavily made up and he had a Band-Aid across his nose. He was fidgety. He said, "We really have to do this clothing line together. I have millions of fans all over the world who are waiting for it." He spoke in the same wispy voice we had all grown accustomed to. "I know you and Andy understand me and my aesthetic. You're into music and fashion like nobody else."

That was good to hear. "Michael," I asked, "what are your expectations?"

"I want to open a store on Rodeo Drive," he said, "and in Las Vegas and Paris and other cities."

I told him these were not decisions I could make on my own and that I would check with my partners when I got back to New York.

As Michael and I were saying goodbye, one of his managers pulled me aside and told me to wait at the bottom of the staircase in the main entry. "Michael never introduces his children to anyone," he told me, "but he wants you to meet them."

Prince and Paris came barreling down the stairs dressed as characters from a Broadway show or *The Sound of Music*: velveteen knickers, dirndl jumper, ruffled blouses, patent leather shoes, each in full makeup, their hair bleached blond with dark roots. Blanket was an infant in a nanny's arms. I said hello, got on the train back to the helipad, and flew back to Beverly Hills. Back at the hotel, I answered my cellphone and discovered it was a call from Michael himself.

"We're doing this," he said, "right?"

"Michael, I really have to see what my partners think of the idea."

"How could they not like the idea?" he said. "I'm the most famous star in the world. I have fans begging for it!"

But it wasn't meant to be. When I presented the idea to my partners, they had no interest whatsoever. The Tommy Hilfiger Corporation was throwing off huge profits, and we had lots of cash on hand to make an acquisition or buy back stock. They had bigger deals in mind: at the very same moment I was talking with Michael Jackson, they were negotiating with Barry Schwartz and Calvin Klein to buy the much more developed Calvin Klein business. In the end, we were outbid (by a hair) by Phillips–Van Heusen (PVH). Looking back now, it was a regrettable mistake not to have offered more. It would have been a steal.

Michael continued to call and ask us to reconsider, but our decision was firm, and he never did the clothing line. But I was extremely pleased when he appeared on the cover of *Vibe* magazine wearing an oversized sweater from our line, featuring a large "H" on the front, alongside a nice quote from his wife at the time, Lisa Marie Presley, looking very happy.

In 1998, the concert promoter Michael Cohl and the Rolling Stones' financial advisor, Prince Rupert Loewenstein, told me the band was seeking sponsorship for their twenty-four-city No Security tour. I loved the Stones, I loved their logo—how could I say no? I gathered the forces and told them, "The Stones are the biggest band in the world, and we will have our logo with their logo." As part of the deal, we made clothes for the band to wear onstage and for the crew to wear backstage—clothes that were very different from our preppy all-American look. Mick Jagger was quite a chameleon, an inspiration to rock stars and fashion people throughout the world.

Our thought process was to give him and the entire band something that would move them even more forward. This was going to be a treat!

Early on, when the Stones became *the Stones*, Keith Richards had been way, way, way out there with skull-and-crossbones and black as the color of hard cool. Over the years, he was instrumental in creating the looks of hard rock, glam rock, biker rock, heavy metal, and even punk. We developed our own take on Keith, which involved animal-print shirts, jackets, and scarves, but we never told him how to put it all together. Keith was his own stylist!

We went to Keith and Patti Hansen's home in Weston, Connecticut, to show him our ideas. This visit was set up by Keith's assistant, Jane Rose, who was always most helpful and informative. When we arrived, Keith had just returned from the studio and was entrenched in that day's music. He was on rock-and-roll time and spent most of the afternoon listening to one song over and over, and at first it was hard to get him to check out the clothes. Toward the end of the day, however, Patti got him to focus.

First they showed me a lot of stuff from his closet, which was like a living museum of rock style, filled with animal prints, particularly leopard. Keith was more interested than I thought he would be, and also incredibly respectful, fun, and funny. He pulled out his favorites—lots of longish coats, a few shirts—and then said, "Show me what you've got." I presented sketches and swatches, and it was no surprise that he liked the leopard and other animal prints the best. He knew specifically what he wanted to wear on this tour— longer coats and skinny jeans—so that's what we made.

Charlie Watts was always dressed in tailored clothing and bespoke suits with John Lobb shoes. He looked and carried himself like a proper English gentleman. We dressed him in simple T-shirts and bomber-type jackets. Ronnie Wood came to the band from the Small Faces with a shag haircut and a funky vibe. I think he added a lot of energy with his guitar playing, his prancing onstage, and his very individual cool English rock look.

Mick Jagger has always been a step ahead of fashion and very influential on the industry itself. We were just entering the age of athletic performance fabrics: very technical and almost feather-weight, flexible thanks to four- and six-way stretch, breathable to wick away perspiration. The Stones work hard onstage, and rather than a shirt drenched in sweat, they wanted one that showed—and felt like—no perspiration at all. Mick was into a sporty, streamlined look at the time. He wanted tight-fitting T-shirts and very slim trousers so he could move lithely onstage.

My creative director and assistant, Susie's cousin Stephen Cirona, and I visited Mick at his house in France. I chose Stephen to work directly with Mick and the boys because he is very organized and creative, with great taste, and I suspected we would need exactly that kind of approach with a group this spectacular. Stephen had done all the sketches, and we arrived with designs and color charts. Mick was quite particular. The first time we brought samples, Mick eyeballed them on the rack and knew instantly what made the cut and what didn't. He had a sure and absolute vision of the music, the stage set, and the band in his mind. After our fittings, we went back to the design studio, made corrections, and then trotted across the globe to meet him somewhere else.

We found nuances and necessities that were not commonplace in our world. For instance, we made a very cool jacket in a reflective metallic fabric that we were hoping Mick would find appealing. He tried it on and found it didn't have a lot of movement to it, but the larger problem was that when photographed onstage, the fabric would reflect both flashbulbs and stage lights back onto the camera lens, and the pictures would come up blank. It would be like shooting light itself.

So we scrapped that design, and Mick stuck to simple basics. Sometimes over the course of the tour, he would wear a special jacket or shirt just to look good when he hit the stage, then get rid of it before the second song.

On opening night at Candlestick Park in San Francisco, the crowd was huge, and there was a lot of nervous tension backstage. I found that when Mick walks into a room, the vibe changes drastically. Conversations halt, people fall silent, and all eyes move toward him, because hey, it's Mick Jagger! And before a concert, he's fidgety.

Very fidgety. He can't sit still. He'll pace the backstage area rapidly, quick steps, not unlike the way he prowls the stage, ducking his head into Ronnie Wood's dressing room and Charlie's—he's got the keys—saying in his recognizably arch British accent, "Hey, Ronnie, are you all right?" His head turns and his eyes dart quickly: "What's going on in here?" Inquisitive, not accusative. Spying a newcomer: "Hey, what's your name?" Not waiting for an answer: "All right, see you soon." And out he goes.

He'll pop into the backstage area where corporate sponsors are talking idly, watching the door, waiting for their meet-and-greet, and walk up to unsuspecting people with drinks in their hands and say in rapid succession, "Hello. Are you all right? Are you ready for the concert? You've got good seats, I hope." Making small talk with people who, taken unawares, are unable to fully respond—they have a chance to talk to Mick, but all they can get out is their seat number. Mick will respond, "Oh, is it way out there or is it up close? Up close, I hope. I hope I don't get water on you. I hope it doesn't rain, is it going to rain?" And then he'll move on to somebody else, notice his baseball cap, for instance, and say, "Where did you get that hat? What is that, a grizzly bear?" And before the man in the cap can answer, Mick has gone to the next person. Because he is obliged to be present and accessible, but doesn't really like to engage in conversation with people he doesn't know, Mick will say something vaguely witty and keep moving. The first time I saw this it was funny. After that I was just fascinated by how he could make contact with people every night without actually making contact.

If there are pretty girls around, however, Mick is right on it. He lights up. "Hello, what's your name? I like those trousers you're wearing. Turn around and let's see the bum!" And of course they twirl!

When the Stones hit the stage that night, I was mid-orchestra in the sound booth with lighting designer Patrick Woodruff. The view of the stage from there is just amazing. Monitors in the sound booth showed different sections of the stage up close or from a remove.

I brought my brothers—Bobby, Andy, and Billy, rock and rollers all. We hung out backstage, got our pictures taken, and talked with the guys. Billy and Andy left the opening night after-party around two in the morning, but Bobby and I stayed out all night with Keith and Mick. It was the Hilfiger brothers' dream come true. I don't mind saying it was a thrill.

Sponsoring the No Security tour led to friendships with some of the guys. My sister Ginny and I were in London months later and called Ronnie Wood to see what he was up to. He and Jo, his wife at the time, had just opened a private nightclub/restaurant/spa in Kensington and invited us over. After dinner and drinks, we went to Ronnie's studio, where he played us all the old Faces and *Gasoline Alley* tracks, and we stayed there most of the night listening to him play mandolin and guitar. Ronnie is a good-time presence onstage, often overshadowed by Keith's aura. I know certain Stones and Faces fans are aware of how talented he is, but I'm not sure everyone really knows that Ronnie Wood is one of the best guitar players in the world!

In person, Ronnie was like a kid, laughing and full of energy, a real sweetheart. Jo was saying, "Come on, Ronnie, we've got to go to bed, it's getting late," but he was so passionate—and we were so shameless about egging him on—that he didn't quit. "Play another. What about 'Maggie May'?" Who'd've thunk it, sitting in our little apartment in Hyannis in the summer of 1969, that I'd be calling out cuts live with the guy who made them famous? My life was becoming filled with these perks!

Ronnie and I remain close. He's the sweetest guy, totally funny, totally sincere. He's also a talented painter, and I've collected some of his work, which I cherish. He's now married to the beautiful Sally Humphreys, who is perfect for him. I'm happy to have him as a friend.

Around the time of the Stones tour, we built a set in Hollywood, put a model who looked like a rock star onstage, and shot him from behind facing an audience of screaming models. Peter Arnell created that campaign for us. We called it the Freedom Tour, and launched the fragrance Freedom by Tommy Hilfiger.

After that, we said, "Let's do something new, fresh, and different."

Peter Arnell said, "I've got just the idea. Why don't we shoot at the White House?"

That was ridiculous. They were never going to let us shoot at the White House. But he said, "No, no, no, let's go to Hollywood and build a set that looks like the White House! We can have models on the White House lawn, in the Roosevelt Room, and the Rose Garden, going to visit the president. The president and First Lady will be these hip, beautiful people!"

I said, "Let's go for it. Let's do something outrageous!"

We got to work, studying hundreds of photos of the Oval Office, the White House lawn, the Portico, and the East Room.

Building a set in Hollywood costs hundreds of thousands of dollars, if not millions, so we used ones that had already been built for the movies *Dave* and *The American President*. Rebecca Romijn was a wildly beautiful, sexy supermodel, with long, flowing blond hair— just incredible. We shot Rebecca, Tyra Banks, and the models Jason Shaw, Clayton Hunter, and Alex Lundqvist disembarking from a Tommy Hilfiger–logoed helicopter and running across the White House lawn, and then sat Rebecca in a very provocative pose on the president's desk in the Oval Office. We ran the ads in magazines such as *GQ*, *Vogue*, *Elle*, and *Vanity Fair*. The campaign showcased the optimistic spirit and energy of classic Americanism. Our White House was all-inclusive. Anyone could be president!

And the ads worked! They moved product!

The Monica Lewinsky scandal had surfaced a couple of months earlier, with the president's Oval Office desk as a centerpiece. The image of the White House is in the public domain, we felt, like Mount Rushmore and the American flag. However, we did get a letter from someone fairly high up in the Office of the President directing our attention to a policy against the use of likenesses of the White House or the president for commercial purposes and telling us that they would appreciate it if we would refrain from running ads that were distasteful. We had not intended to make any political statement or commentary, and we complied.

In addition to the Stones, we sponsored tours by Lenny Kravitz, Sheryl Crow, Jewel, and Pete Townshend. Pete began the U.S. leg of his Psychoderelict tour at the Beacon Theater in New York, and for the occasion my brother Andy and I wore striped English schoolboy jackets and shirts with ruffled cuffs and high collars—the sixties Who look that I have always loved. We saw Pete before the show, and he stopped mid-stride and said, "You guys look like English pop stars." *Pete Townshend* said we looked like pop stars!

Nineteen ninety-nine was the Tommy Hilfiger Year of Music. I produced the book *Rock Style*, a series of photographs and stories about the style of rock stars from the 1950s on. In New York City the venerable Metropolitan Museum of Art ran its "Rock Style" exhibition, named after my book and featuring clothes worn by Bowie, Madonna, Hendrix, the Stones, the Beatles, Lenny Kravitz, The Who, Elvis, Stevie Nicks, the Ramones, and the Sex Pistols. Anna Wintour and I co-hosted the Metropolitan Museum of Art Costume Institute Gala, and our guests included Debbie Harry, and Steven Tyler and Joe Perry of Aerosmith. For someone whose prized possession is his childhood vinyl collection, this was a labor of love—and incredible fun.

# CHAPTER SIXTEEN

# HIP-HOP COMES TO HILFIGER

*A Whole New era in Fashion*

I am a commercially minded designer. Although there are people who think good design ought to be more ethereal and esoteric, I am not embarrassed by that description. But there was a moment when I was.

Several years after the Hangman campaign, I was feeling almost entirely unaccepted by the design community. Ralph Lauren, Calvin Klein, Perry Ellis, and the other industry leaders were barely speaking to me. I was derided for my common tastes and the fact that I was selling to the everyman, not only to men with exquisite taste. This was not the life I had hoped to be living.

I turned to my partners for solace. Silas, Lawrence, and Joel very quickly helped me come to my senses. Silas had given my predicament a lot of thought. He had been manufacturing sweaters since he was a young man, and with Ralph Lauren he had combined good taste with great amounts of money. He understood my dilemma and had reached his conclusion. "Profit is sanity," he told me. "The other is vanity. It's frou-frou!"

Lawrence, who tolerated nothing but the best in all things, thought I was nuts. Tommy Hilfiger defined affordable luxury. He said, "Tommy, don't be crazy. We have the perfect position in the world. Why screw with it?"

Joel, more than anyone else, addressed my personality. He said, "Who cares? Do you really want to hang out with those people? So what happens if they accept you? Will that make you a better designer or a happier person?"

It didn't take much convincing. After my moment of doubt and pain, I came to the conclusion that he was right. What was I doing? Why would I even waste my energy, time, or effort on people who didn't respect what I held dear? Why shouldn't I just keep on track, keep doing what I'm doing, and build it and grow it and strengthen it and multiply it? So that's what we did.

Not that it was always easy to tune out the bullshit. In the fashion business, when the press gets all hot and heavy, people often believe their own hype, and it does have an effect. I knew from experience that when you win a design award, it's quite spectacular. I got my first taste in 1984, years before we formed Tommy Hilfiger, when I was honored with the Abraham & Straus American Spirit Award in recognition of American fashion designed for Americans. I went up to the podium in front of the entire industry, like a very big high school assembly, and they gave me a trophy and talked about how great I was. What a powerful high! "Wow, I'm being recognized for my work. Maybe I could become a world-famous designer someday. Maybe this is all going to happen!" I didn't really think I was great, but I knew I was good.

I didn't win another award for more than ten years, until 1996, when we won the four Fragrance Foundation Fifi Awards. At the ceremony I thanked my fabulous team, knowing we all deserved the award and the attention. I was onstage, being handed the trophy by Christie Brinkley, thinking, "This is unreal!"

The temptation is to celebrate like crazy, and we did: we went to the parties and the after-parties, we drank champagne, and we had a great time. But the next morning we went back to work. Let's get real: an award looks good on the shelf, but it does very little for your bottom line. Having gone bankrupt once, I never wanted to go back.

In 1996, when I won the Catwalk to Sidewalk award at the VH1 Fashion Awards, I was excited as hell because it brought me even closer to the music world. In the latter part of the event, after I had gone to the podium, collected the award, and thanked my partners, Lawrence tapped me on the shoulder and said, "Let's get the fuck out of here. I'm thirsty, and this is getting boring."

"I can't leave now!" I told him.

When we met up at the after-party later that night, with models and celebs and all sorts of people milling around, Silas, Lawrence, Joel, and I sat in a corner and had a deep discussion about how to grow the business and become more profitable. I loved it! I prided myself on being realistic and grounded, and our line reflects it.

Tommy Hilfiger is not flamboyant or overdesigned or couture. We simply sell all over the world. To everyone.

We have hired designers over the years for whom that is not enough, who wanted to defy the brand's DNA and impose their own highbrow taste upon us. I have had discussions, arguments, and all-out fights with creative people who have wanted our brand to look like Calvin Klein or Armani or Ralph Lauren. "Why?" I asked. "If Ralph Lauren is doing tartan plaid shirts, ours should be different, not the same. And why should our line be black and charcoal like Armani's when I want it to be red-white-and-blue or preppy green with orange and white?"

In some cases, our high-level hires didn't like what we were doing. They were earning a paycheck, not designing clothes they loved. I wanted people to be passionate about working at Tommy Hilfiger, to love the logo and the image and strive to make it better. Certain designers along the way fought it. I would review their sketches and say, "Let's add trim and detail," and I'd get answers like, "Not everyone wants trim and detail."

I'd say, "I do. Please do it! Guys, my name is on the label. Either you design what I want or there's the door." A design team is like a sports team; some people are all-stars, some are team players, some are troublemakers.

I n 1991, my brother Andy was watching a Formula One race on TV and saw the Lotus car fly by with the Hilfiger flag on it. He called. "Tommy, you're sponsoring Lotus Formula One?"

"Oh, yeah, yeah, yeah, I forgot to tell you. Lawrence gave them clothes for their pit crew." Andy and I had loved Formula One at Watkins Glen when we were kids. I asked him, "Do you want to go to the races and give out T-shirts and hats and stuff? We need someone to do that."

"Definitely."

Andy went to the Grand Prix in Montreal as our promo man and was very successful. He was great with people, and he knew racing. We had signed a contract to make Lotus uniforms and pit crew gear but hadn't gone into production yet. I asked if he'd like to come with me to Hong Kong and get involved, and he jumped at the chance.

On the way back, we took the red-eye from L.A., and as we stood at the baggage claim around six in the morning, Andy saw a bunch of hip-hop guys in Tommy Hilfiger clothes—and some Polo as well—waiting for their luggage, too. Andy recognized them. He knew about these things; I didn't. "That's Grand Puba and Brand Nubian," he said. "They're the guys who are rapping about you." He told me there was a line in their song "360° (What Goes Around)" that went, "Girbauds hangin' baggy, Hilfiger on the top." We were also name-checked in Grand Puba's song with Mary J. Blige, "What's the 411." I said, "Let's go meet them."

We walked over. Andy said, "Hey, this is Tommy Hilfiger."

"This is Tommy Hilfiger?" They couldn't have been more surprised or nicer.

I said, "You guys look great in my clothes. If you need some stuff, why don't you come to the showroom? We have a new line."

Two days later, the whole crew came down, and we gave them clothes. They were happy, we were happy. They started wearing our line in their videos, and we saw a groundswell of Tommy Hilfiger awareness and sales to the urban customer.

All of a sudden, hip-hop stylists and artists all wanted Tommy Hilfiger, and Andy was in charge of product placement. "You're going to do a video? Come on up!"

A year or so later we were at the American Museum of Natural History, dressed in rock-and-roll velvet at the Grammy Awards after-party for Atlantic Records, and Andy said, "Tommy, that's Snoop Dogg! He's the new biggest artist on the West Coast. He's like Dr. Dre." He introduced us, and we got to talking. The guy was very engaging!

We stayed out until three in the morning, and when Andy got to the office at noon the next day, there was a message. "Yo, Andy, it's Snoop Dogg, we met last night." Andy called him back, and Snoop and his crew came to the showroom. I showed them around and gave them a bunch of clothes before they went back to L.A.

Two weeks later, Andy was sitting in his office on a rainy Friday evening, and the phone rang. "Yo, Andy, it's Snoop."

"Hey, man, what's up?"

"We're in New York and we need more gear."

"Come on up."

"I can't. I'm rehearsing for *Saturday Night Live.* Can you come to my hotel tonight?"

"When?"

"Midnight."

"Sure."

Andy got a bunch of stuff from the showroom, went to Snoop's suite—the code to get in was "Gin 'n' Juice"—and it was like the Wild West. The Dogg Pound was there in force. Guys were playing video games; there was smoke all over. Snoop came out of the adjacent room and said, "Yo, Andy, what's up? Where's my gear?"

"Here, Snoop."

"Cool, cool. You want to hang out?"

Andy joined the crew for a while, and as he was leaving Snoop said, "I'm going to wear this tomorrow."

Saturday night around midnight, Joel called to tell me to turn on *Saturday Night Live.*

Snoop was onstage in a red-white-and-blue rugby with TOMMY blasting huge on his chest. He kept turning around and showing HILFIGER on the back.

When we got to the office on Monday there were calls coming in from salespeople around the country saying, "Did something happen? We're getting reorders all over the place. Everybody wants more clothing because of some musician, some Snoop something." That was the night that made Tommy Hilfiger supremely cool with "the youth." We were trending. We were legit.

Then Russell Simmons, a brilliant entrepreneur, told me that urban kids aspired to the upscale, preppy New England look, but they couldn't afford it. Tommy Hilfiger was within reach. At the time, they were wearing Adidas and Reebok athletic wear, but they didn't have their own designer to follow. I became the designer of choice for young hip-hop street kids, rappers, skaters, all different types. It was very exciting, going to this new level. We backed it up with advertising: In every city in the United States, you would see our billboard and the name Tommy Hilfiger writ large.

And it wasn't just urban kids. It was every kid. Okay with us! When we developed Tommy Hilfiger underwear, I put the label on the front of the waistband in a nod to the classic Everlast boxing trunks. It seemed like an entire generation was walking around with baggy pants hanging way low, advertising our brand where it counted. Word started getting around that if you wore Tommy Hilfiger underwear and fragrance, maybe you'd get laid. In one year, sales increased by $100 million!

Russell Simmons then wanted to start a line. He told me, "I don't know what I'm doing—could you help me out?" I brought him into our design studio, showed him where to buy denim fabrics, and how to get clothes manufactured. I gave him a fashion business tutorial. He and I became friends.

Puff Daddy, as Sean Combs was calling himself at the time, came and said, "Let's do this together." He wanted me to partner with and back him. I would have been very pleased—he is another wildly successful businessman with an extremely creative mind. I asked my partners whether I could do this on my own or as a division of Tommy Hilfiger, but they wanted me to focus on Tommy Hilfiger and Tommy Jeans exclusively. This made sense and I had to respect their wishes. I told Puffy that I couldn't work with him, but because he was a very smart, young, aggressive guy from the music world with a great sense of style, I felt he would make it in the fashion business. I introduced him to Brett Meyer, a friend and attorney, who connected him with an Indian family that could provide manufacturing and backing. When they asked my thoughts I told them Puffy had great vision and that I knew he would make it work. I didn't ask for anything in return. I didn't think, "If I get him going, it's going to take business away from me." I honestly thought there was room for everyone. I was wrong. Two years later, Puffy had a $200 million company in Sean John and in competition with us, and it took a big piece out of our urban business. Yet we've always had a good relationship. I respect what he built from nothing but a dream.

# CHAPTER SEVENTEEN

# THE RUMOR

Setting the record straight !!

n 1997, a rumor began to work its way around the Internet. This email went viral:

> *I'm sure many of you watched the recent taping of The Oprah Winfrey show, where her guest was Tommy Hilfiger. On the show, she asked him if the statements about race he was accused of saying were true.*
>
> *Statements like "... if I'd known African-Americans, Hispanics, Jews and Asians would buy my clothes, I would not have made them so nice. I wish these people would \*NOT\* buy my clothes, as they are made for upper class white people."*
>
> *His answer to Oprah was a simple, "YES." Where after she immediately asked him to leave her show.*
>
> *My suggestion? Don't buy your next shirt or Perfume from Tommy Hilfiger. Let's give him what he asked for. Let's not buy his clothes.*
>
> *Let's put him in a financial state where he himself will not be able to afford the ridiculous prices he puts on his clothes.*
>
> *BOYCOTT PLEASE, & SEND THIS MESSAGE TO ANYONE YOU KNOW!!!!!*

I thought it was nonsense, and that anyone who read it would know it was slander. For one thing, I'd never said, thought, or felt anything remotely so repugnant. For another, I'd never appeared on *Oprah*. "If I just ignore this," I figured, "it'll go away."

The opposite happened. It metastasized. Pretty soon the list of people I supposedly hated extended to Indians, Filipinos, gays, and others. It hit me hardest when Joel came to me and said, "People at my synagogue are telling me . . ."

The Internet was in its infancy—and the idea that people could say just about anything and get away with it was brand-new, too. "Welcome to the Wild West," someone told me. "When a rumor hits, there's no going back." I realized I was in trouble, so I spoke to my mentor, Leonard Lauder, who said, "Let's meet with Jules Kroll." Kroll ran one of the world's best corporate investigation firms. "Jules will help us figure it out."

After several months, Kroll's company thought they had it traced to a college campus in the Northwest, but they couldn't come to a definitive conclusion. We went so far as to try to get the FBI involved. They didn't take the case, just asked questions like "Is it somebody playing a prank? Have you had a disgruntled employee?" We hired the most noted public relations firms and asked, "What do we do about this?" I wanted to go out in front of the public and tell them it was all bullshit, but they said, "No, no, no. If you address it, you are going to make it worse. It'll spread the word and sound like you're guilty. Let it go." I took that advice, but I'm still not certain that was the right course of action. On a personal level, I still tell people every chance I get that it's ridiculous and not true.

The rumor cost us money, but it didn't ruin our business. In fact, between 1997 and 2000, sales continued to increase dramatically. It hurt my heart, though, and my integrity, because at the end of the day, that's all you have.

About ten years later, the *New York Times* wrote about plans to build a memorial for Dr. Martin Luther King, Jr. near the National Mall in Washington, D.C. Joel Horowitz called. "You know," he told me, "my parents marched with Dr. King. It would be amazing if we did something. What do you think?"

"Yes, it would be amazing. I think we should."

The Tommy Hilfiger Corporate Foundation, whose president is my old junior high school friend Guy Vickers, was the first organization in corporate America to make a donation. We contributed $6 million and stepped in to help the King memorial project raise money from other donors as well. We held a benefit golf outing, raised $2 million at a benefit concert starring Aretha Franklin and Stevie Wonder, and paid the salary for a Tommy Hilfiger staffer to help organize the project's offices in Washington, D.C. In 2011, the Tommy Hilfiger Corporate Foundation served as co-chair of the memorial's dedication ceremony. It was the right thing to do.

While raising money, we were given a list of potential contributors who had not yet donated. Oprah Winfrey was on the list. I was asked to contact her.

Oprah was more than kind. She said, "I'm building a school in Africa and putting a lot of time and effort into that, but I will do whatever I can to help." She was instrumental in our raising significant funds. In the course of our conversation she also said, "By the way, you should really come on my show, because there is that stupid rumor that we should squash." I told her I would love to, but I really didn't want it to look like this was a quid pro quo. Oprah said, "Look, this rumor has been floating around for ten years, and you have never been on my show. Come on the show." I called Quincy Jones, who said, "Tommy, Oprah will dispel that stupid bullshit. Do it." I was thrilled at the opportunity.

As I sat facing her, Oprah turned toward the audience and said, "I thought that this really horrible rumor had been laid to rest many, many years ago. . . . We're setting the record straight once and for all." Sitting beside me, she asked, "In the twenty-one years that we've been on the air, have you ever been on the show?"

I said, "Unfortunately not. I've never been here before." As to the racist comments, I added, "I would never say that."

"Tommy has never been here before today," Oprah told the audience. "I could not possibly have asked him to leave the set. So that is what I call in the category of a 'BFL.' That's a big fat lie! That never happened!"

Shortly afterward, the Anti-Defamation League issued a statement saying, "Based upon our investigation, it is apparent to us that you never made the statements that attribute racist remarks to you. ADL has investigated the matter in response to the requests of constituents and other community members. We have concluded after careful investigation that the malicious rumors circulating about you and your company are without merit and lack any basis in fact."

Although they simply stated what I knew all along to be true, the vindication was satisfying.

And yet the rumor persists. Friends tell me they still hear at the synagogue that I'm an anti-Semite, and at church that I'm a racist. Even though it's been a decade, the accusations still burn at times. I have my own suspicions about who set this whole thing in motion and why, but without proof I won't say more. There's no effective way to deny the rumor—even quoting Oprah and the Anti-Defamation League might sound like protesting too much—except to say that it's a slander, my life stands in contrast to the accusation, and I am offended to be thought of as a bigot.

# CHAPTER EIGHTEEN

# STAR BRANDING

## STAR ★ BRANDING

*When a hobby Comes to life*

From 1995 to 2000, Tommy Hilfiger was ubiquitous. On every street corner you would see young people, old people, fat people, thin people, Asians, Hispanics, blacks (despite the rumor), white people of all economic strata, gays, straights, lawyers, athletes, musicians, actors, models, skaters, and garbage collectors wearing clothing with Tommy Hilfiger logos, some counterfeit, some real. In the mid-1990s the logo craze expanded, as did the size of the logos themselves. Hip-hop kids displayed TOMMY HILFIGER as a sign that they had arrived, and we were happy to be the brand to which everyone aspired.

Tom Curtin always said, "What can I do to help? What do you need?" I needed someone to run my life, so he introduced me to Sheila Cox. Sheila became my right and left arm and my right and left brain. She is my personal assistant, which is to say she runs my business meetings and manages my travel, reservations, letters, and phone calls. Juggling my schedule is the work of Houdini, and there is nothing she cannot handle. But most important is the infinite trust my family and I have in Sheila. She has such positive energy; nothing negative surrounds her at all. And she has actually somehow learned to read my mind. I'm not sure if that's good or bad, but it sure works for all of us who benefit from her insight. Sheila has become the eighteenth Hilfiger, except she knows more about everyone and everything in our family than the family's actual members do.

I was so busy that Susie thought I had a girlfriend. And I did: the company. I was traveling all the time, my mind immersed in the business. My children were the most important part of my life, but the company ran a close second. I would head into the city early in the morning and come home late at night, and when I was around, I wasn't really present. Susie felt that I had forgotten her, that because I loved my work so much it was like I was playing ball every day, or going to a concert, or being out with the boys instead of spending time with her. She became very resentful.

Susie had always been a good designer, and as a way of feeling involved in my life, she suggested ideas for the brand. "Why don't you make some loden jackets?" she said. She thought Irish tweed would be a successful fabric for us. I told her, "We tried those a couple of years ago and they didn't sell because they were too heavy." Most of our business in America was in warmer climates where tweed didn't work. I think she was insulted that I didn't take her advice. She made other great suggestions that I did put into the pipeline, but when they got watered down, which happens, she took it personally. I think she felt abandoned and underappreciated.

As for me, I felt like a winner during the day, highly respected and achieving great things. But when I came home, I felt I was disappointing Susie by loving my work so deeply. After a while, I couldn't wait to get out of the house in the morning and get to work, where I was doing at least something right. I thought we had exciting projects in our home life, like building the house in Mustique and decorating our home in Connecticut. But between our parental responsibilities to Kathleen as a special-needs child and trying to balance the proper amount of time with our other children, too many projects going on at once, and me not being as available as Susie thought I should be, the tension in our relationship began to fester.

We had practically been childhood sweethearts, and in the early days of our marriage, we were very much in love. Susie was an incredibly creative woman and a wonderful mother. Sadly, we grew apart and could no longer find the goodness in each other that had united us. Unfortunately, we decided to end our marriage.

Ally was fourteen, Richard was nine, Elizabeth was seven, and Kathleen was five. I told them I was going to be in New York doing business and took a hotel room in the city. Then I rented a house near our home under a fictitious name and told the real estate agent it was for an employee. Then the house right across the street from ours came up for sale, and I bought it. Our home had a white picket fence on top of a stone wall going all the way around the property, so

I put the same fence on top of a stone wall all the way around my new one. I wanted the kids to feel at home there, too.

It took seven years to finalize the divorce. Our separation was overwhelming and difficult for both of us. But ultimately, Susie and I came to an equitable agreement, and we remain close and respectful of each other, always putting our children first.

Despite the troubles in my personal life, my business was growing and we were innovating constantly. My brother Andy had brought me Puffy long before he started Sean John, and he'd brought me Britney Spears a moment before she became mega-famous. It was apparent that celebrity branding was going to become a large area of economic and cultural opportunity and that Andy had the creative and marketing acumen to pursue it as a full-time gig, so in 2001 I told him, "Why don't you resign from Tommy Hilfiger? I will partner with you and fund you." I suggested he look up my old People's Place partner Larry Stemerman, who knew how to get things made, and my go-to business guy, Joe Lamastra. We named our company Star Branding.

When we started negotiating with Britney, her manager, Larry Rudolph, asked for $5 million up front. Not long before, they had asked for $5,000 to keep them afloat! Out of the question. We passed.

At the same time, Andy introduced me to another performer who wanted to do her own fashion line, Jennifer Lopez. She wasn't asking for $5 million; she wanted to go 50-50 but didn't want to put up any money. We took that deal. I invested $5 million in the company, and Andy, Larry, Joe, and I created a partnership with Jennifer. We hired some designers, opened a showroom, hired a great salesman, Johnny Calvani, whom I knew from years back; got a chief operating officer to run the day-to-day business finance; and pulled the trigger. They did the work, and I advised from afar.

We created a brand we called J.Lo. Initially it was built around velour and terry-cloth sweatsuits, which Jennifer was wearing at the time. It was very similar to a brand called Juicy Couture, but J.Lo's look was a little blingier. Jennifer was a sweetheart. She was pretty, young, fashion forward, involved. She knew what she wanted, knew the colors she wanted. Her business manager, Benny Medina, was the liaison. And it took off.

Next we did a fragrance license with Coty. Jennifer wanted to call the product Glow by J.Lo, but there was a boutique near Santa Monica called Glow that sold its own beauty products, and we told her we thought the owner might sue. She said, "No, I want to name it Glow." We went back and forth a few times, and finally, since it was Jennifer's line, we did what she wanted. The store owner did sue, and we had to pay a couple million dollars to settle. Glow by J.Lo became the number one women's celebrity fragrance many years in a row.

Jennifer wasn't loving the clothing. She didn't think it looked sufficiently upscale. We explained that if we were going to be in the urban lane, the product had to be at a certain price point; if she wanted to create a Loro Piana cashmere sweatsuit, it would have to be made in Italy, and we wouldn't be able to sell it.

The business didn't grow like it should have. Jennifer wanted to be in Bendel's and Barneys and Bergdorf, so we hired a designer to create a second, more elevated brand we called Sweetface. We held a major fashion show, but the stores thought the clothing wasn't sufficiently chic. In truth, I feel this was the team's fault; product is everything in this business, and if the product isn't right and the stores don't want it, whoever is making the product is to blame. The design ideas were Jennifer's, but I have to believe they weren't executed properly. So I told Andy, "We need a new designer. This girl by the name of Heather Thompson is working over at Sean John, but she wants to leave. Hire her—she's going to leave anyway. But somebody has to tell Puffy, because he's a friend, and I don't want any trouble."

So Heather Thompson came onboard, and soon I got a call from Puffy. "What the fuck are you doing? You're taking one of my best designers!"

I told him, "Look, Puff, I thought they told you, and I thought she was going to leave anyway."

Lauren Bush for
Tommy Jeans campaign

...son Lewis in
...antucket for the
...rtan campaign

Jason Lewis

Me and my brothers Bobby, Billy, an
Andy with the Rolling Stones

Tommy Hilfiger presents Jewel in concert

Michael Fredo for Tommy Jeans campaign

Mark Ronson and Aaliyah

Enriqué Iglesias for the *True Star Men* campaign

TRUE STAR MEN
ENRIQUE IGLESIAS

Beyoncé for ;
*True Star G*
campa

-Tip for ommy Jeans campaign

Beyoncé for the *True Star* campaign

TOMMY HILFIGER PRESENTS THE ROLLING STONE SOLD OUT

Tommy Hilfiger presents the Rolling Stones

true star

*Beyoncé*

A FRAGRANCE BY TOMMY HILFIGER

TOMMY JEANS

David Bowie nd Iman

Tommy Hilfiger presents the Lenny Kravitz Freedom Tour

Tommy Hilfiger presents the Rolling Stones, 1999

OMMY HILFIGER PRESENTS

With David Bowie and Iman

Tommy Jeans *Sons & Daughters* campaign

Spring 2016 runway show

Meet the *Hilfigers* campaign

TommyXGigi,
fall 2016 campaign

GiGi
TOMMY ≡ HILFIGER

Tommy Hilfiger
Kids campaign,
fall 2013

TOMMY ≡ HILFIGER
UNDERWEAR

TOMMY ≡ HILFIGER

Rafael Nadal,
fall 2015 campaign

Ally Hilfiger

Ally on her first
day of school

Ally and Elizabeth Hilfiger

With my son
Richard in 1991

Ally and Richard Hilfiger

Elizabeth and Richard Hilfiger

Richard Hilfiger

Sebastian Hilfiger

With my mother and kids

Kathleen Hilfiger

Backstage with Elizabeth, Richard, and Ally at the Spring 2009 fashion show

Raleigh Hotel, Miami

Alex and Julian

Ally Hilfiger

Kathleen and Elizabeth Hilfiger

With Dee at our Plaza residence in New York

Home in Miami

With Dee in Mustique

Home office in Miami

Pool in Mustique

Home in Mustique

At home in Miami

With my brother Bobby at Ally's book launch party

With my mother and Richard

Kim and Andy

With Dee

Season's Greetings

SUSIE AND TOMMY HILFIGER
ALEXANDRIA, RICHARD
RAIMONDO AND KATHLEEN ANNE

Susie Hilfiger

With Richard Hilfiger

Sebastian Hilfiger

With Ally at the Global Lyme Allian Uniting for a Lyme Free World Inaugu Gala, October, 200

Merry Christmas

The Hilfiger Family
sends their greetings and best wishes

#COCOFORDICKS

The family

ly's daughter, Harley

Elizabeth Hilfiger

Dee and me with Nancy Davis (Chair of Race to Erase MS), Kenny Rickel (Nancy's husband), and their daughters

ith my brother Andy

My sisters Ginny and Betsy

With Steven Tyler
and Joe Perry

Kate Moss at the
Tommy Hilfiger show at
London Fashion Week, 199

With Lenny Kravitz

With Beyoncé

Andy Hilfiger with
Lenny Kravitz

With P. Diddy and
Erica Kennedy

Gisele Bundchen at the Tommy Hilfiger fall 2000 fashion show

With Christie Brinkley

With Barbara Davis at the 16th Annual Race to Erase MS Gala

Andy Hilfiger with Marky Ramone and Jimmy Kunes

With Samuel L. Jackson and Russell Simmons

With Quincy Jones

With Bob Kraft and Dee

With Dee and Tommy and Thalia Mottola

With Mark Ronson

With Anna Wintour

With HRH Prince Charles

Gigi Hadid at the Tommy Hilfiger fall 2016 runway show

Andy Hilfiger with Kendall and Kylie Jenner

With Karl Lagerfeld

With Rafael Nadal

With Lawrence Stroll,
Silas Chou, and Joel Horowitz

With Emanuel Chirico
and Fred Gehring

With Mohan Murjani

With Tom Curtin

With Guy Vickers
in Uganda for
Millennium Promise

With Daniel Grieder

With Joseph Lamastra

"I don't give a shit if she was going to leave. You didn't have to take her."

I told him, "Let me talk to Jennifer." I didn't know what else to do.

He as much as shouted, "You tell her she's messing with the wrong person!"

Jennifer and Puffy had been an item—they had walked the Grammy Awards red carpet together when she wore her famously revealing Versace green silk chiffon number—and had broken up a few years prior. When I told her what had happened, she said, "What? Who the fuck does he think he is? He can't own somebody! You leave it in my hands. I'm going to fix his ass."

Next thing I knew, Jennifer called me back. "Everything is okay. We're cool." And the next time I saw Puffy, it was all cool.

So Heather Thompson came to work for us. But the brand still wasn't doing it. Jennifer wasn't wearing Sweetface—she was wearing Cavalli and Versace and appearing in a Louis Vuitton ad worldwide. Her fan base was saying, "She's not wearing the clothes; she doesn't care about us." So I sat down with Benny and Jennifer and said, "The brand needs to go more mass—Penney's, Sears, Kohl's, Kmart, Walmart—where your customers and fans really live. You can do tons of business there."

She didn't want to do it. She never said it out loud, but I suspect she simply did not want to be associated with a downmarket product.

I told Andy, "You guys have to go back to Macy's and plead with them to expand the business, because otherwise this whole thing is going under." Macy's was a big account. My investment by that time was up to $7 million, and even though the fragrance royalties were funding the business's infrastructure, sales for the fashion had fallen from $50 million to $20 million, and then to $18 million.

Macy's wasn't buying, and our relationship with Jennifer was strained. I felt that she had lost interest and that the strategy of selling to better department stores was not well conceived. I was very frustrated and wanted to see this corrected. Andy was frustrated because he had to get every single thing approved by Benny and Jennifer, and they were often unavailable. Either Jennifer was on tour or she was with her boyfriend at the time, Ben Affleck. She was in Beverly Hills one day, Paris the next, and it was very difficult to nail her down and get answers. In the earlier days, everything was spontaneous—"Tommy, I'm going to dress so-and-so group for their video," or "We're going out to some clubs tonight and give T-shirts and polo shirts away," or "We're going to have a big party at the Playboy mansion," all of which I said okay to—but during the Jennifer and Benny days, the conversation was more like, "We have an opportunity for Jennifer to do an article on the new line with *Glamour*, but the deadline is the tenth. Can Jennifer come to New York?" "Yeah, but you have to pay for a private jet from Beverly Hills, and she needs her hair and makeup people, and she has to stay in a suite at the Peninsula, and . . ."

I understood why—she was a superstar in Hollywood and the music world, and she deserved it—but it was draining us. And that was only when she would agree to do it!

But the bottom line was that business was floundering, the product was nothing to be proud of, and I was the one who had put up the money. Something had to be done. I asked for a meeting with Benny and Jennifer in New York. This was not long after she had married Marc Anthony. I understood that they would be very upset with us.

I opened by saying, "I apologize for everything that has happened that has pissed you off. I don't blame you; as a person with his name on the label, I understand how devastated you must be. Obviously, the right team wasn't in place to make this a success; they didn't execute the way they should have. The trends also changed, and the company's infrastructure wasn't working. And to be honest with you, I have not been able to be as involved as we all would have liked."

Having accepted my share of the responsibility, I offered a solution. "The way I see it, we can do one of three things: close the business, sell the business—it's not worth much—or do a new deal. We are 50-50 partners now, but we are willing to give you majority ownership if you will allow us to take the brand to a more mass-consumer base and do a bigger business. This would be my suggestion. If you accept the added equity and give us that permission, I will make the connection with my friends at Li & Fung, who have experience in exactly this area, to turn this around. I don't believe failure is an option. I don't want to be associated with an enterprise that fails."

Jennifer and Benny agreed, and we remade the contract and moved forward.

I had already formed a partnership with Li & Fung called Music Entertainment Sports Holdings (MESH) to do celebrity brands. They held 75 percent ownership, and my group held 25 percent. We did a deal with Steven Tyler, selling shirts and scarves for a very short amount of time, and a line of rock-and-roll gear that we named after my brother, Andrew Charles. Neither was super successful. I went to Li & Fung's CEO, Bruce Rockowitz, and the U.S. CEO, Rick Darling, and said, "Guys, let's do a deal with Jennifer Lopez and take it to Sears or Kohl's. I will share my ownership with you, and we will become partners with Jennifer." Bruce said, "Let's call [Kohl's CEO] Kevin Mansell and see if he's up for it." He made the call then and there.

"Kevin, what if we were to bring you Jennifer Lopez and give it to you exclusively?"

Mansell knew the line was still in Macy's, but not that they didn't want it anymore. He said, "Yeah, but I don't really need women's brands. I need a men's brand."

"Bruce," I said, "put him on hold for a second." With Mansell waiting, I said, "Let's get him Marc Anthony."

"Kevin," said Bruce, "I'll call you back."

This was starting to shape up pretty well. "Why don't we get him Marc Anthony *and* Jennifer?" I said.

"Would Marc do it?"

I called Benny, who put me in touch with Marc, whose representatives had previously spoken to Li & Fung about making a deal. We went back to Kohl's. Within twenty-four hours they were in. We delivered Marc and Jennifer, then sat down to do the numbers.

Kohl's had approximately twelve hundred stores in forty-nine states. They made their calculations as to how much merchandise they would need for Marc and Jennifer combined. We had to slice it and dice it a few different ways—Kohl's would manufacture some on their own and Li & Fung would manufacture the balance—but at the end of the day it came to be one of the largest celebrity agreements in the history of retail: a $3.5 billion deal! We announced it big.

A few months later, headline news: Marc and Jennifer were divorcing. I'm not sure whether he had an insight on this or not, but Benny Medina had insisted on their deals being separate. The divorce didn't affect the business, which continues to be a success to this day. A few years ago, my group sold the balance of our shares to Li & Fung for a handsome profit.

The new Jennifer Lopez is Thalia Sodi, music business legend Tommy Mottola's talented and beautiful wife, who has recently exploded on the fashion scene, hitting one hundred million dollars the first year out of the box with a huge Macy's collection, a deal which Tommy engineered. He and I have become close friends, Thalia is one of our closest friends, our children play together, we're neighbors in Greenwich. Tommy inspires me with stories about musicians and the music business that only he could tell. As former chairman of Sony Music he has an incredible business mind. We have developed projects together and become like family.

# CHAPTER NINETEEN

# THE BAND'S BREAKING UP

*on my own again !!*

As a precaution, the company had taken out a sizable amount of life insurance on me. Right after my separation from Susie, I took my routine physical and then got a call from the insurance agent. "Your blood test looks a little suspicious. Have you ever had hepatitis?" No, I said. "Would you please go get another blood test?"

The second test confirmed it; I had a trace of hepatitis C. "Have you ever had a blood transfusion?" the specialist asked. I had, in the early 1970s, after a motorcycle accident. He asked, "Did you ever shoot drugs? Because dirty needles, you can pick it up." No. "Maybe it's from water. Rusty, dirty water somewhere. You can't detect the disease right away. But a blood transfusion, for sure you could have gotten it from that."

I was sent to a second specialist, who prescribed a treatment that he said was highly likely to cure me. It would make me feel like I had the flu every day for a year, but it could save my life.

I started taking the medication and got very sick. I lost twenty pounds, I couldn't eat, my head ached constantly, I wanted to sleep all the time. My work suffered, my life suffered; I was distracted and dysfunctional.

Three months into this treatment, Mohan Murjani sent me to a Dr. Zhang, who gave me a bunch of herbs that he said would alleviate my symptoms. He was right: I was able to eat again, and I wasn't quite as tired and flu-ish. Six months after I took Dr. Zhang's herbs, my blood test showed not a trace of hepatitis C. I consider myself extremely lucky.

At the same moment my marriage was dissolving and my body was breaking down, Silas and Lawrence decided it was time for them to sell their shares and leave Tommy Hilfiger. Most investors have an exit strategy, but the timing could not have been less welcome or more difficult.

Silas and Lawrence are inventive and extremely successful investors. They nurture their investments. Silas has told me that they buy a business in its infancy and sell it at puberty. "When a baby is three years old, you can see if it is smart or not smart, healthy or not healthy." They bought Tommy Hilfiger for $20 million in 1989, and by the time they sold in 2001, the public company was worth more than $1 billion. "We do not wait until adulthood, because then there is no growth. We sell at puberty, so there is still growth in the market. There is no risk."

Silas and Lawrence bought the Tommy Hilfiger brand when I was thirty-nine. They had bought Ralph Lauren Europe when he was around 40. Silas says there is a reason for this: "Designers at forty have energy, but their experience means they have had some financial trouble. At twenty or thirty years old, they may still be dreamers. When they are forty, they are not dreamers anymore. They are still full of energy, but they are more realistic. They understand the meaning of money."

Michael Kors was at this very stage when I introduced him to Silas and Lawrence in 2000. Michael came to Mustique over New Year's. He was staying at the Cotton House Hotel, and he came to my home and seemed concerned about his business. He told me that it wasn't great and he didn't know what to do. He was on the humble side of life, and it seemed to me that he really needed money. He had gone twenty years without becoming über-successful and was ready to do what it took to get there. I knew Michael's clothes from Bergdorf Goodman. Simple elegance. He had great taste. I said, "Why don't you meet my partners?" Lawrence and Silas were on their way out, but I thought, "Maybe we can buy Michael Kors. It could give the Tommy Hilfiger Corporation some new growth."

Lawrence and Silas thought differently. "We own so little of Tommy Hilfiger now," they told me. "If the company buys Michael Kors, it's not going to help us any."

I said, "Why don't you guys do it on your own?"

"Do you want to become partners with us?" they asked.

"I can't—it conflicts with my contract."

Lawrence wasn't sure whether they should get involved. "It's a small business, it's expensive. I don't know. What kind of guy is Michael?"

"I think he can be the next Ralph Lauren," I told him, "or the next Calvin Klein. He's got great talent. He's going to be a great name." I told Lawrence and Silas that I could not invest, but that they should, absolutely. I made the introduction and the deal got done.

They brought in John Idol, a superstar in the business who had worked with Ralph Lauren and Donna Karan and had ownership in Anne Klein, as CEO and partner. They were the new team in town. In the beginning, the brand was mostly apparel and some shoes, handbags, and accessories (belts, scarves, and so on). For the first three years they invested a lot of money but it didn't take off. They created a secondary, less expensive line called Michael by Michael Kors—no go. Still, they were very smart businesspeople. They saw the Coach business exploding with handbags and accessories, so they decided to take Michael Kors more heavily in that direction, while still keeping the fashion halo over the brand.

That did it. Thanks to a combination of great design, great price points, great positioning, a super team, and fortuitous timing, Michael Kors exploded. The strong accessory and handbag business made the fashion look better, and vice versa.

You can tell when the timing is right; the customer tells you. At first you sense it. You start selling out of things. Then you start getting hot items. Then the customer goes into a frenzy.

They started opening smaller stores stocked primarily with handbags, shoes, belts, and wallets, with a couple of items of clothing. Then they logoed it.

I know Lawrence well enough to be certain that he is the one who insisted on the logo. I believe Michael himself was hesitant, even though he probably knew a logo would be important. Many designers are anti-logo; they think it's too commercial, it's not cool. But Lawrence knows how to build a business, and he knew that the logo was necessary to knock this one out of the park.

Lawrence and Silas invested more than $20 million to buy Michael Kors's brand. Michael was forty-two years old at the time. They owned the majority of the company's equity when it went public in 2011, valued at $4 billion. They sold their interest in 2014, by which time the value of their Kors stock had more than quadrupled. At one point it went to almost $18.5 billion. I was very happy for my former partners. Multibillionaires are in a totally different league, and Lawrence and Silas are wealthy in the extreme. *Women's Wear Daily* asked what I thought of the deal. I praised Silas and Lawrence and Michael, and said, "Anybody who doesn't invest in Michael Kors would be foolish." Unfortunately, although I was invited, because of my position at the Tommy Hilfiger Corporation, I could not invest in what was deemed the competition. I was extremely disappointed, but I did not want to jeopardize my situation with Tommy Hilfiger and our parent company, PVH.

Silas and Lawrence contributed in so many ways to the overwhelming success of the Tommy Hilfiger brand. Without their acumen, vision, intimate knowledge of the field, and unrelenting push to succeed, we never would have achieved our level of influence, our international effect, or our degree of wealth. Their departure would mean an immediate drain on the brand's financial, manufacturing, and visionary fronts, but it would also mean we wouldn't see each other as often or in the same way as we had for the past eighteen years.

Then Joel decided to retire. He had told me years prior that at some point he was going to leave, but when I received an official letter of resignation from him I felt like I was in the middle of the Atlantic on a melting iceberg. I got a lump in my throat. The band was breaking up. I was the only one left.

The combination of all three disembarking was a huge disappointment to me because at about the same time, the business started to sink.

Tommy Hilfiger had been such a roaring success that it was bound to crest. A careful reading of our inventory should have told us that something was going to happen. We were losing momentum. Our products were not selling as quickly as they had in the past, and many stores were coming back to us, asking for markdown money.

Why did we start to come apart?

Between 1995 and 2000, everyone was wearing Tommy—all the hip-hop kids, street kids, skateboarders, jocks, preppies. In response, I designed more athletic, brightly colored, sporty looks and made them way oversized, because kids who wore normal sizes were coming into the stores and saying, "Do you have that in XXXL?" We were more than happy to give them what they wanted. Pants with waistlines that hung at crotch level were all the rage. (I learned that this style originated in prison, where pants hung low because inmates' belts had been confiscated.) Teamed with hockey and rugby jerseys, all with XXXL-size logos, our line dominated the street style conversation. In certain circles it was hard to be cool without us. We had about a four-year run in which I had never seen merchandise sell so fast in my life.

But high visibility implies risk. While a brand is on the cusp, everything is great. When you walk into a restaurant and of the five super-cool people inside three of them are wearing your brand, you're on the winning end. But if people who are not and never will be your core consumer are everywhere wearing your brand, you can lose the cool factor and the core factor at the same time. We got too big too quick. We lost our core customers, the men, women, and children of every size and shape who wanted the old Tommy.

Perhaps they thought I no longer stood for the oxford shirts and the chinos we had been so aggressive in providing. Many young professionals who had been wearing my basics went to other brands that were copying our classics: the May Company, the Gap, Banana Republic, Express, and even stores such as Dillard's, Macy's, and Bloomingdale's, which had private-label departments. They were selling all of that basic merchandise—our button-downs with the lining in the neck, the lining in the pants, the prep crew sweater, the jackets. The perception of our brand was changing. To the outside world, it looked like we had abandoned preppy classic gear and given birth to street fashion, when in fact we were selling them in parallel.

In 2000, the business started slowing down. Partners and company executives were all saying, "What's wrong, what's wrong, what's wrong?" What was wrong was that we had become ubiquitous.

We hired Bain & Company, a management consulting firm out of Boston, and their research told us that the brand's message was confused. "Is it preppy? Is it hip-hop? Is it rock and roll? Is it men's? Is it women's? Is it too expensive? Is it not expensive enough?" Our womenswear line, launched in 1987, closed two years later, and reopened in 1996, was looking stale and not selling well. Our jeanswear was underachieving. The men's sportswear was boring and safe. But anytime we tried something exciting or different, merchandisers and salespeople were afraid it wouldn't sell.

Then all of a sudden it seemed that every hip-hop kid in America was Tommyed out. They'd spent a few years with us, and, as trendsetters and -followers do, they moved on to the next thing. Big logos were going out of style. People had seen enough of the red, white, and blue. They started wearing urban brands like Ecko and Cross Colors. Jay-Z had Rocawear, Puffy had Sean John, Russell Simmons had Phat Farm. FUBU defined itself as For Us By Us.

As a public company, we needed sales volume and profits to keep the stock price up. Every quarter, Joel would get on a conference call with the Wall Street analysts and hear them say, "Wow, that's great. What are you doing next quarter?" When your growth rate is accelerating, the multiple (the price/earnings ratio, or stock price divided by earnings) that you get on your stock keeps expanding. In order to make the numbers on a monthly basis we had to keep money coming in. If the growth rate slows down, the multiple starts to shrink, and then the stock price falls and you hit a downward cycle. You can crash. That's what analysts are afraid of. The financially sound thing to do would have been to control our sales and pull back, but that train had left the station and we really didn't feel we could stop. Wall Street doesn't understand the concept of pulling back to correct, and they don't care. Their questions are "What happened this quarter?" and "Where are you going next quarter?" A lot of investors started pulling out.

As our numbers became public, rumors and questions and bad

press abounded. "Are they over?" "Here today, gone tomorrow." "Has-been." *Women's Wear Daily* and *Daily News Record* used to print "Best Sellers for Fall," "Best Sellers for Christmas," "Best Sellers for Spring." Tommy Hilfiger's carpenter jean and our Prep crew sweater had been perennials on those lists, but no longer. What to do?

Prada and even Calvin Klein were becoming cleaner, more minimalistic, and more modern. So, thinking the preppy, all-American, bright color blocking and red-white-and-blue logo gear were gone, I tried to modernize. We did that for a couple of seasons, but the customer said no. I began doubting myself.

I also learned that certain people in our organization were getting pressure to produce basics at opening (pre-discount) price points equivalent to those of the department stores' private labels, the Gap, and other retailers with less expensive goods. I felt the loss of Lawrence at that moment. He would have gone nuts. I didn't. Rather than stand up for the quality upon which Tommy Hilfiger had made its reputation, I rationalized. "Okay, well, they're not wrong, the stores do need lower price points. So let's give them that and let's also have a line that is more sophisticated, more expensive, and what I would really want to wear."

With our head men's sportswear designer, Michael Sondag, and my sister Ginny leading the team, we created a line called H. It was beautiful. We had David Bowie and Iman to headline the advertising. The clothes were cool, crafted mostly in Europe, meticulously made, and more expensive. Tailored sportswear. Better fits. We put higher collars on the shirts, used European checks and plaids and stripes and a slimmer cut. It was wonderful merchandise. And people loved it.

As our sportswear and jeanswear business continued to deteriorate, we decided to put the H line in department stores. Macy's buyers bridled. "It's too expensive," they told us. We couldn't ignore them; we needed sales. In response, we chose to no longer make H in Europe but to transfer production to Asia, where the price points were lower. The look was similar, but the quality was not the same. We hurt the business and were now competing with our regular line.

When it seemed that our jeans business was cannibalizing our sportswear business because they were vying for the same customer, we directed Tommy Jeans to sell a cheaper quality just to hold on to the biz. Tommy Jeans had been selling millions of garments with big Tommy Hilfiger logos. Now they were of lesser quality and were being discounted, so people were buying our jeans at 40 percent and 50 percent off.

It came down to Business 101: supply and demand. When you oversupply, the demand stops.

The big discounters, including T.J.Maxx, Century 21, and Costco, all wanted designer brands, and in order to continue building volume and pumping up the sales, we began selling them a lot of goods. All of a sudden Tommy Hilfiger, once known as affordable luxury, was on sale in discount houses and knocked off on the streets in Chinatown. It was all over the place, cheap. As a result of this flood of merchandise, there were markdowns in the regular stores. When everybody is discounting a product, the value falls out of the brand, which is what happened to us. We had steered ourselves into a self-fulfilling negative spiral. I saw the writing on the wall but did not know what to do about it.

With Silas, Lawrence, and Joel gone, we needed a new CEO. We went on a worldwide search, looking for people with Lawrence's big thinking, Joel's solid business decision making, and Silas's financial acumen. There were a lot of very smart executives around, but being a smart executive and having the combined vision we had all developed together were two different things.

In August 2003, we brought in David Dyer, who had done a great job as CEO of Lands' End, a subsidiary of Sears. We were in desperate need, he had a lot of experience, we thought Wall Street would respect him, maybe he would help us fix this.

Dyer arrived when Tommy Hilfiger was probably at its worst. There were inventory problems, bloated expenses, ways of doing things that in his mind were antiquated. We had tinkered with e-commerce, for instance, but hadn't really put it in place. The team running our European division thought what we were doing sucked. Company morale was at an all-time low, and I was personally miserable on several fronts. For the first time since I'd gone bankrupt in my early twenties, I felt like a loser. All eyes were on me. "Tommy, it's your fault. You lost your touch. The designs are terrible, otherwise we would be selling. You followed the trends and didn't stick to your roots. The advertising went from preppy all-American to rock and roll to plain Jane to plain vanilla. You cheapened the brand. You are all over the discounters."

And the fact was, they were pretty much on target.

Maybe David Dyer had the silver bullet. Maybe there was a way to bring Tommy Hilfiger back.

Unfortunately, as soon as Dyer got in the saddle, I felt the energy go even more negative. It seemed to me that his perspective on everything was, "Wow, you guys really screwed this up." There are positive and negative ways of changing group dynamics, and he seemed most comfortable with the negative.

Wall Street insists that public companies have an independent board of directors, so our hand-picked board members could not renew their contracts because they were not sufficiently at a distance. We replaced them with professionals from other companies: a woman who worked in marketing from Verizon, a corporate consultant, executives from various walks of life. While they were all eminent in their fields, they knew nothing about the apparel business. I would sit in board meetings and cringe at their comments because they all gave advice based on the balance sheet and the numbers rather than on an informed view of our specific industry. And I felt Dave Dyer was doing the same.

Dyer wanted to close the jeans division. I had my doubts, but we had jeans in sportswear, so I agreed. The jeans division was eating up a lot of cash, and if we shut those doors we would have more money for advertising, which I thought would reignite the business.

Dyer did try to appease me in some areas. I felt our company was physically scattered, with no central hub. Lands' End had been voted one of the Best Places to Work in America, and when he and I visited its headquarters in Wisconsin I was very impressed with the modern and extremely well-organized campus; clearly some top-level strategic thought had gone into its setup. I thought, "If David Dyer can do that with Lands' End, he certainly can do it with Tommy Hilfiger. I would like us to be one of the Best Places to Work in America." That would attract new talent and go a long way toward retaining what we had. He gave me a list of items to be made excellent, everything from health insurance to proper lavatory facilities. It all sounded great.

Our building at 485 Fifth Avenue had become a bit run-down. The one on 25 West 39th Street was beautiful but bulging at the seams. I would take the elevator to the sixteenth floor and feel depressed that Joel and Lawrence and Silas were no longer there.

I visited the offices of Deutsch Inc., our advertising agency at the time, and found they occupied an entire floor of a building at 15th Street and Eighth Avenue. The design was industrial, with a very cool open feel and spectacular views of downtown Manhattan, the Hudson River, and New Jersey. It ran an entire city block. As I walked from one end of the floor to the other, I could see everyone at work on separate but integrated projects, and I thought that could work for us. If we sold our properties, we could lease space in one of the vintage buildings being renovated on the Far West Side and put our entire company on one floor. We could greatly improve communications; everyone would know what the rest of the company was doing; and we could all be comrades and work together and create an exciting new energy. I immediately called my friend Bruce Surry, one of the top honchos at the real estate firm CBRE, and asked him to show me similar space.

We sold 25 West 39th, which we had bought for around $25 million, for around $70 million. We thought we had made a good deal, but the next week the buyer flipped it for something approaching $100 million. How that happened we will never know. It was a big fiasco. When we sold the other building, we included a clause saying that we would share in the profit if it was flipped within a given amount of time.

We leased space that Bruce Surry showed us at 601 West 26th Street, the landmark Starrett-Lehigh building with 150,000-square-foot floors, the largest in New York City. I thought this was very cool. We could all be together and get rid of the negative energy hovering in our former buildings. Dyer suggested installing a gymnasium for the employees, and a nice cafeteria, since there weren't a lot of good restaurants in the area. It was a new day. I believed it would, in fact, become one of the Best Places to Work.

But while our trappings were coming along, I was not happy with what the clothing design teams were showing me. We had lost the vibe and the charisma. When I tried to give them direction, they told me, "But that's not selling. It's too expensive," and gave me inferior ideas for replacement. The sales and merchandising teams were all trying to make the brand moderate. I hate mediocrity! The bloom had fallen off the rose in the jeans business, going from approximately $500 million annually to $400 million, then $300 million, then $200 million. The European team didn't like what we were showing them and wanted to design their own product. Our PR program wasn't clicking. There was no excitement, only numbers. I did a designer reality TV show on CBS called *The Cut*, which received a lukewarm reception. The producers wanted me to act more like Donald Trump, to be mean and tough, which really isn't me. I continued to feel like we had lost our way.

And the store buyers themselves were changing. Years earlier, they had been real garmentos. Now, on any given day, the person in charge of purchasing men's sportswear for a store might have spent the prior season in electrical appliances. These new people were looking at the history of what had sold *recently*—what colors, what sizes—and what hadn't. They rarely took their eyes off the spreadsheet. They'd say, "Whatever sold last year, we're going to sell again." We called that "last-year-itis." That doesn't move the business forward! Risk taking, the knowledge and foresight to buy new cool items that may click and connect—that's how you get new styles moving! At regular prices, not discounted!

Sadly, we didn't have any of that going on.

I tried to redesign the line. I had been shopping at Fred Segal in L.A. and seen very cool military cargo pants with studs on them. Also T-shirts with studs and rhinestones. I liked the studs. Maybe we should stud some of our jeanswear, could be a cool trend coming up. I didn't want to be locked into a trend for a long time, but I thought, "Maybe let's just throw some out there."

With assistants, I redesigned the whole jeanswear line, every single item. I said, "Let's twist it. Let's mix up the stripes. Let's make it brighter, let's make it more fun, let's put on some logos, let's put on some numbers, let's make it sportier, let's make it a little more streetwise and hip."

The line went out to market, and most of what I felt from the executives was fear of markdown. John Karakus, president of jeanswear at the time, came back and said, "This is a disaster. They're not selling. Nobody wants it."

"Just try it," I told him. "Just get it into the stores to try. Nobody thought the hockey jerseys were going to sell, either. Or the oversized oxfords with a crest on them and the green buttonhole—there were doubts that they were going to sell. Buyers told us to take off the logo, but when we put the logoed goods in, they sold. I mean, come on, let's just try."

"Tommy, they don't want it. It's too expensive with the studs, people aren't going to wear it."

My proven philosophy was that if you put merchandise in the stores with lots of colors and a big display—and you look like you believe in it!—the customer is going to think, "This is what I want. This is the thing to buy." I thought it would still hold true. But everyone was running scared. They were only going to push what the retailers wanted, which was what had sold last year. There was no positive energy; the basic corporate emotion was fear. This just wasn't my way of doing business. I ended up saying, "Well, if you're not going to try, you're not going to try." Unbolstered by company enthusiasm, the line didn't sell.

# CHAPTER TWENTY

# WE ARE FAMILY

We are Family

My partners were leaving, my wife wanted a divorce, I had hepatitis, and the business was tanking.

What the hell else could happen?

My brother Billy fainted one day and went to a hospital in the Catskills for a CAT scan. They told him they didn't see anything wrong and said to come back in a year. Not long after, he started to have seizures. This time Billy went to a New York City hospital, where he was told he had a brain tumor. The entire family was devastated. Billy was a musician and an all-around fun guy. This just wasn't possible.

We found a very good neurologist, who told him he needed surgery. We found a top-flight surgeon and prayed.

They shaved his entire head, then cut around one side, lifted the skull off, and took out the tumor. It was cancerous, a blastoma, the worst kind. They told us these tumors usually grew back, but that they had had enough margin that the excision would not affect his eyesight or brain function, and that Billy would be monitored. We were hopeful.

My brother was supposed to heal within a couple of weeks and get a little bit better month by month, but after they stitched him up and bandaged his head, he began having severe headaches. We were told this was normal, that Billy should take some Tylenol and they'd continue to watch him. But the headaches worsened and his head blew up. He was so uncomfortable they had to shoot him full of cortisone to reduce the swelling. He was on all these drugs, and they were hoping that they got all the cancer, but they didn't know. Billy was miserable. He had another operation, and they removed another tumor. More discomfort, swelling, headaches. Terrible pain. Then he got spinal meningitis.

Billy had continued to play guitar in bands all his life. He played his Gibson Firebird in Glass Head, and then in Fright. He was in a band with Andy and a couple of guys from Blue Oyster Cult called the Cult Brothers, and with Richie Stotts and Marky Ramone in King Flux. Since 1993, he'd been in a band called the Brain Surgeons. You can't make this stuff up! He went back to Elmira regularly to play with Andy in the "family band" they called Hippo, our father's nickname.

Billy died on September 15, 2001, four days after 9/11, at the age of forty-three. He was a great man, a great talent, a great brother, and I miss him dearly. So sad. What a waste. We were all devastated. I had never seen my mother so brokenhearted, not even when my dad died.

At his wake, Billy's friends and bandmates gathered and played Mountain and Cheap Trick and Stones songs.

Damn.

I went on a bit of a wild streak. I figured, "My world is collapsing, I'm going to go out and have a good time." Dating, partying, clubs. In 2006, my brother Andy said, "Let's go to Plumm," a New York nightclub. "It's going to be a really cool night. Axl Rose and Lenny Kravitz are going to be there. Kid Rock, a bunch of people." So we went. We were sitting on a banquette and some guy came over and bumped into me and spilled our drinks. Then he tried to push past to get near one of the girls. I said, "Hey, watch it!"

He said, "Fuck you!"

"Well, fuck you!"

"No, fuck you!"

"No, fuck *you!*"

So Axl Rose pulled his fist back. He looked big and tough. His hair was set all in braids and dreads, and his fingers were full of huge rings. If they ever hit my face I was a goner. I thought, "Either I'm a dead man, or I've got to throw the first punch." So, *boom,* I stood up and hit him, which only served to enrage the man.

I'm clearly not a fighter. But he came at me, and I swung again. It was a classic celebrity non-brawl: my bodyguard Rosie—275 pounds of muscular giant—pulled me away from him, and his body-guard pulled him away from me. Rosie lifted me up and hauled me out of the club. I'll always be thankful to him for saving my life! The fight didn't turn into a brawl but it was still a big ruckus. Made the front page of the *New York Post*. Later, when he got up and played, he introduced "Welcome to the Jungle" by saying something to the effect, "This is dedicated to my friend Tommy Hilfiger." We've since made up.

Larry and Laura Stemerman introduced me to a woman, Lizzie, who was fifteen years my junior—young, but not too young—and the first woman I seriously dated after my separation. She was a lot of fun, but life got complicated quickly. She had two boys; I had my children. My children were not happy with her or her children, and I'm sure her children weren't happy with me and mine. We'd go out, break up, go out, break up. By the summer of 2005, we had broken it off completely and I said, "This is it—I'm going to go away and have a great time, and decide what the hell to do some other time. For now I'm just going to enjoy myself." So in the middle of July, I chartered a yacht, gathered my unmarried, unattached, crazy-fun party friends Alex Garfield and Henry Pickman, and my fitness instructor, the former model Joe Pilewski, whom we called "Yoga Joe," and headed off for two weeks in Saint-Tropez.

Jerry Hall had just gotten divorced from Mick, and she was in Saint-Tropez already, so I invited her to join us on the boat one evening. "Come on, we'll have dinner, we'll have fun."

That afternoon, we went to the place where all the gorgeous girls and cool people go for lunch: Club 55, or Cinquante-Cinq. We anchored and took a tender from the boat to the dock. I told the guys that Jerry was coming that night and suggested they find some women so she wouldn't be the only female on the boat. Yoga Joe started walking around the beach, trolling for women. No problem for Joe.

"Guys, look what I found! Come over and meet the girls." We

walked on the beach and said hi to two attractive women. I was looking forward to talking with Jerry that evening, but when we got back on the boat I was concerned about the composition of the dinner table. I asked, "Are the girls coming tonight?"

He said, "Yeah, well, I don't think so. The one has kids and she doesn't think she—"

I said, "Have her bring the kids."

"I don't know. You want—"

"Give me her number. What's her name?"

"Dee Ocleppo."

I got on the phone. "Dee, this is Tommy Hilfiger. We just met you on the beach and my buddy Joe tells me that you can't come tonight because you've got kids." She said, yes, she was sorry, she couldn't make it. "You know, we've got a chef onboard, he'll make chicken fingers for your children, they can watch a movie. Come with us!" I think she appreciated the gesture; it couldn't have been easy for a single woman to go out for an evening in Saint-Tropez with children at her side.

Later that afternoon, Jerry Hall, Dee, and her friend Melissa Roen came aboard. I was happy to spend time with Jerry, but when I saw Dee I thought, "Wow, she is very pretty!" She seemed very nice as well. We had drinks on the boat, then left the kids with the chef and a babysitter and went out to a restaurant. Drank a lot, partied a lot, went back to the boat that night, and partied some more. It was a fun evening but ended early because Dee had to go home and put her children to bed.

I thought maybe Alex or Henry had eyes for Dee, too. The next morning, I asked each of them if it would be all right if I asked her back. Alex as much as laughed at me for tiptoeing around. He said, "Tommy, we're here for you. I think she might have liked you—she kept trying to talk to you all night but you were so fucking shy, sitting on the other side. Go ahead!"

I called her. "Where are you?" She and her friend and kids were on the beach. She didn't know anything about me other than that I was a designer, so she automatically assumed I was gay. She told me later that when she had seen me with Jerry Hall the night before she'd thought, "Oh, maybe he's bi." Still, it's fun on those boats, so she'd accepted my invitation. She thought the whole evening was kind of weird.

Over lunch at Club 55, we struck up a conversation. Dee didn't realize I had been married and separated, she didn't know I had children, she didn't know anything about me—it was a discovery lunch. We started talking about our kids, kind of dancing around any major revelations. But when Dee's boys had come onboard the night before, I could tell that one of them was very similar to Kathleen. And then I realized we were dealing with the same issues. There is little more profoundly and soulfully connecting than honestly discussing one's children's difficulties with someone who understands. We spent the entire day together, and as we shared stories and the overwhelming affection we felt for our children, we developed a noticeable bond.

She told me she was from Rhode Island and had been a model. She'd moved to Paris and married an Italian professional tennis player, but was now divorced and living in Monaco. I thought, "This is a great woman, I've had fun with her, but we could never have a long-distance relationship." Still, it was worth a try.

Dee had to return to Monaco that night, but I arranged for her car to be driven back so she could stay a few hours longer, and at dusk I chartered a helicopter to take her and her children home. Toward evening, I looked at her and said, "You know, I should be with somebody like you. We would have so much fun together. Let's be in touch. You've got to come to Mustique!" After being single for three years, she had gotten very jaded about men and relationships, so she took everything I said with a grain of salt. We made a date for August, but as it turned out, she was right to be wary.

When I returned to the States I was drawn once again to Lizzie and we agreed to give it one more try. I sold the house across the street from Susie and bought another one in Greenwich that wasn't quite so close. If I was going to have a girlfriend coming over regularly, I didn't want to be in such close proximity to my almost-ex. A few months later, Lizzie moved in.

Dee and I had no agreement; we barely knew each other. But

something in the way we had responded to each other compelled me to call and tell her what was going on. I said that I had gotten re-involved with my girlfriend, but that it had been great meeting her and I would still like to be friends. She resisted the urge to call me a son of a bitch, told me Lizzie was a lucky woman, and left it at that. It turned out she was coming to New York soon. I said, "Well, at least let me take you to lunch."

The day of our date she called and said, "I am so sorry. I have to cancel."

"Oh." I found myself very disappointed. I'd been looking forward to seeing her again.

"I'm going to Turks and Caicos."

"Who are you going with?" I asked.

She hesitated. "Um . . . some friends."

"Really? Who?"

"Uh, Prince Albert."

I also found out that while she was in New York she had gone on a date.

"Anybody I know?"

"I don't know if you know him."

"Try me."

She said, "Bruce Willis."

I thought, "You know what? Prince Albert, Bruce Willis—she's not going to pay any attention to me."

I told my kids that Lizzie and I were going to try living together. The night she and her two boys moved in, Elizabeth and Richard, who were splitting time between my house and Susie's, said, "Dad, can we talk to you? Is she going to live here with her kids?"

I told them, "Let's just give it a try. You never know." They weren't too happy.

I quickly found that I wasn't happy, either. I felt a weird negative vibe between Lizzie, her kids, and my kids. Lizzie expected that we'd get married, but I wasn't divorced from Susie. It took a couple of months for me to be certain, but between the tension among our children and the lack of a marriage proposal, they moved out and we broke up for good.

I invited Dee to spend a long weekend with me in St. Bart's, and she accepted. It wasn't like she could just pick up and go; there was preparation involved. For starters, she got her mother to fly over from America to stay with the kids. And then, three days before we were to meet on the island, I had to cancel. I got cold feet.

Dee was not happy. Understandably, she thought I was a total flake.

Three months later, I was being honored by the We Are Family Foundation along with Nile Rodgers and Quincy Jones, and I wanted to take somebody. I may not have been a prince or a movie star, but this was shaping up as a notable occasion, so I called Dee. Despite our previous fits and starts, there was clearly something connecting us that was worth exploring, and she agreed. I offered to dress her and put her up in a hotel, but she preferred to stay with a girlfriend and not feel obligated to return any favors.

This time, I didn't cancel.

She flew over and we attended the event together. This was the first time I saw her dressed up—Saint-Tropez had been very casual—and she looked absolutely fantastic! She was a gracious and beautiful woman with real class, the kind of woman I knew I should be with.

We went to an after-party at Cipriani Downtown with Lenny Kravitz and a bunch of people, and had a lot of fun. When I finally dropped her at her friend's house, I said, "I have another event coming up. Why don't you stay for the weekend and we can go to that together, too?"

I was very pleased when she agreed, and I asked if she would like to stay at my house in Connecticut after the event. She accepted, and when we got home that night, we sat downstairs and talked for hours. It was clear to both of us that we liked each other, so I said, "So what about us?"

"Well, what about us?"

"We should go out."

Dee stayed the night, and we officially started to date. When she flew back to Monaco, I hoped she would consider coming back again soon.

Silas invited Dee and me to stay on a boat with him for the Cannes

Film Festival. Even though we stayed out partying until three a.m., I was up at six every day. (I wake up very early each morning; my mind just switches on.) Finally Dee said, "This isn't going to work. I need more sleep than you do." There was no way I was going to let my sleep pattern interfere with my relationship with this wonderful woman, so I lay in bed and waited however many hours were necessary so we would wake up together.

We became closer and closer. That summer we brought our kids together on a boat in the south of France. The more time I spent with Dee, the more I realized she was the type of woman I needed in my life: balanced, grounded, emotionally stable, fun to be around. We had a similar sense of humor. We each had a child with special needs. We understood each other's trials and tribulations. She told me that she had met several men after her divorce, but none of them could understand what she was going through.

She moved in with me in autumn 2006; her boys were in school in Italy and stayed with their father. In December 2007 I asked her to marry me. We planned a wedding for August 8, 2008— 08/08/08—in Mustique. Leonard Lauder threw us a huge engagement party. Dee bought a wedding dress, brought in her "glam squad," arranged her family's travel plans. We spent July in Europe and were coming back to the States when I received word from my ex-wife that Ally was going to the hospital with a severe setback in her Lyme disease.

Ally had started getting joint aches when she was a teenager. Her pediatrician thought it might be growing pains, but we thought it might be Lyme disease, so we saw another doctor, but Ally tested negative. The pain persisted and we saw a third physician, who told us that Ally had fibromyalgia, that she should take it easy and take some Advil because, you know, sometimes these things go away. It didn't go away, so we took her to a specialist at Harvard, who had her tested for Lyme (negative again) and said she might be suffering from preadolescent arthritis—or MS. That sent chills down my spine; my sister Dorothy has MS, and I knew the terrible trials that disease entails. As it turned out, that doctor was wrong.

Another doctor said, "It's all in her head." Another suggested she be tested for Lyme one more time. Again the results were negative. The joint aches and headaches and pain went on for a decade. Dizziness, night sweats, brain fog. We suffered, knowing what our daughter was going through, but despite all the experts and specialists we consulted, we could not help her.

Thirteen years after our first inquiry, as Ally was suffering a particularly difficult bout of illness, we had her tested for Lyme disease for a fourth time. Tests were much more accurate by now, and this time we were told that all the previous results had been wrong; Ally had been suffering from Lyme disease for more than a decade. On the one hand, we were furious that our wonderful daughter had suffered so needlessly; on the other, we were relieved to understand what she had.

But Lyme disease is tough. We took Ally to specialists who pumped her full of antibiotics, and while she got a little better, her stomach was a mess, and the drugs she took to quiet it weakened her in other areas. I'm sad to say that all these years later, the problems have not entirely abated.

With Ally in the hospital and in such a bad way, I didn't feel I could concentrate on creating a new family. One morning in July I came out of the shower, put on my bathrobe, sat on the edge of the bed, and told Dee, "I can't go through with this." She was shocked.

"What's her name?" she said.

"No, no, no, no. It's not that." I had a hard time explaining. "My family . . . my family has been through a lot, I can't do this to my family right now. I just can't go through with it." It did not occur to me to say "Let's not get married, but let's stay together," or "I can't get married right now, I'm under so much stress, let's put it off for a while," or "Let's just live together and not get married." I couldn't explain my feelings to her properly because I didn't fully understand them myself. In hindsight, I was feeling a decade's worth of guilt for not finding the source of Ally's pain, and while that pain was flaring up again, I had been on vacation in the south of France, coming home to get remarried, my life absolutely wonderful. I was abandoning my kids . . . again.

I wasn't thinking clearly and didn't feel I had the strength to deal with anything else. I said, "I will go to Mustique with my kids and you can move out whenever you can."

Dee was completely blindsided and furious. "I don't need any time." She got movers on the phone, found an apartment to rent, and was gone within a day and a half. We had lived together for three years, and when I walked back in, there wasn't a trace of her. Her dad wanted to kill me. Dee's friends rallied around her. She went back to Europe and I went to Mustique. We tried to email each other, but she was heartbroken, and so was I.

Ally needed and deserved my attention, and I gave it to her willingly, but I was terribly distraught over my breakup. My work continued to be unrelenting. Ally and Richard were out of school, and Elizabeth was going to Convent of the Sacred Heart High School in New York, so I rented an apartment where she and I would live. The plan was for Susie to stay there when I was traveling, but sometimes we were there at the same time, and it appeared that we were living together. That wasn't our intention or the reality, but it was confusing to the kids. And to Dee.

I received a succession of calls from Dee's mother and friends: "What are you doing?" "Are you sure?" "You're making the biggest mistake of your life!" It was all very dramatic. Finally, Dee and I spoke by phone at the end of August. She had been physically ill, could barely swallow food, and had lost almost twenty pounds, but she was beginning to feel slightly stronger. I was drained, too. She told me she thought she had turned a corner and was going to be okay. I wasn't so sure I had made the right decision.

Six weeks later, I was in New York doing a Fashion Rocks event. Dee had been invited and came with a girlfriend. As she was leaving, I met her at the door. Seeing her was a bit shocking; neither of us was in great shape. I told her I had something I wanted her to read.

While I was in Mustique after our split, I had sat down every night and handwritten Dee long letters explaining how distraught I was over the illness of my daughter, how important family was to me, how much I loved Dee, and how proud I felt when I was with her. I had never done anything like this before. Ever. I wanted to let Dee know how I felt but I could not convey such intimacy in an email or phone call. I had a stack of pages two inches thick, the size of a book. Now I placed them in an orange Hermès box and sent them to her apartment. She undid the ribbon, took out the letters, and read the last page first. I had ended with "I'm so sorry, but at this time I can't be with you. Love, Tommy." So she had her answer.

But we started talking on the phone again, and the conclusion I had reached in Mustique didn't seem so solid in New York City. "I miss you," I told her. "Let's get together, let's talk." When we met, Dee gave me a big hug and we started to cry. I knew with total certainty that I couldn't be away from this woman.

I began to drop by Dee's girlfriend's apartment each morning, and we started to find each other again. We rented an apartment for just the two of us on 62nd Street between Fifth Avenue and Madison, and decided we needed to be together forever. A couple of months later, we found that she was pregnant. To be safe, I said, "Why don't you take every test you can to tell whether you're healthy and the baby's healthy?" She passed with flying colors.

We went back and forth: Should we have a baby? Should we not? We decided we should! It was exciting. I thought, "This is fun. It'll keep us young!"

Soon enough, our children understood the relationship between Dee and me, as well as that between Susie and her boyfriend, Jeff. In November, Susie went off to Las Vegas and got married. It was the biggest gift she could have given us, because it cleared the path for Dee and me.

I proposed. Again. Dee was so afraid and said, "Let's not. We can live together and still be happy." She had been through a horrible divorce and was not champing at the bit to marry a second time. Plus, I had broken her heart by calling it off, and she did not want to go through anything remotely like that again.

But the more she refused, the more ardent I became. Finally she said, "I don't want any engagement parties. I'm not going to send out one invitation, I'm not going to make one plan. If you want to get married, you call the justice of the peace and we can do it simply. We'll throw a party after the fact."

We were married at home in Greenwich on December 12. Four people attended: Dee, me, the justice of the peace, and the security guard on duty that day. Our children were spread out around the world, and we couldn't wait to tell them. It would have been fun to celebrate in Mustique, but saying those vows was most intimate. Dee and I are partners, best friends, and lovers.

Our son, Sebastian Thomas Hilfiger, was born in August 2009. Ally came to the hospital. Susie arrived with our daughters Elizabeth and Kathleen. Dee's ex-husband, Gianni, came with Dee's boys Alex and Julian. We all celebrated together. Dee and I had both wanted to include everyone, so much so that we asked Gianni and Susie to be Sebastian's godparents, and they accepted.

Sebastian was a beautiful bouncing baby boy with big hands and big feet. He came out at almost ten pounds and his back looked like a little linebacker's! All the girls wanted to hold him. Even the boys wanted to hold him! Rich was in L.A., and I called him right away. Sebastian's baptism a few weeks later served as a family connector—everyone wanted to be a part of it.

We all loved Sebastian like crazy. He was a beautiful, blond-haired, blue-eyed boy and got about as much attention as a child could bear. He was the perfect union of Dee and me.

Which made our discovery all the more difficult. After about a year and a half, we sensed something was wrong. For instance, we would call his name, and he would not respond. A nanny said, "You should get his hearing checked." We had done that with Kathleen and it had proved worthwhile. Sebastian was one and a half years old when we had him tested. The results came back: he was on the autism spectrum.

Our hearts dropped. I felt out of breath and sick to my stomach. I thought, "This has to be a nightmare. It's not true." Dee had had every test under the sun while she was pregnant. Every single one. She ate organic food, didn't eat sugar, didn't drink a drop of alcohol, didn't stay up late. She was a complete health freak! The news was rattling. Driving home, we both just stared straight ahead at the highway, not talking. Dee was crying. I was crying.

But Dee and I are both positive thinkers. When something negative happens we say, "But look how lucky we are." We leaned on each other. We told each other that Sebastian had been born into the right family. We had been there before, we understood the entire situation and what it entailed, and we were extremely fortunate to have the wherewithal to get Sebastian the right help. Rather than wallowing in sadness and depression, we said, "Okay, what are we going to do? Whom can we call?" We were going to do everything in our power to help our son.

We took Sebastian to an array of specialists and tried many approaches, from diet to applied behavioral analysis, in which speech and language techniques are used to move the child along. We were told that early intervention was best, so we surrounded him with occupational therapists and speech therapists. In addition to his nursery school, Sebastian had at least twenty-five hours of therapy every week, and the progress was notable.

Our dear friends Laura and Harry Slatkin, who have a severely autistic child, introduced us to Dr. Catherine Lord, a world-renowned specialist. Fortunately, Sebastian's case was not severe. While he remains on the spectrum, we are happy to report that after a tremendous amount of applied behavioral analysis, occupational therapy, speech therapy, and a small dose of physical therapy, Sebastian is progressing very nicely.

Dee and I joined the board of Autism Speaks, an organization headed up by Bob and Suzanne Wright that has raised millions of dollars, created tremendous awareness, and funded intensive research into a disease that remains mysterious. Sadly, there is no government funding of autism research to speak of. We still don't know why or how people become afflicted. A child may be developing properly, and then all of a sudden he regresses. At a year old, for instance, Sebastian was counting steps as he was going up the stairs. Then one day he just stopped. So something happens in those formative years. Is it genetic? Probably. Is it environmental? No one knows. At one point, people thought autism developed in reaction to a vaccine, but that was proved to be wrong. There are a lot of theories going around, but in reality no answer has been found.

Autism Speaks is one of the most important charities with which we are involved. The Night of Too Many Stars, produced in support of the New York Collaborates for Autism charity foundation, has become an annual institution. It is heart-wrenching to think that there are families out there who don't know that their children have the disease, or don't know what to do once they know their child is afflicted. A lot of families just think their child is "off," "retarded," or "stupid." That breaks my heart. Having been written off as stupid myself, I am keenly aware of the responsibility adults have to help their children in need.

Autism is the world's fastest-growing serious developmental disability. Ten years ago, 1 in 166 children were on the spectrum; today, it is 1 in 68. About 1 percent of the world has autism, including more than three million Americans. According to Autism Speaks, in the United States the prevalence of autism in children increased by 6 percent to 15 percent each year from 2002 to 2010, a total increase of 119.4 percent; each year an estimated fifty thousand teens with autism age out of school-based supports and services; nearly half of all twenty-five-year-olds with autism have never held a paying job and 84 percent remain living at home with their parents; and the cost of autism across a lifetime averages $1.4 million to $2.4 million.

According to some reports, one of the reasons autism may be so prevalent is our industrial use of pesticides. Most of the animals we are eating are themselves eating grains produced with pesticides. Most of the fruits and vegetables on our tables are sprayed with pesticides. The plastic containers we're drinking and eating out of are all basically toxic.

I feel very fortunate and grateful that I am able to take care of my children. But what of others who do not have my wherewithal? What do you do when autistic children become adults? They don't have jobs; they can't take care of themselves. It is a major problem, and so many families are affected by it. Certainly the government is not overly helpful. Until the government recognizes the degree to which it is affecting the country and views it as an issue of importance, the problem will continue.

I'm honored and proud to be a part of Autism Speaks. Its Autism Response Team members are specially trained to connect families with information, resources, and opportunities. Dee and I also donate to organizations that are researching cures for MS and breast cancer. We recognize that we are blessed with good fortune, and we do our best to spread that blessing. We have our priorities, and autism is on top of the list now, but so many causes are worthwhile. ALS, AIDS, breast cancer—where does one concentrate one's generosity? Our decisions are based on which issues affect us most directly and where we feel we can be most helpful. I believe health-related causes are vital. Societal issues are also significant. We have supported the Fresh Air Fund and are now, through the corporation, involved with Save the Children.

Over the past twenty years, under the guidance of president Guy Vickers, the Tommy Hilfiger Foundation has donated more than $50 million to causes and organizations around the world. We have also been very involved with Millennium Promise, an organization affiliated with the United Nations whose mandate is to empower communities to lift themselves out of extreme poverty. Its core belief is that extreme poverty can be cut in half, even in some of the poorest, most remote places in the world. For example, the Millennium Villages Project uses a holistic, science-based approach to benefit more than half a million people across sub-Saharan Africa. In 2010, the Tommy Hilfiger Corporation donated $5 million to the project and matched contributions by our employees dollar for dollar. We sponsored Hilfiger employees to travel with Millennium Promise personnel and bring clothes and medicine. We went to Ruhiira, Uganda, where people were living under extreme conditions, poverty like nothing I had ever encountered. The village death rate had been staggering because of their lack of medicine, health care, and sanitary facilities, and we helped gather money and people and know-how and assisted in bringing water and electricity into the village. We helped rebuild the school and hospital, and participated in teaching villagers how to grow sustainable crops to subsidize themselves. It was eye-opening.

When I first started to make a little bit of money, I knew one of my main goals was to give back. In the late 1980s, I had the opportunity to contribute to building the Ernie Davis Community Center in Elmira, which provided day care, afterschool programs, and many other programs for less-fortunate children in my hometown. When we learned that the Fresh Air Fund took fifteen thousand children out of New York City every summer and put them into summer camps, we built Camp Tommy next door to Mariah Carey's Camp Mariah. Fresh Air Fund children go there every summer and do everything from computer training to canoeing to sleeping under the stars to cooking and camping. My sister Betsy has been instrumental in these efforts. The Tommy Hilfiger Foundation sponsors the Race to Erase MS, organized by my friend Nancy Davis, who has worked tirelessly for almost twenty years to find a cure and has funded many doctors who are working on discovering a breakthrough. My company's contribution to the Dr. Martin Luther King, Jr. memorial on the National Mall is very important to me. I realize that I have made several fortunes, and I am pleased to have the ability to use some of those proceeds to help other people's lives.

The writer and filmmaker Mary Pat Kelly was directing a feature film called *Proud*, which I financed and co-produced, about African American sailors who had been mistreated on the shores of America, performed heroically at sea during World War II, and happened to land in Ireland, where they were treated like gold by the

Irish. Ally, a teenager at the time, was studying acting at New York City's Professional Children's School, and I gave her the opportunity to be on set, to learn about how films were made. She became the movie's producer. Parts of *Proud* were filmed in Elmira, in a beautiful old Tudor mansion in Strathmont, one of the houses I always used to ogle while I was delivering newspapers. Years later, when that house came on the market, I bought it and was over the moon. It was a childhood dream come true!

At around the same time, Ally had the opportunity to be in one of the first reality TV shows, on MTV. I thought it sounded like a cool idea. She had just had a part in an off-Broadway musical, *Abby's Song*, also directed by Mary Pat Kelly, and enjoyed it and wanted to follow her acting dreams. The MTV show was presented to me as a portrait of New York City private school teens in general, and we were supposed to have creative approval, but that never happened. One thing led to another, and it became a show about Ally and one of her friends.

After the deal was struck, the producers wanted to name it *Rich Girls*. I should have known then that there would be problems. Nobody from our side liked the title, but the producers said, "Let's just film the show and see what it's like. We can always change the name later." I was naive enough to agree. I told my daughter, "I think you should do it. It would be a lot of fun."

But instead of presenting a real-life look at New York kids, Ally and her friend were encouraged to be obnoxious on camera to create an edgy show that would bring a lot of eyeballs. They came across as spoiled, snippy, snotty rich girls who have everything and think nothing. We tried to change the edit and the title, but there was a firestorm: "Sorry, you agreed to it." You'd have thought, after my years dealing with the media and lawyers, that I'd have known better. We paid the price, she much more than I. It was a disaster.

Ally got very stressed from people's negative reaction to the show—and to her!—and started drinking. I also think she was affected by Susie's and my divorce, and as the oldest child, she had taken on a lot of responsibility with her siblings, much like I had.

Then I found out she was also smoking pot. She was getting out of control; she was at a breaking point. So I forced her into rehab. Tell a seventeen-year-old girl to go to rehab, and she'll say no, no, no. She was not happy with me.

During thirty days at Silver Hill Hospital, however, she realized she needed help and accepted it. She was in good shape when she was released, but then, her Lyme disease flaring, she started to slip back and self-medicate.

Lyme disease can be devastating. Over the course of her life Ally has gone through years of treatment. We took her to doctors in upstate New York, Boston, and Connecticut, most of whom put her on antibiotics. If you catch it early enough, antibiotics can kill Lyme. If you don't, the drugs never really do the job. Nothing worked until Katrina Borgstrom, a makeup artist who is very close to our family, went to a holistic doctor and was impressed with the practice. She told my assistant Sheila about it, and Sheila told Ally. Ally started to cleanse, and for the first time in many years began to feel better. She then went through chelation and all sorts of hydrating and revitalizing. She rehabilitated herself through holistic cleansing and meditation.

After that, to her tremendous credit, Ally made a decision to go back to twelve-step meetings and clean herself up completely. She decided she really wanted to change her life. Ally cleansed everything out of her system and has been sober and clean and clear and incredible ever since.

And she has a baby! Her partner, Steve Hash, was an art director at Warner Music, and now he's the brand manager for the DJ Skrillex and other musicians and artists. They live in Los Angeles, and she is in remission. Steve and Ally could not be happier together, and we are all happy for them. I am very proud of my daughter; she is everything I always thought she would be. And I am crazy about my granddaughter, Harley Elizabeth!

My son Rich and I always had an incredibly close relationship. We were the boys. We loved to go to sports events, hike in the woods, play outdoors. I loved taking him to hockey practice when he was a kid and lacing up his skates at four-thirty in the morning. He was always creative, beginning when he was seven years old and drawing cartoon figures; at age fourteen, he started writing music. A lot of fathers might see their kid wanting to do hip-hop music and rap, or wear street style, or get tattoos, and say, "No way!" But because my dad was so tough on me, I wanted to give my son the opportunity to realize his dreams. Rich is an amazingly creative human being. He moved in with me after Susie's and my separation, which made our relationship even stronger. Although I've talked to him about the fashion industry many times, he is more inclined toward the music business, which makes me terrifically pleased and proud. Although there have been some obstacles, including a stint in rehab, he is now healthy and happy. Rich is currently creating animation and characters for an animated TV series, *Slickville*. He has a great sense of style. He's fun and funny. He loves his family, and his sisters and I adore him.

My daughter Elizabeth has never stopped marching to her own cadence. She graduated from Sacred Heart in NYC and went to the Rhode Island School of Design, and soon was surrounded by students who were creative and artistic in a wide variety of disciplines—architecture, animation, sculpture, fine art. Elizabeth became increasingly intellectual and artistically sophisticated there. She is creative and unique, thinks things through deeply, and takes her art seriously. She is interested in sustainability and technology, which is the future. Elizabeth recently graduated from RISD and, using her nickname, has developed her own designer label, Foo + Foo.

Having eight brothers and sisters, I know from extensive experience that everyone in a family is different. Each person is born with a given personality, and Elizabeth was born confident, social, and responsible. Whereas some children of privilege feel entitled and act rashly, when Foo Foo makes a request, she has considered all its ramifications.

Elizabeth lives in L.A., but she is considering a move to Hong Kong or London to continue with her label. I am very proud, very happy with my little Foo Foo.

My daughter Kathleen has been such a beautiful, loving, sensitive, adorable daughter. Words cannot describe how proud I am of her.

Sebastian is a great addition to our family! He is now seven years old, with beautiful Harley as his favorite and only niece. Sebastian is attending a wonderful school and learning every day, loving every moment, and meeting new friends. He loves dinosaurs, farm animals, boats, and planes. And music too! A real Hilfiger!

My stepsons Alex and Julian—Dee's boys—are now men. Alex teaches tennis to young kids and also works at his dad's factory in Italy, driving forklifts and learning the business. Julian is the tennis star—a member of the Association of Tennis Professionals, and on tour all the time. He is disciplined and serious about winning, but at the same time fun and funny. We are blessed, grateful, happy, delighted—and appreciative of all the children!

# CHAPTER TWENTY-ONE

# GOING PRIVATE IN PUBLIC

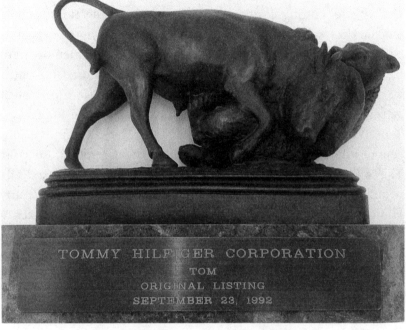

TOMMY HILFIGER CORPORATION
TOM
ORIGINAL LISTING
SEPTEMBER 23, 1992

*Bye Bye Wall Street for Now*

Our new CEO, David Dyer, had come from Lands' End in 2003 and begun doing what any red-blooded CEO would do: cutting costs, closing divisions, getting rid of people while trying to maintain and grow the business. Longtime employees who provided value, enthusiasm, and institutional memory were being fired because they were too expensive. We closed H, which was all of the better sportswear. We did several things I regret, such as selling our buildings. Most important, Dyer wanted to position Tommy Hilfiger as a mainstay mass brand, a far cry from the concept of affordable luxury that had been at the core of our success. The soul of a brand needs to be understood by the person who leads it, and I began to see that Dyer didn't understand the soul of Tommy Hilfiger, and when he started understanding it, he didn't appreciate it, because the business was in freefall.

I followed his lead for quite a while. We cut the advertising budget; we cut the travel budget. Instead of growing and blossoming, everything was shrinking and wilting. I thought, "He's an experienced CEO. I know the business is ill; we've got to take medicine to fix it. These are hard pills to swallow, but we must heal our wounds." We discussed how to grow the business. We thought, "Maybe we're not going to grow from within right now, but we've got a lot of cash in the bank. Why don't we make some acquisitions?"

A short while later I was asked by *Harper's Bazaar* to be photographed by Karl Lagerfeld in his studio in Paris. Karl and I hit it off. I liked the fact that he took himself seriously but had a sense of humor that took the pretense out of his work. He invited me to breakfast at his home the next day, and as we were sitting over coffee and very little food, I asked, "Tell me, how did you make Chanel the world's most exclusive luxury brand?"

"It's very simple," he told me. "I just went into the archives of

Coco Chanel and I took everything she had originally created and made it more relevant for today."

That made sense to me. He asked how I was spending my time. I told him, "My brand has slowed down and we need more growth. We're thinking of buying a brand."

He said, "Buy mine!"

Within two months, we had made the deal to buy Karl Lagerfeld's namesake collection. I loved the fact that Dave Dyer listened to me and agreed.

Unfortunately, the first season was not great. And the second season was not great. Dyer put fashion industry veteran Anne Acierno in charge, and it still wasn't great. A Lagerfeld fashion show didn't succeed, and the brand was put on hold. Tommy Hilfiger was still shrinking, and the stock kept sinking.

The stock price was dropping daily. I asked myself, "Should I cash out as well?" I would not make the fabulous money that my other three partners had when they divested, but this was a fortune not to be ignored. I asked Joe Lamastra, my go-to guy on all such financial matters, and he advised me, "Don't sell." The *Wall Street Journal, Barron's*, all the financial journals were saying the company was doomed. But Joe repeated, "Do not sell!"

The stock continued to plummet. Months later, I told Joe, "You gave me the worst advice ever!" The stock, which had peaked at 41, was at 6, then 5. I asked him, "Is it going to one? Is it going to zero? Do I sell now?" He was extremely nervous, but sometimes in life you have to go with what you believe, and Joe was following his gut. I trusted him, but I saw my life's work disintegrating. I was miserable.

For years, Fred Gehring, CEO of Tommy Hilfiger Europe, had had a perspective that none of us in America had considered.

Fred was born in Amsterdam, came to the United States to work in the diamond business, and stayed to consult for European companies wanting to enter the U.S. market—companies selling flowers, bicycles, dairy products, and ultimately fashion. He had met Silas, who encouraged him to move back to Europe, where Fred had ultimately risen to CEO of Polo Ralph Lauren Europe. He had been aware of Tommy Hilfiger and liked our freshness and rebelliousness of spirit. Fred had participated with Silas in the purchase of a management stake in Pepe Jeans, of which he became CEO. Pepe Jeans USA was the licensee for Tommy Hilfiger, which is where he and I first met, mostly on a social level. Fred and Silas brainstormed about how cool it would be to establish Tommy Hilfiger on the Continent. Fred was eager to move forward, but Silas, the disciplined strategist, said, "No, no, no, too early, too early."

For a long time, European tourists would return home from vacation in the United States with a suitcase of Ralph Lauren for the family. Now they were beginning to go home with a suitcase of Tommy Hilfiger. We were the newest thing. We developed a cachet in that market, and in 1996 the time arrived. Fred and Silas signed a license to launch Tommy Hilfiger Europe.

Pepe Jeans had its home office in Amsterdam. Fred and I had several conversations about moving it to London, but Fred convinced me that the European continent was the right place to base Tommy Hilfiger Europe.

This was 1997, when Tommy Hilfiger had become extremely streetwear-focused. That style didn't sell in Europe. Fred believed that for Tommy Hilfiger Europe to develop longevity, we needed to present the original DNA—the original concept of affordable luxury, which he felt was more in keeping with European sensibilities.

From my first purchase of bell-bottoms on St. Mark's Place, I have been pleased to involve myself in trends, but Fred felt that trends set you up for failure, and often quicker than you think. "Stay short of hype" was his credo. He felt that the new jeans-driven business attracted customers who pushed out the original consumers who had been comfortable shopping with us. His first two years with Tommy Hilfiger Europe were complicated because his was the voice telling us we had it all wrong. But ultimately, he turned out to be correct.

There were conversations between Joel and me on one side and

Silas and Lawrence on the other, in which Joel and I would say, "Why are we giving Fred all this authority? It's wrong. Tommy Hilfiger should be one brand around the world!" Silas would counter with his core business philosophy: "Give him a blank check, give him total authority and ownership, and let him deliver. He is as invested as we are. Let's have discussions on the larger picture, not on individual product. Just let him take it!"

Silas won that debate.

There were the other dynamics as well. Because of our need to satisfy Wall Street, everything had to be *big*. We opened a huge flagship store in a luxurious location in Beverly Hills that needed its own dedicated product because the new Tommy Hilfiger merchandise was too inexpensive. We opened a 20,000-square-foot store on Bond Street in London for the Tommy Hilfiger Europe 1996 launch, but it was a complete debacle because it was way too big, and it closed in 1999. With those experiences in mind, Fred's argument got traction. He wanted to bring to Europe the core Tommy Hilfiger concept that had existed before the hype: affordable luxury, classics with a twist.

Tommy Hilfiger Europe began tweaking the American product. Under normal circumstances, a company can create economy of scale by combining orders. By manufacturing American and European clothing in the same factories at the same time, we could save significant amounts of money. However, Europe often found they needed to substitute fabrics for better fabrications. Sometimes American designs eliminated quality details that needed to be reinstated for European consumption. Because of the difference in concept, everything had to be done at a higher level. At first, Europe didn't create their own designs but took Tommy Hilfiger designs and raised the quality. It was the original Tommy Hilfiger, but a little more sophisticated, a little more expensive. The battles with Europe were always about "We need it better."

It worked. The European business was profitable and grew nicely. Once Tommy Hilfiger Europe demonstrated that their tweaks were resulting in higher performance, the discussion got easier.

By the late 1990s, we agreed that the brand's development in the United States and in Europe were so different that European needs could not be solved from America. Amsterdam, it was decided, would be entirely independent; their decisions need no longer be submitted to U.S. headquarters. No other brand had ever done that. Fred said, "I want to hire people from New York as creative director, marketing director, and creative services director. Do not send me people; propose people to me. I will interview, choose and hire, but they will have your blessing." I thought this was masterly; Fred would have his hand-picked organization, and the American team managing the company's core would have people on the ground in Europe with whom it felt comfortable.

Fred hired Avery Baker, a relatively junior person, to head up communications. She had been a public relations marketing assistant in New York, and when Fred took over, I said, "I think she would be great on the team because there needs to be some cross-pollination." Avery proved herself to be a superstar. Today, she's the company's chief global marketing and brand officer. Alice Flynn was named a creative jeanswear/children's wear designer. Daniel Kelly became a creative director, doing all the showrooms and stores. The corporation gained peace of mind because we knew and approved of these people, and Fred got peace of mind because they weren't pushed on him; they weren't, as he feared they might be, moles. Tommy Hilfiger Europe was put in control of its own design, production, marketing, licensing, finance. It became a stand-alone.

Tommy Hilfiger Europe resisted hip-hop fashion, which was hot in England, and streetwear, which was having its moment on the Continent. Instead of being a discovery brand, something cool kids would pick up in trendy boutiques that showed the latest gear but might have trouble paying their bills, TH Europe was sold at leading department stores such as Peek & Cloppenburg, Galeries Lafayette, El Corte Inglés, Selfridge's, House of Fraser, and thousands of well-established luxury independents. Rather than appearing in jeans shops next to Diesel, Replay, or Levi's, our clothes would sell alongside Ralph Lauren, Hugo Boss, and some of the Italian brands. A year later, research showed American consumers saying, "Tommy's gone. He's everywhere now." Tommy Hilfiger Europe resisted that overexposure and became everything the original brand had become in America before the fall. It had continuity of authenticity. It didn't go outside the DNA. It became a wild success.

From 2000 to 2005, Tommy Hilfiger saw a constant escalation of success in Europe and deterioration in the United States. American sales fell annually, and European sales grew approximately 50 percent every year. In 2002, when Joel left, Dyer arrived, and new members joined the board, the dynamics changed even further.

When David Dyer became CEO in 2003, he and Fred Gehring did not see eye to eye. Fred had his European vision, which was a big success. Dyer and the board kept focusing on trying to regrow U.S. revenue and profitability. I was comfortable with Fred in ways I was not with Dave. Fred, for his part, could never work with the guy. From day one, the leaders of Tommy Hilfiger were driven by passion and love for the brand. Dyer showed no emotion; he was just doing a job. The business had shrunk from $1.5 billion annually to $500 million; without other pillars to lean on, it would collapse and go under.

About nine months after the new CEO's introduction, at a two-day meeting in Amsterdam with Dyer and the Tommy Hilfiger Europe management team, Fred argued that Dyer was, understandably, marketing in America to solve the American problem, but Tommy Hilfiger Europe didn't have the American problem and needed marketing that supported its particular issues. Dyer told him to do his own. Fred said that marketing was the one thing that should be global, that without global marketing, Tommy Hilfiger would stop being a global brand. A consumer would not know that the company was issuing different designs in different parts of the globe as long as they all had the same feel. But branding, the logos, the marketing—that had to be consistent. Dyer disagreed and refused. Our sense was that he would have liked to fire Fred, but he couldn't because the European business was throwing so much profit off to the main company. Fred was indispensable for all the right reasons. He was a powerhouse and he'd set up a powerhouse team. And he had positioned the brand perfectly.

The meetings were a disaster. Europe's management looked shaken. Fred sat with CFO Ludo Onnink and said, "We have got to do something." They began thinking of alternatives. As Dyer staffed up for his acquisition strategy, Fred started to build a shadow business plan.

When he began his calculations, he didn't have access to anything other than the publicly reported numbers. He looked at them from a new angle. Tommy Hilfiger America was hemorrhaging, but *what if it didn't exist?* What then? Tommy Hilfiger Europe was independent; if the American brand didn't exist, it would have no bearing on that part of the company, so he deducted that from his calculation of losses. Tommy Hilfiger Canada was also relatively independent, because it created its own product. Deduct that. Licensing had minimal operational costs. Deduct that. The U.S. retail outlet stores, under the excellent purview of Gary Sheinbaum, a consummate pro who has become CEO of Tommy Hilfiger Americas— there is not a more passionate or loyal Tommy Hilfiger team leader—were fully vertically integrated; every style sold in Tommy Hilfiger outlet stores was specially designed and produced for those stores. No excess there; deduct that. What was left was the combination of U.S. wholesale, corporate costs, and public company costs— all the problem areas. Fred felt that the first four buckets were all compellingly successful; the fifth bucket was filled with poison.

In essence, David Dyer and the new board were doing everything in their power to reclaim the ground the company had lost when revenues slid, but Fred thought, "That's never coming back, so why not just acknowledge those losses and move forward? Why not solve the isolated disease of the American business by shrinking it massively?" And how else to do this but buy the company and take it private? Without the pressure to please stockholders, the need for earnings increases each quarter would disappear. The brand could pull back as it should have done in the first place, regroup, and move forward in increments, all the while being supported by the success of the company's other components.

Fred went to Silas, who said, "That sounds like a good plan, but you are going to need private equity." Buying Tommy Hilfiger would demand significant funds. Fred interviewed private equity companies and eventually found Apax Partners, which was based in Europe, where the brand was strong. Silas was ready to invest, too.

And then they came to me. Fred said, "Let's buy the brand. Let's take it private. I have some bankers who are willing to back us, but I will only present it to the board if you support it. Let's buy it together—we will turn the whole thing around." I was terrifically interested.

It was April 2005. I spent long hours talking my decision out with Joe Lamastra. Should we go with David Dyer's vision and make Tommy Hilfiger a mass brand, or should we pursue Fred's vision and try to reestablish it as affordable luxury? Would David Dyer's plan work, or would it ultimately kill the brand and leave us with nothing? Of course, if the company was sold, I would come home with a lot of money, but I would no longer have an ownership stake. My name would be on the door, but I would have no clout. Could I live with that?

Then there was the matter of pride. Joe said, "You know, there is also a legacy issue for you." This was a brand called Tommy Hilfiger. How did I want to be remembered in the design world? As a man who had a real effect on American fashion in the twenty-first century, or a guy who sold a ton of clothes at Walmart?

Joe's gut and mine said to go with Fred. Fred's argument rang truer, and he had so much confidence that we didn't doubt him.

We were going private.

# CHAPTER TWENTY-TWO

# BOARDROOM
# BLOODBATH

*Finding my
Strength*

D yer nearly choked on his food when, over a meal, Fred Gehring said he was prepared to buy Tommy Hilfiger. Management buyouts are typically initiated by the CEO of a company, but here was the CEO of a subsidiary office coming in to dispossess the chief. Dyer was hostile to the idea when it went to the board, where the notion of selling the Tommy Hilfiger Corporation and taking it private was met with a lot of resistance: "Fred Gehring? He has no business trying to do this! Who does he think he is?"

The boardroom battle took place in Bermuda. Rather than deal with the offer, the board suggested cutting expenses to make the company more profitable. But expenses had already been cut to the bone. "No," I was told in essence, "we *really* need to slice expenses." What they meant was cut my salary; their compensation committee had met and decided that the company's failings were all about me making too much money.

It got ugly. The board basically ganged up on me. Board members I had thought of as friends turned on me, and while those friendships didn't entirely disintegrate, there was certainly personal and financial tension. I said, "Look, I gave up my name when I founded the business. What I am earning is a payout for me founding the brand and putting my name in the deal." Their position was that I had been paid out already and they didn't like the way I was doing my job, though they were vague about what exactly my failings had been. That line of economic hostility didn't go anywhere because my contract was locked in, and I was not about to abandon my position.

It's interesting that I can't recall exactly what was said in that room. In many cases when things are negative, I choose not to remember them. What remains vivid is the fact that there was a blowup, and I felt under siege. There were a lot of fingers pointing toward me and the former regime. I felt that they hated the idea that Fred might buy the business and oust them.

I did have some allies. At one of the last meetings before his contract expired, board member—and my great friend—David Tang stood up and gave a speech that basically told them they were crazy.

Joe and I considered Fred our new best friend. We saw things the same way, but almost all the finance people at Tommy Hilfiger seemed to be in David Dyer's camp. Of course, Joe and I had moments of doubt: "Are we missing something here? These are smart people; they are successful in their own realms. Why are we seeing something they aren't?" But I believed in Fred.

Ultimately, rather than consider the offer itself, the board voted to put the company up for auction. The prevailing sentiment was that if the company was sold to a group that included insiders, we could all be sued for malfeasance by shareholders who might question the price. Many lawyers navigated the process in order to be fair to all shareholders.

The company hired J.P. Morgan to be the lead investment bank, in charge of amassing the book of corporate information and soliciting potential buyers. Through the summer of 2005, the list narrowed to three bidders: Iconix, Sun Capital, and Apax. Each had a different strategy for Tommy Hilfiger's future.

Iconix was a brand management company with a diversified portfolio, kind of a bottom-feeder. Their plan was to keep me involved in the company in some capacity and to take Tommy Hilfiger to Walmart. They believed that they could turn Tommy Hilfiger into a behemoth with $10 billion a year in retail sales, which comes to approximately $6 billion wholesale. Under my lifetime contract, which paid me 1.5 percent on top-line revenue, my annual earnings would have been in the neighborhood of $100 million—maybe more if the brand thrived. It was hard to argue with their economics. Of the three proposals, this was by far the most lucrative for me personally.

The second bidder was Sun Capital, a private equity company based in Florida that was buying a lot of consumer brands at the time. Sun was not interested in keeping me around; their philosophy was that Tommy Hilfiger was a brand and they really didn't need the person. They didn't come out and say it, but I believe they wanted to take the brand to a JCPenney or a Kohl's, something clearly lower in both quality and cachet than our standard of retailer.

Apax shared Fred Gehring's vision. A European private equity company, Apax viewed Tommy Hilfiger as the international affordable-luxury brand it already was on the Continent. Not only did they want to make the brand more luxurious, they wanted to expand its international footprint and get me more involved. From a nonfinancial point of view, Apax was certainly the most appealing.

All three were making their bids, and it was their money. I could have said to Sun Capital and Iconix, "I am going to exercise my trademark veto rights [the right to veto any use of my name that could demean its value] as strongly as I possibly can," which might have dissuaded them from putting forward their best offer, but after consultation with lawyers I chose not to pursue what could have turned into an expensive lawsuit. But I certainly could give my opinion as to the company's best future, which I did.

And I could root! Joe and I were hoping that Apax would come up with the highest bid. Because of quality and the kind of world I wanted to live and work in, I was prepared to take a pass on a $100 million annual income. Gary Fuhrman of GF Capital, whom I had met when he worked with Edgar Bronfman on my deal to invest in the Warner Music Group, acted as an advisor and agreed with Joe and me. Of course, no matter which bidder was successful, at the end of the day I was going to have a tremendous amount of money. But still—$100 million every year!

As part of the process, each potential new owner had to deal with my contract. In 1988, when Silas bought out Murjani, he offered me a unique lifetime employment agreement. But at that time, people worked differently than they do today. Nowadays people work until they die; back then, "lifetime" meant until you stopped working. I'm guessing that Silas thought, "Tommy will work until he's sixty-five and then retire." That wasn't going to happen!

Also, in 1988, Tommy Hilfiger was a small menswear company in the United States, so the agreement didn't mention revenue streams such as licensing and foreign distribution, which by six or seven years later had become high-performing elements. For instance, in 1993, we made our license deal with Estée Lauder for fragrance and beauty products. If Lauder made $100 million in sales, was I to receive any of that? Joe had tried to renegotiate my contract with Silas, but when the company went public, there was hesitation about changing it because of a law restricting the amount of tax deduction for salaries of over $1 million a year. My contract had been grandfathered in, so whatever I was making was fully tax-deductible; any changes to our agreement would eliminate that deduction for the company. So the problem lingered. When David Dyer came in, Joe and I ran into the same roadblock. Joe kept telling me, "You are being underpaid. This was not the intent. It's unfair." Now we finally had a chance to get things right.

Iconix wanted to keep the contract as it was. They didn't care about foreign distribution because they were pursuing the Walmart deal. And since I would be earning as much as $100 million a year, I didn't see the need to pursue it further. Sun Capital, which was interested in the brand, not the person, wasn't inclined to make any changes. They said essentially, "We don't even need Tommy."

Apax had a different view. They said, "We want to grow this company to be a global brand. We want you to be motivated to get on a plane and go to a store opening in Shanghai. And we know you're a wealthy guy who doesn't need to work, so we want you to be fully incentivized to do this. We definitely want to change your contract; we don't like it, either!" Joe Lamastra negotiated a new deal under which, instead of 1.5 percent of wholesale sales, I would receive 10 percent of licensing revenues. I would also earn 0.5 percent on retail sales at Tommy Hilfiger stores and 1 percent on wholesale sales throughout the brand. Forever. *This* was a lifetime contract. Apax was open to fixing the contract, and we agreed in principle on a salary of approximately $22 million a year for the first three years.

Dyer objected. Way too high, he said. In 2000, I had been making $20 million, but because I was being paid on the top line, and the top line had dropped steadily for five years, by 2005 my salary was $12 million. Dyer told Joe, "You can't go from twelve to twenty-two." We said, "What do you care? You're selling, you are gone, Apax is going to own the company." The board cared, he told Joe. They thought my salary could affect Apax's bid price. If I was paid less, they thought, Apax would bid more.

We brought Apax into the room. "No," said their representatives. "Our bid price is mutually exclusive from Tommy's salary. What we are paying Tommy has to do with the fact that we need him to fly around the world and open up stores in India, China, South America." Theirs was a plan of incentivization.

I was on the board of the Tommy Hilfiger Corporation, but because I had expressed an interest in remaining with the company and so had a vested interest, I was not allowed to attend the meeting in Bermuda where the final decision was to be made. We had to wait outside while they met.

It was a grueling day. I huddled in a nearby hotel lobby with Joe Lamastra and Jeff Weinberg, an attorney with Weil Gotshal who had been introduced to me by Leonard Lauder. We had to be ready for anything. What if the board came out of that room and said, "Iconix won the bid at $19 a share, but they want to renegotiate your contract, Tommy, and cut it in half"? Just as a baseball player needs to know what to do with the ball before it comes to him, we had to consider what each bidder's victory would mean for us.

What would happen if they chose Iconix? Having grown up in Elmira, I understood the Walmart culture, and I got how the Tommy Hilfiger red-white-and-blue, all-American brand completely matches it. And I couldn't deny the fact that having such a vast amount of money would open up new worlds. But I enjoyed my glamorous life and the culture, scenes, and people I encountered because of it, and I wasn't certain I would be enthralled with going to Bentonville, Arkansas, and servicing that client solely. I felt the integrity of the brand would be dissipated.

Sun Capital was the easiest scenario. Clearly they showed little interest in keeping me, so this would be a cash-out. I'd be done. I'd have a tremendous amount of money that could never be taken from me; coming from Elmira, I would have fulfilled a lifelong quest for security. But what would I do each morning? What would chapter two in my life be? I was fifty-four years old, I was healthy, I wasn't a golfer, I didn't have other hobbies. I thought, "What would I do for the next forty years?" I wasn't going to sit on the beach and watch the waves roll in; I would have to dig deep and find my next passion. My immediate thought was to reinvolve myself in the fashion industry; it was what I knew and loved. But I had a noncompete clause, so I'd have to sit out a couple of years. I was an entrepreneur, and as early as 2000, Joe and I had talked about owning a hotel. However, neither he nor I knew anything about the hotel business, so that wasn't a truly viable option at our fingertips.

My agreement with Apax was based on what Joe called "nebulous handshake thoughts." In December 2005, as the decision on the buyer was being made, we had only a general sense that the direction we were going in was acceptable to Apax. Things could have broken down after the fact—"Oh my God, we thought we were on the same page, but we're not!" We were trying to predict the future based on gut feelings and handshakes with people we hadn't known very long. The stress was real.

Ultimately, it boiled down to cash. Iconix never entered an official offer—they withdrew at the very last minute. Sun Capital came in at about $14 a share. Apax came in at about $16 a share. We won!

And then, in a twist, the board rejected both offers.

Big fight. The board, in the voice of David Dyer, said this was going to be a busted process if Apax didn't come up from $16 and I didn't agree to a lower salary. A game of high-stakes chicken began in the hallways and lobbies of several Bermuda hotels.

Joe did the talking. He and I had picked the $22 million number out of thin air—there was no mathematical formula behind it. So we resorted to old-fashioned nose-to-nose negotiating. Our task was to instill in the board an understanding of the risk they were running if they rejected all offers and the company went bankrupt in two years, which was entirely possible. We had to inject litigation risk into these people's minds; that was our chess game. So as they were pounding their chests saying, "We can reject any offer we want!" Joe said, "Oh, really? So then when Fidelity, who is a major shareholder, sues the board—individually, by the way—for not accepting a bona fide full-value offer, are you willing to accept that risk in your life?"

Outwardly they blustered and told us they weren't afraid. But in their private moments, it had to affect them. So they had risk, and we had risk.

It was an intense couple of days. We were huddling in the lobby with our lawyers, thinking like crazy. Joe was worried about me. There was such a connection between my life and the Tommy Hilfiger Corporation that he feared that no matter what I did next, I would never be as happy as if I stayed. Joe knew me very well. He was right.

Sometimes in mediation you have groups in separate rooms with a mediator running back and forth trying to make both sides feel weaker so each will compromise. There was no official mediator in this scenario; the bankers took on that role. J.P. Morgan wanted the deal to happen, and their lead banker was telling us, "Tommy, they are right, you have to go down." I'm sure in the other room, he was saying, "You're going to get sued; this is better than demanding a full-value offer and not getting it." The banker would ask us, "Tommy, would you accept sixteen million instead of twenty-two?" And to them, "Guys, if Tommy does sixteen, will you take it?" That's the banker's role: make the deal happen. And it did.

The deal closed in May 2006 for $1.6 billion. Apax came up to $16.40 a share, and my annual salary was set at $17.5 million. (By 2016 it would be north of $33 million.) In addition, I was allowed to reinvest into Apax, a decision that was ultimately very wise. After all of my crying about cashing out and his insisting that I hold steady, Joe Lamastra turned out to be a genius.

I know, I know—I was about to trade approximately $70 million a year for my legacy. I was pleased to do it. Joe kept saying, "Tommy, you can be rich as hell. Where do you want to stand when you are eighty years old looking back?" I lead a life I love. I want for nothing; my family is secure. I surround myself with exquisite art, I live in wonderful places, I meet and interact with extraordinary people, and my work is fun. My decision was not easily made, but I am happy with it.

# CHAPTER TWENTY-THREE

# TURNAROUND

*my Saviors*

As a part owner of Tommy Hilfiger, I could have sold my shares to whichever bidder won, gotten my check, and ridden off into the sunset. This is what Calvin Klein chose to do when he sold his brand, and I don't know why. Instead, when Apax asked me to roll my equity, I was happy to accept their offer. Because I was going to stay with the company, I took some of the money and reinvested it with them. Doing so, however, opened a series of legal issues. Under the rules of the U.S. Securities and Exchange Commission there is higher scrutiny on a management buyout than on one that is unattached. We passed that test.

More than any other factor, what made Joe and me tip toward Apax was our extreme confidence in Fred Gehring. Fred was focused on the fact that because Europe was rocking and rolling we could do the same in South America and Asia. It was not that we didn't need the United States, but we could put ice on it, let it chill, and revive the brand when it was ready to be revived. We would stabilize and shrink the American operation while we grew the company around the world. This resonated with each of us as the right strategy.

Which is not to say we were without our anxious moments. There was a beautiful Tommy Hilfiger store in Short Hills, New Jersey, and another in Dallas. We had similar stores all over the country, and to see them close one by one was heart-wrenching. From 1990 to 2000, we'd had ten years of high success, but now we were in a low that was achingly familiar. It was like walking past People's Place the day after. Not fun. *There used to be a ballpark here.* I actually hurt!

Dyer was gone; the shareholders were all bought out. (I was one of the largest shareholders and received tens of millions of dollars.) I had a new lifetime contract with a new regime. Fred became CEO of the Tommy Hilfiger Corporation, moved to New York, and began the reorganization of the U.S. business. We stopped selling to discount-

ers, and he eliminated $100 million in overhead pretty much over-
night. The Dyer regime had staffed up for acquisitions; we staffed
down. He fired leadership, letting the costly people go. A major, back-
office investment in e-commerce, including logistics systems, was
scaled down. The Karl Lagerfeld brand was put on hold (to be re-
invigorated in 2013). By taking the company private, we were able to
lose the public company structure. Fred moved the head office to
Amsterdam, which allowed us to start over in New York very lean.

We had been doing business with the Dillard's and Belk chains
and a large number of department stores around America, but when
we examined the devolution of annual sales from $1.5 billion to $500
million to $250 million, we saw that for many years 75 to 80 percent
of our business had been with Macy's. Joel Horowitz, who was an
investment partner in the new group, said, "Why don't we sell to
Macy's exclusively? We'll have one department store home, and we
can do a great job there." The idea had merit.

We started talking to Terry Lundgren, Macy's chairman and
CEO, one of my greatest friends and supporters and one of the most
visionary thinkers and smartest retail businessmen I have ever met,
at the 2006 wedding of Joel's daughter Leigh in Montauk, Long Island. Lawrence, Silas, Joel, Fred, Terry, and I were there with our
wives, and everyone had been drinking a lot when the conversation
started. Although they had sold the vast majority of their ownership,
Silas, Joel, and Lawrence still had a keen interest in the success of
the business. Terry had always believed in the brand, and he grasped
the idea instantly.

Fred executed. We had a new band, and Fred, being a drummer
in real life, kept the beat and became our bandleader. At a series of
meetings he told Terry, "Why don't we just become super-important
for each other? When both companies can be focused on each other,
there's no distraction. We deal with your consumer; you give us the
best locations and the space. We jointly build shops to create a stage
for us to perform on, and we take the noise out of the air."

And so we did. When it was papered, the deal was historic. Never
before in the retail business had a designer joined with a retailer in
an entirely exclusive arrangement such as this.

We built and rebuilt shops in Macy's around the country. We tried raising the price points again, but we were still in the department store business, and you can't just jack up prices overnight. We added layers of merchandise at higher price points—more jackets and sweaters, more cashmere instead of wool. Advertising and promotions helped rebirth the business. It didn't happen overnight, but ultimately we succeeded.

Globally, we put a halo over the international brand via one of our best advertising campaigns. Trey Laird of the advertising shop Laird + Partners had worked for the Gap and Donna Karan for many years, and each time I saw him I'd say, "Trey, we need you!" When his contract was up, I asked him to come talk to us. Fred Gehring is very particular; he deals only with people he likes and relates to—a requirement I admire and respect completely—and I was hoping they would get along. Fred vets people by having his whole team meet them. Trey went to Amsterdam, met everybody, and came back with the job.

Under the aegis of the talented CMO Avery Baker, the ad campaign was inspired by the Wes Anderson film *The Royal Tenenbaums*. A diverse, quirky family of old people, young people, black, white, Asian, Hispanic, gay, straight people. The inspiration also came from the Hilfigers: a large family with different types, personalities, and tastes. It launched in 2009 and brought a lot of eyeballs to the brand again, and it continues to be incredibly successful.

Fred took the reins, and I felt tremendous relief to be in such good hands. He went on a mission to open beautiful anchor stores around the world: Fifth Avenue, Beverly Hills, Paris, London, Tokyo, Rio, Munich, Düsseldorf, Amsterdam, Milan, Florence, and Athens, and smaller shops in other cities as well. Internationally, we began selling a line designed for the European customer: higher-priced and more sophisticated, with more cashmere, more fine fabrics, slimmer fits. The design work was done in Europe, but it was derived from my design philosophy and DNA. I didn't love everything the company did, but there was enough I did like to satisfy me.

And I had trust and faith in Fred. He had succeeded wildly as CEO of Tommy Hilfiger Europe, and I knew that if he started doing in America what he had done with the European business, we would get to a better place. Which is exactly what happened. More press, more respect, better sales, cooler image again. We started to get some traction.

Fred rescued the brand from oblivion. The dream came alive again!

And then came 2008. The housing bubble burst, the stock market crashed, and everyone started getting very, very scared. The collapse of the economy seemed imminent. Bear Stearns and Lehman Brothers went under. What did this mean for us? Would we have to close stores? Would we have to fire half our people again?

But it turned out to be an incredible year! Not only did our business hold up, it grew, making 2008 and 2009 two of our best years ever! It became clear to me that price-wise, image-wise, style-wise, position-wise, and in the locations of our stores, Tommy Hilfiger was right in the fashion world's sweet spot. We were still a designer brand, we still connoted status, and at the same time we were affordable, accessible, desirable, inspirational. I was praising the heavens. Like a man on the verge of death who had miraculously been revived, I was loving every day.

I was also enjoying myself, because with fewer business responsibilities, I had more time to experience life. I enjoyed Dee, enjoyed my family, visited my son in California, spent more time with my other children. I had the one treasure most executives sacrifice in pursuit of fortune: more time!

One night in 2007, Terry Lundgren invited me and Dee to a dinner at Macy's penthouse. During cocktails, I spotted Manny Chirico, CEO of the clothing company Phillips–Van Heusen. PVH had bought Calvin Klein and at one point had looked at Tommy Hilfiger, back when Mark Weber was PVH's CEO. During our presentation, Weber had been condescending and rude. I wasn't there, but I was told that he gave us a look of disgust, as much as saying, "I want nothing to do with this," and walked out. Because Weber did not believe in us, he had missed out on an incredible opportunity, which infuriated the Apax partners, who were heavily invested in the PVH-Calvin Klein deal and thought our acquisition would be great for their company. Within a short time he was no longer CEO. Now Manny Chirico had taken his place.

Private equity firms make their money by buying companies, turning them around, and selling at a profit. The Tommy Hilfiger Corporation was a great success, and eighteen months after taking us private, Apax was ready to exit. The timing was good. Fred and I had been thinking of taking the company public again, and we'd begun filing papers and planning the road show for a new initial public offering.

Now Manny Chirico introduced himself. I shook his hand and joked, "When are you going to buy our brand?"

His response surprised me. "I talked to Fred about it not too long ago, but I didn't know if you guys were interested."

I said, "We are lining up an IPO, so if you want to look at it, now is the time."

During dinner, I was seated next to Manny's wife, Joanne, who had smiled when I first mentioned the idea. I told her, "Your husband should really buy this. It would be great for him to add to his Heritage Brands portfolio." PVH owned Izod, Arrow, Bass, Van Heusen, and Calvin Klein, and Tommy Hilfiger was a good fit for two reasons. First, I wanted to capitalize on the brand while our momentum was building. Second, I thought that being part of a large American public company could be very positive because PVH had clout with department stores and with manufacturing. It could be good for everybody.

"Why don't you call Fred?" I told Manny. Then I considered whom I was talking to and what I was asking, and said, "Better yet, I'll have Fred call you."

I emailed Silas and Joel for their opinions and put Fred in touch with Manny. The negotiations started, and in May 2010, the public company PVH bought Tommy Hilfiger for $3.1 billion. Considering that Apax (with me, Fred, Silas, Lawrence, and Joel as minority partners) had bought it for $1.6 billion four years earlier, using about $400 million in cash, we ended up making over an 800 percent return on our money. Again I kept my contract and my stock, and today the company is still growing, still rolling. I have some equity, but the real benefit is in my lifetime contract; I will be paid a royalty on everything with the Tommy Hilfiger name for the rest of my life.

Under PVH, I became the Tommy Hilfiger ambassador. Daniel Grieder is the new dynamic CEO of Tommy Hilfiger Global and is my current partner as we take the company forward. With his modern perspective, tech savvy, and outlook on how to grow the brand we make a great team with a shared vision. It is an exciting time for our business to leap to the next level. He replaced Fred Gehring, who stepped up to vice chairman of PVH and strategic advisor to Manny Chirico. I started cutting ribbons at new stores, making personal appearances, and giving magazine and newspaper interviews. We started producing spectacular runway fashion shows every season, and for that I credit CMO and Chief Brand Officer Avery Baker, who pushed for them. By handing over the baton, I gave the brand the opportunity to take my DNA and my signature and make it better. I am very proud of the job they have done, and we work very well as a team.

However, I can't help myself. I send pictures, ideas, samples. I visit the design studios and showrooms. I give my opinion on a regular basis, and the Tommy Hilfiger designers are responsive. The difference is that now I make suggestions rather than give directions.

I am no longer sketching out the styles, picking the colors and buttons, adding the stripes. I miss the days when I could touch everything, but because of the size of Tommy Hilfiger—we are talking thousands of styles being designed every single day—it would be impossible for me to participate in every design meeting. I have basically let go, and I am somewhat relieved not to have the pressure on a day-to-day basis. There is a whole team in place. They listen to my ideas, and on occasion we argue and I get frustrated, but they work hard and come up with great stuff. I have become the editor/advisor, making adjustments along the way. I feel incredibly proud. I am gratified that our team has been so passionate about making the brand so powerful. I couldn't be in a better position. And I do the fun stuff! The fashion shows. Flying to Shanghai to open a store. Determining the direction of our advertising. Collaborating with stars like Gigi Hadid, Zooey Deschanel, and Rafael Nadal to keep the brand fresh.

I was very grateful to receive in 2012 the Geoffrey Beene Lifetime Achievement Award from the Council of Fashion Designers of America. It was a long road from the Hangman ad, and I truly appreciated Anna Wintour's words at the ceremony. She called me "the most grounded designer working in fashion today" and said I "not only represent the best of American fashion, but the best of American values."

I have also branched out personally into the hotel world, with the development of the Raleigh in South Beach, Miami. Through Star Branding, after successfully launching Jennifer Lopez's J.Lo in partnership with Li & Fung, I introduced David Beckham first to Belstaff as the face of the brand and then to Global Brands Group in partnership with Kent & Curwen, owned by Li & Fung's Trinity Group. I was honored to be asked to join the Li & Fung retail board of directors. It is not only a pleasure to work with Victor, William, and Sabrina Fung, it gives me tremendous insight into the global retail community and specifically the Asian marketplace, the fastest growing in the world. The Li & Fung Group is the exclusive manufacturer of all Tommy Hilfiger products, as well as many others worldwide. In 2000, Silas came up with the genius idea of selling our Asian buying offices to the Li & Fung Group. We have enjoyed a great partnership ever since.

As an investor and advisor to Sandbridge Capital, I've seen lots of momentum investing in great brands such as Derek Lam, Karl Lagerfeld, Thom Brown, Bonobos, Topshop, and others. I continue to learn about brands and various businesses to keep my mind relevant and fertile. It's a passion I've always had and hope I have forever.

And I'm not the only entrepreneur in the household. Dee has invented a new customizable handbag with a detachable, reversible cover. She has been very successful at the high end, selling to Saks

Fifth Avenue and Harrods, among others, and is beginning to build a big business. She recently sold her patent for the reversible covers and Bag Bar concept to Kate Spade. She will always be grateful to Marigay McKee and Lisa Manice for helping to get her brand off the ground. I am very proud of Dee and the success she has earned in such a short amount of time.

I am honored to still be involved in the growth of the Tommy Hilfiger brand. It is my creation. It's my baby. I couldn't be happier that the DNA is intact, and the dream I conceived all those years ago, with no money in my pocket and an armful of sketches, is still alive. As a boy in school, dreaming, I thought I had big things in store, but I didn't know how my dreams would ever come true. I hoped and prayed that they would. I'm grateful to be a dreamer, and always will be.

# ACKNOWLEDGMENTS

Thanks and praise to my dear mother, Virginia Gerrity Hilfiger, who gave me tons of love and confidence while sharing herself with so many others. Thank you, Mom. I'm sure I wouldn't be where I am today without your love and support. I miss you terribly. You were a saint. I will love you forever.

Throughout my life I have had the great fortune to be surrounded by incredible people. They have guided and supported me, inspired and driven me to be the best version of myself in life, and served as teachers and partners in my work life. To my wife, Dee; my children Ally, Richard, Elizabeth, Kathleen, and Sebastian; my stepsons Alex and Julian; and my granddaughter, Harley. To my siblings Kathy, Susie, Betsy, Billy, Dee Dee, Bobby, Andy, and Ginny; my sisters-in-law Joanne and Kim, and my son-in-law, Steve Hash; my nieces and nephews Molly, Jane, Michael, Joe, Jamie Lynn, Lauren, Rachel, Jonathan, Andrew T, Andrew H, Will, Audrey, and all my cousins, too numerous to mention. Very special thanks to Susie Hilfiger, Gianni Ocleppo, and Pat and Vedat Erbug.

To my partners at Tommy Hilfiger: Mohan Murjani, Joel Horowitz, Silas Chou, Lawrence Stroll, Fred Gehring, Daniel Grieder, and Manny Chirico.

To Aaliyah, Bryan Adams, Teri Agins, Tevfik Akdag, Jonathan

Allen, Emmanuelle Alt, Imran Amed, Nandie Anderson, Marc Anthony, Jazz Armstrong, Peter Arnell, Amy Astley, David Bailey, Glenda Bailey, Avery Baker, Tyra Banks, Fabien Baron, Tina Bateman, Barbara Bates, Swizz Beatz, Bob Beauchamp, Linda Beauchamp, Jonathan Becker, David Beckham, Victoria Beckham, Richard Beckman, Amanda Beecher, Bender, Jessie Bennett, Beyoncé, Leilani Bishop, Tim Blanks, Jeff Bloom, Brenda Bomasoid, Katrina Borgstrom, Lloyd Boston, David Boswell, Bubbles Bott, Herman Bott, Joe Bouchard, David Bowie, Mark Bradley, Dawn Brandl, Sandra Brandt, Jordana Brewster, Gary Brody, Jeff Brody, Ethan Brown, Joy Bryant, Maja Hoffmann Buchtal, Stanley Buchtal, Martyn Lawrence Bullard, Giselle Bündchen, John Burke, Robert Burke, Jimmy Cacala, Naomi Campbell, Christian Carino, George Carrera, Graydon Carter, Gia Castrogiovanni, John Catrambone, Paul Cavacco, Gretha Cavazzoni, Andrew Cesari, Antonia Cesari, Camille Cesari, Carina Cesari, Henry Cesari, Lucy Cesari, Mary Chely, Eva Chen, Angelica Cheung, Soon Young Choi, China Chow, Stephen Cirona, Alina Cisek, Grace Coddington, Shari Cohen, Kenneth Cole, Jack Colgrove, Jim Colgrove, Lily Collins, Sean Combs, Peter Connolly, Samantha Conti, Coolio, Jane Cortill, George Cortina, Chris Cortez, Chris Cox, Justin Cox, Sheila Cox, Malcolm Crews, Sheryl Crow, the Cult Brothers, Bill Cunningham, Fran Curtis, James D'Adamo, Jeannine D'onofrio, Sante D'Orazio, Rick Darling, Helen David, Brandon Davis, Clive Davis, Nancy Davis, Godfrey Deeny, Jeffrey Deitch, Kevin Delaney, Cara Delevingne, Patrick Demarchelier, John Dempsey, Donnie Deutsch, Seth Dinnerman, DJ Cassidy, Babeth Djian, Ken Downing, Carlo Ducci, John Duka, Rhea Durham, Pat Durkin, Lia Duvall, Steve Eichner, Arthur Elgort, Edward Enninful, Abdel El Hamri, Matthew Fairchild, James Fallon, Dow Famulak, Linda Fargo, Eliane Fattal, Nabil Fattal, Patricia Field, Jay Fielden, Ed Filipowski, Ruth Finley, Pamela Fiori, Nian Fish, Catherine Fisher, Alice Flynn, Bridget Foley, Bill Ford, Ariel Foxman, Ron Frasch, AJ Fratarcangelo, Mike French, Virginia French, Kim Friday, Douglas Friedman, Etta Froio, Mike Frost, Anne Fulenwider, Bonnie Fuller, Simon Fuller, Sabrina Fung, Victor Fung, William Fung, Stephen Gan, Nina Garcia, Pattie Garrahy-Robertson, Gabrielle

Giardina, Robin Givhan, Marie-Claire Gladstone, Robert Gladstone, Richard Glasser, Roe Glasser, Morris Goldfarb, Grand Puba, David Granger, Rogan Gregory, Timothy Greenfield-Sanders, Efraim Grinberg, Mindy Grossman, Bob Gruen, Nicola Guarna, Tom Gwynn, Jefferson Hack, Bella Hadid, Gigi Hadid, Cody Hammond, Bert Hand, Katie Hand, Sarah Hand, Pamela Hanson, Andre Harrell, Gilbert Harrison, Debi Hartland, Jackson Hartland, John Hartland, Kendall Hartland, Heavy D, Koshawn Henry, Stan Herman, Donald Hilfiger, Paris Hilton, Dustin Horowitz, Cathy Horyn, Michael Houghton, Todd Howard, Kate Hudson, Rosie Huntington-Whiteley, Enrique Iglesias, Iman, Eddie Irvine, Constance Jablonski, Georgia May Jagger, Jimmy Jagger, Lizzy Jagger, Mick Jagger, Jay Z, Marie Jose Jalou, Dana Jamwant, Tim Jeffries, Kendall Jenner, Tiffin Jernstedt, Jewel, Richard Johnson, Dylan Jones, Kidada Jones, Rashida Jones, Quincy Jones, Spike Jonze, John Kamen, Carmen Kass, Kim Kassel, Faith Kates, Liya Kebede, Kezia Keeble, Douglas Keeve, Kathleen Keller, MaryPat Kelly, Beth Kent, Alicia Keys, Kid Rock, Jaime King, Staci Kipnes, Richard Kirshenbaum, Kwong Lung Kit, Karlie Kloss, Steven Kolb, Selma Kon, Robert Kraft, Reed Krakoff, Kevin Krier, Rich Kronengold, Vivien Kronengold, Jimmy Kunes, Karolina Kurkova, Tony Kurz, Karl Lagerfeld, Trey Laird & Partners, Olivier Lalanne, Sanjay Lalbhai, Joe Lamastra, Mirian Lamberth, Lauren Bush Lauren, Dan Lecca, Choong Keol Lee, Larry Leeds, Annie Leibovitz, Donovan Leitch, Cindi Leive, Amy Lemons, Jo Levin, Steve Lewerenz, Jason Lewis, Kelly Lewis, Meredith Lieberman, Li'l Vicious, Angela Lindvall, David Lipman, Margaret Lo, Mark Locks, Lisa Lockwood, Lindsay Lohan, George Lois, Jennifer Lopez, Teresa Lourenco, Terry Lundgren, Tina Lundgren, Cheng Chi Lung, Lynyrd Skynyrd, Susan MacLeod, Irv Maldonaldo, Fern Mallis, Dovie Mamikunian, Maggie Mangan, Lisa Manice, Gerard Mankowitz, Julia Mannion, Anne Marino, Daniel Marks, Kurt Markus, Bill Marpet, Lisa Marsh, Karen Martin, Sid Mashburn, John Mather, Kevin Mazur, Patrick McCarthy, Craig McDean, Kevin McDonald, Kyle McDonald, Marigay McKee, Patrick McMullan, Dave McTague, Benny Medina, Anne Menke, Suzy Menkes, Metallica, Mobb Deep, Charlie Modlin, Michael Mombello, David Mongeau, Jim Moore, Mandy Moore, Joe

Moretti, Maggie Morrisey, Courtney Moss, Kate Moss, Thalia Mottola, Tommy Mottola, Virginie Mouzat, Kevin Mullaney, Robbie Myers, Rafael Nadal, Chris Nakatani, Nancy Boy, Edward Nardoza, Enrico Navarro, Deborah Needleman, Jim Nelson, New Edition, Jonathan Newhouse, S.I. Newhouse, Joel Newman, Camilla Nickerson, Dewey Nicks, Bob Nielson, Don Nowill, John Olsen, Kristina O'Neill, Ludo Onnink, Jeff Palmese, Danielle Panazzo, Scott Parker, Peter Paul, Jay Penske, Daniel Peres, Bill Phillips, Scott David Pickle, Jonny Pigozzi, Dino Pisaneschi, David Pisor, Brittany Podell, Johnny Podell, Chris Pollucci, Candy Pratts Price, Sharon Pritchard, Q-Tip, Marc Quinn, Anita Rausa, Frankie Rayder, Missy Rayder, Jona Rechnitz, David Remnick, Simon Rex, Anyitsi Reynolds, Billy Reynolds, Bobby Reynolds, Craig Reynolds, PJ Reynolds, Jack Rich, Keith Richards, Terry Richardson, Nicole Richie, Ken Rickel, Steve Rifkind, Cindy Rinfret, Lisa Rinna, David Rivas, Jose Rivas, Maggie Rizer, Mick Rock, Bruce Rockowitz, Robert Rodriquez, The Rods, Carine Roitfeld, Xavier Romatet, Rebecca Romijn, Mark Ronson, Charlotte Ronson, Samantha Ronson, Paula Rosado, Bob Rosenblatt, Diliana Roussev, Spas Roussev, Matt Rubel, Hal Rubenstein, Margaret Russell, Roberto Russo, Ferit Sahenk, Salt-N-Pepa, Elizabeth Saltzman, Ellin Saltzman, Gina Sanders, Pete Sanders, Francesco Scavullo, Marybeth Schmitt, Chris Schram, Mark Seliger, Rachna Shah, Lynn Shanahan, Steve Shane, Jason Shaw, Pat Sheehan, Gary Sheinbaum, Paul Shindler, Alexandra Shulman, Russell Simmons, Ulrich Simpson, Ingrid Sischy, Harry Slatkin, Laura Slatkin, Anne Slowey, Jourdan Smalls, Carter Smith, Snoop Dogg, Miles Socha, Peter Som, Michael Sondag, Roberta Sorvino, Soul for Real, Franca Sozzani, Marypat Spannbauer, Britney Spears, Simon Spurr, Nick Steele, Gabor Stein, Larry Stemerman, Kimberly Stewart, Ben Stiller, Charlotte Stockdale, Steve Stoute, Tim Street-Porter, Debbie Strobin, Nick Sullivan, Bruce Surry, Lynn Surry, John Sykes, Andre Leon Talley, David Tang, Edward Tang, Sal Tangore, Priya Tanna, Arlene Taylor, Team Lotus, Dom Telesco, Sue Telesco, Karl Templer, Lori Tesoro, Lynn Tesoro, Mario Testino, Lois Theisen, Fru Tholstrup, Liz Tilberis, TLC, Stefano Tonchi, Mike Toth, Pete Townshend, Tam Tran, Ivanka Trump, Tyrese, Usher, Anne V., Vanco Security, Guy Vickers, Ed

Virgadamo, Patty Virgadamo, Celia Visconte, Diane Von Furstenberg, Ellen von Unwerth, Diana Vreeland, Marsi Wadsworth, Sharon Waldron, Andy Warhol, Immy Waterhouse, Suki Waterhouse,
Charlie Watts, Amy Webster, Scott Welliver, Linda Wells, Stan Williams, Paul Wilmot, Eric Wilson, Anna Wintour, Trent Wisehart, Bob
Wolfe, Jesse Wood, Ronnie Wood, Bob Wright, Harvey Wright, Jan-
ice Wright, Susanne Wright, Mike Wronkowski, Wu-Tang Clan,
Steve Wynn, Eileen Youtie, Phil Youtie, John Yunis, Olivier Zahm,
Serge Zalkin, Joe Zee, Rachel Zoe, ZZ Top.

**Special Thanks**

I would like to give special thanks to Peter Knobler who is not only a
great writer, but a patient listener. We spent hours together discussing my life story and I am grateful for the incredible effort he put
into this project. I can now officially call Peter a friend. Thank you to
Alina Cho. This book was something I wanted to do in my senior
years but Alina, with the help of Jim Cirona, convinced me to do it
ASAP. I'm grateful for their advice. Words cannot express my grati-
tude to my editors Jennie Tung and Sara Weiss. Their stewardship,
vision, and impeccable eye for detail made this manuscript sing,
shine, come to life. Thank you also to Nina Shield and the entire
team at Penguin Random House. What a pleasure. Last but not least,
I beg forgiveness of all those who have touched my life through the
years whose names I failed to mention.

**From Peter Knobler**

Thanks to David Black, who made the introduction, and Gary Morris, who helped in the process. To Sheila Cox for endless and unceas-
ingly good-natured facilitating. To Jennie Tung for inspired editing,
Nina Shield for her attention to detail, Sara Weiss for the future, and
Alina Cho for her vision. To Sue Warga for copyediting, and the team
of Joe Perez, Shona McCarthy, Mark Maguire, and Diane Hobbing
for production and design. To Ian Wehrle for his good transcribing.
To Irv Maldonado for transportation and conversation. To Stacey
Grifman for listening.

# INDEX

# ILLUSTRATIONS CREDITS

Dan & Corina Lecca Photo (p. 216), Sante D'Orazio/Trunk Archive (p. 227), Harpo Inc./George Burns (p. 235), Tommy Hilfiger Archives (pp. 3, 32, 44, 66, 77, 107, 152, 181, 283), IM_photo/ Shutterstock (p. 292), Dimitrios Kambouris/WireImage (p. 249), Annie Leibovitz (p. 262: © Annie Leibovitz 2016, courtesy of the artist), created by George Lois and Luke Lois (p. 144), Roger Macuch (p. 119), Kevin Mazur/WireImage (p. 300), Carter Smith (p. 202: courtesy of Art + Commerce), Syracuse University Archives (p. 19)

**First Insert:**
Mr. and Mrs. Hilfiger (Tommy Hilfiger Archives), young Tommy Hilfiger (Tommy Hilfiger Archives), Dorothy Hilfiger Grega (Tommy Hilfiger Archives), the Hilfiger family (Tommy Hilfiger Archives), Mr. and Mrs. Hilfiger's wedding (Tommy Hilfiger Archives), Billy and Andy Hilfiger (Tommy Hilfiger Archives), Hilfiger family home in Elmira (Tommy Hilfiger Archives), Mrs. Virginia Hilfiger (Tommy Hilfiger Archives), notice of violation (Tommy Hilfiger Archives), Tommy's aunt Annie (Tommy Hilfiger Archives), Billy and Michael Fredo (Tommy Hilfiger Archives), Ginny and Bobby (Tommy Hilfiger Archives), Tommy and Billy

(Tommy Hilfiger Archives), Bobby Hilfiger at family home (Tommy Hilfiger Archives), Virginia Hilfiger on bike (Tommy Hilfiger Archives), Tommy's mother, aunt Annie, and Dee Dee and her kids (Tommy Hilfiger Archives), Susie Hilfiger (Tommy Hilfiger Archives), Tommy's mother and sister Kathy (Tommy Hilfiger Archives), Tommy's mother and his sister Betsy (Tommy Hilfiger Archives), Bobby and Joanne's wedding (Tommy Hilfiger Archives), Tommy and mother in Mustique (Tommy Hilfiger Archives), Tommy and mother at table (Tommy Hilfiger Archives), Hilfiger kids (Tommy Hilfiger Archives), Ginny, Dee Dee, and Betsy (Tommy Hilfiger Archives), Tommy with mother and sister Betsy (Tommy Hilfiger Archives), People's Place storefront (Tommy Hilfiger Archives), People's Place key sign (Tommy Hilfiger Archives), People's Place sign, Elmira (Tommy Hilfiger Archives), newspaper clipping (Tommy Hilfiger Archives), Tommy and Larry Stemerman on boat (Tommy Hilfiger Archives), Andy and Bobby Hilfiger with Michael Houghton (Tommy Hilfiger Archives), Tommy and Larry Stemerman (Tommy Hilfiger Archives), People's Place sign (Tommy Hilfiger Archives), People Place, Elmira (Tommy Hilfiger Archives), Tommy hitchhiking (Tommy Hilfiger Archives), Further Adventures Ltd. (Tommy Hilfiger Archives), People's Place ad (Tommy Hilfiger Archives), Further Adventures Ltd. presents B.B. King (Tommy Hilfiger Archives), Cheque Point logo (Tommy Hilfiger Archives), Jacob Alan logo (Tommy Hilfiger Archives), Click-Point business card (Tommy Hilfiger Archives), 20th Century Survival storefront (Tommy Hilfiger Archives), 20th Century Survival logo (Tommy Hilfiger Archives), factory in India (Tommy Hilfiger Archives), Tina Bateman at People's Place (Tommy Hilfiger Archives), Tommy with Susie Hilfiger (Tommy Hilfiger Archives), O'tokyo logo (Tommy Hilfiger Archives), Click Point tag (Tommy Hilfiger Archives), Tommy with Pete Townshend (Tommy Hilfiger Archives), young Tommy headshot (Tommy Hilfiger Archives), Hangman campaign (created by George and Luke Lois), Coca-Cola clothing (Tommy Hilfiger Archives and Coca-Cola), Hangman campaign billboard (Luke Lois), young Tommy (Francesco Scavullo), An American Classic campaign (Luke Lois), the bad boy article (created by George Lois, photo by Carl Fischer), Tommy Hilfiger presents An Evening with Pete Townshend (Tommy Hilfiger Archives), Joe Fredo and Shannon (Tommy Hilfiger Archives), Tommy Hilfiger in suit (Douglas Keeve), Naomi Campbell (Tommy Hilfiger Archives), Boxers in Tartan campaign (Mike Toth/Toth + Co), men's sportswear campaign (Dewey Nicks), waving American flag, (Mike Toth/Toth + Co), Ethan Browne for men's sportswear campaign, (Dewey Nicks), VH1 Vogue Fashion Awards (Tommy Hilfiger Archives), Tommy waving (Tommy Hilfiger Archives), Tommy Jean campaign with Simon Ramone (Dewey Nicks), Camp Tommy (The Fresh Air Fund), Britney Spears's ". . . Baby One More Time" tour (Peter Arnell), Tommy Jeans 1999 campaign (Peter Arnell), Tommy with Naomi Campbell (Alex Lubomirski), campaign with Jason Lewis and Ethan Browne (Dewey Nicks)

**Second Insert:**
Lauren Bush for Tommy Jeans campaign (Carter Smith/Art + Commerce), Jason Lewis in Tartan campaign (Mike Toth/Toth + Co), Jason Lewis (Dewey Nicks), Tommy with the Rolling Stones (Tommy Hilfiger Archives), Tommy Hilfiger presents Jewel in concert (Dan and Corina Lecca Photo), Micael Fredo for Tommy Jeans campaign (Peter Arnell), Mark Ronson and Aaliyah (Sante D'Orazio/Trunk Archive), Enriqué Iglesias for True Star Men campaign (Mario Testino/Art Partner), Beyoncé for True Star Gold campaign (Mario Testino/Art Partner), Q-Tip for Tommy Jeans campaign (Peter Arnell), Tommy Hilfiger presents the Rolling Stones (Peter Arnell), Beyoncé for True Star campaign (Mario Testino/Art Partner), David Bowie and Iman (Ellen von Unwerth/Trunk Archive), Tommy Hilfiger presents the Lenny Kravitz Freedom Tour (Dan and Corina Lecca Photo), Tommy presents The Rolling Stones, 1999 (Peter Arnell), Tommy with David Bowie and Iman (Ellen von Unwerth/Trunk Archive), Sons & Daughters campaign (Carter Smith/Art + Commerce), Spring 2016 runway show (Randy Brooke/Getty Images), Meet the Hilfigers campaign (Craig McDean/Art + Commerce),

TommyXGigi campaign (Mikael Jansson/Trunk Archive), Tommy
Hilfiger Kids campaign (Benny Horne/Trouble Management),
Rafael Nadal, fall 2015 campaign (Mikael Jansson/Trunk Archive),
Ally Hilfiger with Santa (Tommy Hilfiger Archives), Ally on first
day of school (Tommy Hilfiger Archives), Ally and Elizabeth
Hilfiger (Tommy Hilfiger Archives), Tommy and son Richard in
1991 (Tommy Hilfiger Archives), Ally and Richard in riding gear
(Tommy Hilfiger Archives), Richard Hilfiger and teddy bear
(Tommy Hilfiger Archives), Elizabeth and Richard (Tommy Hilfiger
Archives), Sebastian Hilfiger (Tommy Hilfiger Archives), Tommy
with his mother and kids (Tommy Hilfiger Archives), Kathleen
Hilfiger close-up (Tommy Hilfiger Archives), backstage at spring
2009 fashion show (Astrid Stawiarz/Getty Images), Raleigh Hotel,
Miami (Nikolas Koenig/OTTO), Alex and Julian in trunks (Tommy
Hilfiger Archives), Ally at the beach (Tommy Hilfiger Archives),
Kathleen and Elizabeth in sailor outfits (Tommy Hilfiger Archives),
Tommy and Dee at Plaza residence (Trent McGinn/Trunk Archive),
Dee in white gown (Kate Martin), exterior of home in Miami
(Douglas Friedman), Tommy and Dee in Mustique (Kate Martin),
red and blue office in Miami (Douglas Friedman), pool in Mustique
(Kate Martin), exterior of home in Mustique (Tim Street-Porter),
Tommy and Dee in Miami home (Douglas Friedman), Tommy and
brother Bobby at Ally's book launch (Tommy Hilfiger Archives),
Tommy with mom and Richard (Tommy Hilfiger Archives), Kim
and Andy (Tommy Hilfiger Archives), Tommy and Dee on tarmac
(Tommy Hilfiger Archives), Seasons Greetings (Tommy Hilfiger
Archives), Susie Hilfiger on beach (Tommy Hilfiger Archives),
Tommy and Richard (Tommy Hilfiger Archives), Sebastian school
picture (Tommy Hilfiger Archives), Tommy and Ally at Global
Lyme Alliance gala (Dimitrios Kambouris/Getty Images), family
Christmas card (Tommy Hilfiger Archives), Tommy and Dee on red
carpet (Tommy Hilfiger Archives), Dee kissing Tommy (Richard
Phibbs/Art Department), Hilfiger family (© Annie Leibovitz,
2016), Ally's daughter (Tommy Hilfiger Archives), Elizabeth
Hilfiger (Tommy Hilfiger Archives), Tommy in hat with Dee
(Tommy Hilfiger Archives), Tommy and Dee with Davis, Rickel,

and their daughters (Tommy Hilfiger Archives), Tommy and Andy with guitars (Tommy Hilfiger Archives), Tommy and Dee (Tommy Hilfiger Archives), sisters Ginny and Betsy (Tommy Hilfiger Archives), Tommy with Steven Tyler and Joe Perry (Tommy Hilfiger Archives), Kate Moss, London Fashion Week, 1996 (Rex Features/ Shutterstock), Tommy with Lenny Kravitz (Mark Weiss), Tommy with Beyoncé (Dimitrios Kambouris/WireImage), Andy Hilfiger with Lenny Kravitz (Tommy Hilfiger Archives), Tommy with P. Diddy and Erica Kennedy (Tommy Hilfiger Archives), Gisele Bundchen, fall 2000 fashion show (Kevin Mazur/WireImage), Tommy with Christie Brinkley (Tommy Hilfiger Archives), Tommy with Barbara Davis (Tommy Hilfiger Archives), Andy with Marky Ramone and Jimmy Kunes (Tommy Hilfiger Archives), Tommy with Samuel L. Jackson and Russell Simmons (Tommy Hilfiger Archives), Tommy with Quincy Jones (Tommy Hilfiger Archives), Tommy with Bob Kraft and Dee (Tommy Hilfiger Archives), Tommy and Dee with Tommy and Thalia Mottola (Mike Coppola/ Getty Images, Tommy with Mark Ronson (Astrid Stawiarz/Getty Images), Tommy with Anna Wintour (Neil Rasmus/BFA.com), Tommy with HRH Prince Charles (Richard Young Photographic Ltd.) Gigi Hadid at 2016 runway show (Antonia de Moraes Barros/ FilmMagic), Andy Hilfiger with Kendall and Kylie Jenner (Kevin Winter/Getty Images), Tommy with Karl Lagerfeld (James Devaney/WireImage), Tommy with Rafael Nadal (Gary Gershoff/ WireImage), Tommy with Lawrence Stroll, Silas Chou, and Joel Horowitz (Tommy Hilfiger/PVH Archives), Tommy with Manny Chirico and Fred Gehring (Lee Clower), Tommy with Mohan Murjani (Tommy Hilfiger Archives), Tommy with Tomy Curtin (Tommy Hilfiger Archives), Tommy with Mohan Murjani (Tommy Hilfiger Archives), Tommy with Guy Vickers in Uganda (Jay Heyman), Tommy with Daniel Grieder (Mounir Raji), Tommy with Joseph Lamastra (Mike Coppola/Getty Images)

# ABOUT THE AUTHORS

For thirty years, TOMMY HILFIGER has brought classic, cool, American apparel to consumers around the world. Under Hilfiger's guidance, vision, and leadership as Principal Designer, The Tommy Hilfiger Group has become one of very few globally recognized designer brands offering a wide range of American-inspired apparel and accessories.

Hilfiger introduced his first signature collection in 1985 by modernizing button-down shirts, chinos, and other time-honored classics with updated fits and details. The relaxed, youthful attitude of his first designs has remained a distinctive hallmark throughout all of Hilfiger's subsequent collections. Today, the Tommy Hilfiger brand continues to bring preppy, all-American classics to consumers around the world. The business has grown from a single menswear collection in 1985 to a global lifestyle brand achieving over $6.7 billion in retail sales in 2014. There are over 1,400 Tommy Hilfiger stores in over 115 countries on five continents.

PETER KNOBLER has collaborated on several bestsellers, including Sumner Redstone's *A Passion to Win* and James Carville's and Mary Matalin's *All's Fair*. He has written with NYPD Commissioner Bill Bratton, Kareem Abdul-Jabbar, Hakeem Olajuwon, New York City mayor David Dinkins, and Texas governor Ann Richards, among others. Knobler is the former editor in chief of *Crawdaddy*, "the first magazine to take rock music seriously." (the *New York Times*)He lives in New York City.